I0881191

Approaches to Teaching Jacobs's *Incidents in the Life of a Slave Girl*

Approaches to Teaching Jacobs's *Incidents in the Life of a Slave Girl*

Edited by

Lynn Domina

The Modern Language Association of America
New York 2024

85 Broad Street, New York, New York 10004
www.mla.org

To order MLA publications, visit www.mla.org/books. For wholesale and international orders, see www.mla.org/bookstore-orders.

The MLA office is located on the island known as Mannahatta (Manhattan) in Lenapehoking, the homeland of the Lenape people. The MLA pays respect to the original stewards of this land and to the diverse and vibrant Native communities that continue to thrive in New York City.

Harriet Jacobs's signature appears on the cover of this book courtesy of the Department of Rare Books, Special Collections, and Preservation, University of Rochester Libraries.

Approaches to Teaching World Literature 176
ISSN 1059-1133

Library of Congress Cataloging-in-Publication Data

Names: Domina, Lynn, editor.
Title: Approaches to teaching Jacobs's Incidents in the life of a slave girl / edited by Lynn Domina.
Description: New York : The Modern Language Association of America, 2024.
Series: Approaches to teaching world literature, 1059-1133 ; 176 | Includes bibliographical references.
Identifiers: LCCN 2023056826 (print) | LCCN 2023056827 (ebook) | ISBN 9781603296540 (hardcover) | ISBN 9781603296557 (paperback) | ISBN 9781603296564 (EPUB)
Subjects: LCSH: Jacobs, Harriet A. (Harriet Ann), 1813-1897. Incidents in the life of a slave girl. | Jacobs, Harriet A. (Harriet Ann), 1813-1897—Study and teaching (Higher) | LCGFT: Instructional and educational works. | Essays.
Classification: LCC E444.J17 A77 2024 (print) | LCC E444.J17 (ebook) | DDC 306.3/620711—dc23/eng/20240325
LC record available at https://lccn.loc.gov/2023056826
LC ebook record available at https://lccn.loc.gov/2023056827

CONTENTS

Intertextual Approaches

Teaching Strategies

Part One

MATERIALS

Introduction

Any scholar working on Harriet Jacobs and her *Incidents in the Life of a Slave Girl* owes an enormous debt to Jean Fagan Yellin. During the later decades of the twentieth century and into the twenty-first, Yellin committed herself to researching this text and its author, demonstrating that *Incidents* was, in fact, autobiographical rather than entirely fictional, despite its astonishing contents. In the introduction to her biography of Jacobs, Yellin narrates the sequence of her discoveries, beginning with an examination of letters undeniably written by Jacobs, letters whose style was consistent with the style of *Incidents*. She then outlined the details of the family of Linda Brent, as Jacobs is identified in *Incidents*, and the family who held Jacobs and other people in slavery, also identified by pseudonyms. Her sleuthing led her to identify the actual historical individuals whose lives matched those of the characters in *Incidents*, proving that the book was, in fact, an autobiography rather than a novel. Yellin's substantial archival research has also revealed significant information about Jacobs's life, family, social network, and geographic context. Nearly all contemporary work on Jacobs has been made possible through Yellin's earlier books and articles.

Since the 1970s, *Incidents* has been taught in a wide variety of courses, including African American literature, American literature, Africana studies, American history, and women and gender studies classes. It is taught in high school as well as university courses. Among the most frequently taught slave narratives, it is likely second only to Frederick Douglass's *Narrative*. Excerpts appear in the standard American literature anthologies, and the complete text is available in multiple editions.

Part 1, "Materials," includes suggestions from teachers and scholars for secondary material that can enhance student comprehension of *Incidents*. These materials include not only other books and articles but also films, websites, and additional electronic resources. Some of these resources will be most useful for instructors preparing to teach Jacobs, while other materials will be appropriate for distribution to students. The amount of suggested material will certainly exceed most instructors' available time, at least within a single semester, but as with other volumes in this series, part 1 of this volume assumes that instructors will return to this volume as they continue to teach Jacobs.

The initial step in the preparation of this volume was distribution of a survey about *Incidents* to instructors across the country and around the world. Their responses inform the discussion of resources listed below.

Further Reading for Students

Choices regarding additional reading for students will be dramatically affected by the type and level of course in which Jacobs is being taught. In lower-division survey courses, instructors might not have the luxury of several class periods to devote to *Incidents*, and students might not be prepared for substantial secondary reading. In more advanced courses, students will likely benefit from additional material on the slave narrative, nineteenth-century American progressive movements in addition to abolition, and the legal status of women.

Instructors frequently pair *Incidents* with Frederick Douglass's *Narrative*, sometimes relying on excerpts. Douglass's *Narrative* is both engaging and accessible, so it elicits considerable interest from students at all levels, including developmental courses; its historic and literary content, however, from Christian support for slavery to international participation in American slavery and abolition, provides ample material for research and discussion in more advanced courses. Although Douglass also published two subsequent autobiographies, the *Narrative* remains most popular for several reasons, including its brevity. His speech "We Welcome the Fifteenth Amendment," an address he gave to the American Equal Rights Association in 1869, in which he contrasts the need for suffrage among African American men with the need for suffrage among women, is another text students could wrestle with. Instructors will want to contextualize it, however, within Douglass's support of women's suffrage. Most instructors who pair Douglass and Jacobs emphasize the effects of gender within the texts and on enslaved persons' lives. Because Douglass did not have to consider the situation of children, he experienced different psychological and ethical challenges than Jacobs as he prepared to escape. Together the two autobiographies also illuminate different methods of escape, which will be helpful for students to consider.

For additional primary texts to pair with Jacobs, instructors should consult the "Intertextual Approaches" section in part 2 of this collection. The essays in this section describe courses that supplement *Incidents* with autobiographical and fictional texts published in the nineteenth, twentieth, and twenty-first centuries.

Recommended secondary readings appropriate for students include Angela Davis's "Reflections on the Black Woman's Role in the Community of Slaves." Instructors also recommend excerpts from John Hope Franklin's *From Slavery to Freedom* for historical context. Jay Parini's introduction to *The Norton Book of American Autobiography* provides interesting discussion points for considering the slave narrative's position within the genre more broadly. Michelle Burnham's article "Loopholes of Resistance" offers students additional entry points for discussion of *Incidents* as literature.

Editions and Adaptations

Following the adoption of this text in so many classrooms, editions of it have proliferated, from the most basic and inexpensive to those that include significant ancillary material. Like other books in its series, the Norton Critical Edition includes letters and periodical articles contemporaneous with Jacobs's life along with excerpts from several pieces of literary criticism written more recently. Bedford has also published an edition that contains introductory biographical information, including a list of individuals for whom pseudonyms are used in the book itself; this edition also includes letters and periodical material from the mid–nineteenth century. A Signet mass-market paperback, *The Classic Slave Narratives*, edited by Henry Louis Gates, Jr., includes *Incidents* along with the narratives of Douglass, Mary Prince, and Olaudah Equiano. Broadview Press recently published an edition edited by Koritha Mitchell, which includes significant ancillary material and contextualizes *Incidents* within Jacobs's long life. The Schomburg Library of Nineteenth-Century Black Women Writers series, which I discuss further below, includes an edition of *Incidents*. Most other publishers with backlists of American literature also have editions in print. Although some of these editions include brief introductions, most of them are quite similar to each other and will serve most instructors' needs in the high school and undergraduate classroom.

Incidents has also served as source material for additional pieces of literature. Lydia R. Diamond adapted the book for a play, called simply *Harriet Jacobs*, which premiered in Chicago in 2008. The script is available through Northwestern University Press. A version intended for middle school students has also been published: *Letters from a Slave Girl: The Story of Harriet Jacobs*, by Mary E. Lyons.

The major anthologies often include excerpts from *Incidents*, which can limit an instructor's ability to examine specific themes in depth. In addition to discussing the advantages and limits of reading only an excerpt from a text, instructors relying on anthologies can adapt many of the activities described in the following articles, depending on the specific chapters included. Volume B of *The Norton Anthology of American Literature*, edited by Robert S. Levine and Sandra M. Gustafson, includes chapters 1, 7, 10, 14, 21, and 41, which focus particularly on Jacobs's decisions involving sexuality, motherhood, and her escape, the issues that many instructors foreground. Volume B of *The Heath Anthology of American Literature*, edited by Paul Lauter, includes similar but not identical chapters: 1, 6, 10, 16, 21, and 41. The major difference here is that the Heath includes a chapter describing Jacobs's complicated relationship with her enslaver's wife, especially after her enslaver pursued a sexual relationship with her. *The Dover Anthology of American Literature* includes excerpts from chapters 17, 18, 20, 21, 29, 30, 31, and 40 (Blaisdell). These chapters focus much more on the period following Jacobs's "escape" to the attic and subsequent events than on her earlier fraught decisions regarding both Dr. Flint and Mr. Sands.

Hollis Robbins and Gates have also edited *The Portable Nineteenth-Century African Women Writers*, which includes a chapter from *Incidents* in the context of excerpts from several other slave narratives, as well as other memoirs, letters, fiction, and poetry. Instructors searching for additional primary materials with which to contextualize *Incidents* will find this collection useful.

The Instructor's Library

Instructors have a wealth of options to choose from as they enhance their understanding of Jacobs in her social and political context. Significant biographical information has been discovered over the last few decades, and important work has also been published on *Incidents* and other related texts. Instructors can easily zoom out from articles that analyze *Incidents* specifically to books that explore the economic, political, and social ramifications of the American slavery system from its origins to the twenty-first century, and they can just as easily zoom in from broader discussions to specific scenes in *Incidents*, since Jacobs's narrative addresses so many subjects pertinent to nineteenth-century American life.

Biographical Works

Yellin's *Harriet Jacobs: A Life*, published in 2004, is the most thorough and influential biography of Jacobs. In 2008, Yellin published the two-volume *Harriet Jacobs Family Papers*, which contains hundreds of primary documents related to Jacobs and her family. Additional material regarding this project is available at the National Historical Publications and Records Commission website. *Harriet Jacobs in New Bedford*, by Peggi Medeiros, explores the relationship that Jacobs and Cornelia Grinnell Willis, the woman who ultimately purchased Jacobs's freedom, both had with the town of New Bedford, Massachusetts.

Essay Collections

No full single-authored books on *Incidents* have yet been published, with most research and criticism appearing in periodicals or in edited collections devoted to broader topics than Jacobs and her work. However, one collection of essays, *Harriet Jacobs and* Incidents in the Life of a Slave Girl*: New Critical Essays*, edited by Deborah M. Garfield and Rafia Zafar, appeared in 1996.

Uncollected Critical Essays

Hortense Spillers's article "Mama's Baby, Papa's Maybe: An American Grammar Book," initially published in *Diacritics*, is particularly useful for its analysis of gendered relationships. Other articles that also address issues related to Black women and sexuality include "Notes on an Alternative Model—Neither/Nor," also by Spillers; Sander Gilman's article "Black Bodies, White Bodies: Toward an Iconography of Female Sexuality in Late Nineteenth-Century Art, Medicine, and Literature"; and Beverly Guy-Sheftall's "The Body Politic: Black Female Sexuality and the Nineteenth-Century Euro-American Imagination." An article by Patricia D. Hopkins, "Seduction or Rape: Deconstructing the Black Female Body in Harriet Jacobs' *Incidents in the Life of a Slave Girl*," addresses one of the main concerns of this text. A well-known article that links Jacobs's experience with late-twentieth-century events is Lauren Berlant's "The Queen of America Goes to Washington City: Harriet Jacobs, Frances Harper, Anita Hill." Ann Taves's article "Spiritual Purity and Sexual Shame: Religious Themes in the Writings of Harriet Jacobs" gets at the source of much of Jacobs's attitude toward sexuality.

Several articles have also been published on domesticity and maternity in *Incidents*, including Caroline Levander's "'Following the Condition of the Mother': Subversions of Domesticity in Harriet Jacobs' *Incidents in the Life of a Slave Girl*," Stephanie Li's "Motherhood as Resistance in Harriet Jacobs's *Incidents in the Life of a Slave Girl*," Grace McEntee's "The Ethos of Motherhood and Harriet Jacobs' Vision of Racial Equality in *Incidents in the Life of a Slave Girl*," and Xiomara Santamarina's "Black Womanhood in Women's Slave Narratives." Barbara Welter's influential article "The Cult of True Womanhood, 1820–1860" remains pertinent.

Alice A. Deck outlines some challenges presented by texts over which the author lacks ultimate control in her "Whose Book Is This? Authorial versus Editorial Control of Harriet Brent Jacobs' *Incidents in the Life of a Slave Girl: Written by Herself*." Albert H. Tricomi also tackles this issue in "Harriet Jacobs's Autobiography and the Voice of Lydia Maria Child." Another crucial topic is the relationships of authorship to literacy and print, as explored in "Harriet Jacobs and the Recirculation of Print Culture," by Samantha M. Sommers, and "Reading between the Lines: The Black Cultural Tradition of Masking in Harriet Jacobs' *Incidents in the Life of a Slave Girl*," by Novian Whitsitt. "Dismantling 'The Master's House': Critical Literacy in Harriet Jacobs' *Incidents in the Life of a Slave Girl*," by Martha J. Cutter, also considers related issues.

Another theme related to sexuality and maternity is the "tragic mulatta." This stereotypical figure originated in the nineteenth century and appeared well into the twentieth, until negative assumptions about mixed-race identity began to be interrogated and racial identity in the United States and elsewhere began to be acknowledged as more complex than an either-or binary. The stereotypical mulatta character had been categorized as "tragic" because of assumptions that such a person would inevitably suffer depression and isolation, belonging fully neither to white nor to Black culture. Mulatta characters appear in work by many canonical and noncanonical authors, including Lydia Maria Child, William Wells Brown, Kate Chopin, Mark Twain, Charles Chesnutt, and Langston Hughes. Instructors interested in pursuing this theme could consult *The "Tragic Mulatta" Revisited*, by Eve Allegra Raimon, and *The Mulatta and the Politics of Race*, by Teresa C. Zackodnik. Werner Sollors's *Neither Black nor White yet Both: Thematic Explorations of Interracial Literature* provides a broader analysis of related themes. Similarly, Julia Charles analyzes several issues related to mixed-race identity in her *That Middle World: Race, Performance, and the Politics of Passing*, and instructors interested in the figure of the mulatta might find Charles's introduction particularly useful. Individual articles include Nancy Bentley's "White Slaves: The Mulatto Hero in Antebellum Fiction," P. Gabrielle

Foreman's "Who's Your Mama? 'White' Mulatta Genealogies, Early Photography, and Anti-Passing Narratives of Slavery and Freedom," and Heidi M. Hanrahan's "Harriet Jacobs's *Incidents in the Life of a Slave Girl*: A Retelling of Lydia Maria Child's 'The Quadroons.'"

Many other topics are frequently raised in *Incidents*. For ideas to expand classroom discussions, instructors could consult Casey Pratt's "'These Things Took the Shape of Mystery': *Incidents in the Life of a Slave Girl* as American Romance," Sally Gomaa's "Writing to 'Virtuous' and 'Gentle' Readers: The Problem of Pain in Harriet Jacobs's *Incidents* and Harriet Wilson's *Sketches*," and Erin E. Forbes's "Do Black Ghosts Matter?: Harriet Jacobs' Spiritualism."

Background Readings

Given the content of *Incidents*, the racialized history of the United States, historic and contemporary debates about gender roles, and current events such as the Black Lives Matter and Me Too movements, instructors recommend background material that ranges from histories of American slavery to contemporary memoirs. William L. Andrews's *To Tell a Free Story: The First Century of Afro-American Autobiography, 1760–1865* is particularly useful, along with *The Slave's Narrative*, edited by Charles T. Davis and Gates. *The Oxford Handbook of the African American Slave Narrative*, edited by John Ernest, provides updated articles that complement much of the earlier work done on this subject. Though originally published in 1976, Eugene Genovese's *Roll Jordan Roll* remains a standard reference. Instructors also recommend *Out of the House of Bondage: The Transformation of the Plantation Household*, by Thavolia Glymph. Joanne M. Braxton's *Black Women Writing Autobiography* includes a chapter specifically on Jacobs and other material on the slave narrative. *A History of African American Autobiography*, edited by Joycelyn K. Moody, is a comprehensive collection that contains several articles related to slave narratives and other antebellum texts. Although not directly related to Jacobs, *The Hemingses of Monticello: An American Family*, by Annette Gordon-Reed, provides a sophisticated analysis of the relationships between powerful white men and enslaved women, relationships that might have been reciprocal and might have included romantic love.

For materials on African American literature more generally, instructors could consult Hazel Carby's *Reconstructing Womanhood: The Emergence of the Afro-American Woman Novelist*. Frances Smith Foster's *Written by Herself: Literary Production by African American Women, 1746–1892* includes significant material on slave narratives and other genres. Carla Peterson's *Doers of the Word: African American Women Speakers and Writers in the North, 1830–1880* is another foundational study. The work of Gates continues to inform nearly all scholars working on African American materials, especially his *The Signifying Monkey: A Theory of African-American Literary Criticism* and *"Race," Writing, and Difference*. Robyn Wiegman's *American Anatomies: Theorizing Race and Gender* explores literature within a broader context of other types of cultural texts and movements. *Black Feminist Thought: Knowledge, Consciousness, and the Politics of Empowerment*, by Patricia Hill Collins, has proven useful for its theoretical analysis and reflections on more recent writers. Katherine McKittrick's *Demonic Grounds: Black Women and the Cartographies of Struggle* examines space and place and their relationships to race. Several of the essays in *Early African American Print Culture*, edited by Lara Langer Cohen and Jordan Alexander Stein, could help instructors discuss the reading of *Incidents* and the circulation of slave narratives more generally. Instructors who pair Jacobs with Douglass should also consult the MLA's *Approaches to Teaching* Narrative of the Life of Frederick Douglass, edited by James C. Hall.

Instructors foregrounding gender or women's writing in teaching *Incidents* could consult *Sensational Designs: The Cultural Work of American Fiction, 1790–1860*, by Jane Tompkins. Many recommended texts focus on issues of gender and sexuality, not surprisingly given the attention Jacobs herself devotes to these issues. The most widely cited text is Saidiya Hartman's *Scenes of Subjection*. Ann duCille's *The Coupling Convention: Sex, Text, and Tradition in Black Women's Fiction* explores these topics within a specifically literary tradition. Linda Grasso's *The Artistry of Anger: Black and White Women's Literature in America, 1820–1860* helps contextualize many of the issues raised in *Incidents*. Karen Sanchez-Eppler's book *Touching Liberty: Abolition, Feminism, and the Politics of the Body* situates questions of physicality within cultural controversies, as do many of the articles in Kimberly Wallace-Sanders's edited collection, *Skin Deep, Spirit Strong: The Black Female Body in American Culture*.

For discussion specifically of domesticity, motherhood, and maternity, instructors might consult *That Pale Mother Rising: Sentimental Discourses and the Imitation of Motherhood in 19th-Century America*, by Eva Cherniavsky, or *Negotiating Motherhood in Nineteenth-Century American Literature*, by Mary McCartin Wearn. Scholars sometimes analyze domesticity in relation to national events; Claudia Tate's *Domestic Allegories of Political Desire* is a good example.

In addition to the novels and memoirs that the articles in this collection discuss, instructors could work with the remarkable series published as the Schomburg Library of Nineteenth-Century Black Women Writers, much of which is available online. Volumes in this series contain autobiography (including *Incidents*), fiction, and poetry. Shorter narratives are sometimes published together, such as in *Collected Black Women's Narratives*, edited by Gates, which includes material by or about Nancy Prince, Louisa Picquet, Bethany Veney, and Susie King Taylor. Longer novels, including Frances E. W. Harper's *Iola Leroy; or, Shadows Uplifted*, and narratives such as Elizabeth Keckley's memoir, *Behind the Scenes: Forty Years a Slave and Four Years in the White House*, are published individually. Given the frequent attention to gender, motherhood, freedom and enslavement, and other cultural questions, nearly any volume in this series could fruitfully be discussed alongside Jacobs.

Many instructors also pair *Incidents* with a twentieth- or twenty-first-century neo–slave narrative. Most often, these include Toni Morrison's *Beloved* and Colson Whitehead's *Underground Railroad*, although revisions of the slave narrative are being published with increasing frequency, so choices are likely to expand. One critical work that instructors could find helpful is *Neo–Slave Narratives: Studies in the Social Logic of Literary Form*, by Ashraf Rushdy. Background reading in contemporary literature beyond neo–slave narratives could include *Between the World and Me*, by Ta-Nehisi Coates.

Sources focused specifically on teaching controversial or challenging material include *Teaching with Tension*, edited by Philathia Bolton, Cassander L. Smith, and Lee Bebout. The MLA's *Teaching the Literatures of Early America*, edited by Carla Mulford, also contains articles useful for teaching the slave narrative.

Audiovisual and Digital Materials

The development of technological tools over the last few decades has substantially changed teaching and learning as well as reading in general. Instructors have available to them not only new ways of presenting information but new types of information itself. Mapping projects, for example, have become increasingly popular; instructors will often assign students to map the locations described in *Incidents*. The most accessible tool is probably *Google Maps*'s Street View function. One particularly detailed and informative mapping resource is Elizabeth Della Zazzera's "Incidents in the Life of Harriet Jacobs: A Virtual Tour of *Incidents in the Life of a Slave Girl*."

Another very useful electronic source is the University of North Carolina's database *Documenting the American South* (docsouth.unc.edu). This database provides access to numerous maps, photographs, newspapers, letters, memoirs, and other material focused on the American South and the period surrounding the Civil War. A similar resource, more narrowly focused but nevertheless providing extensive materials, including some focused specifically on teaching, is the *Colored Conventions Project*, originally produced by the University of Delaware and now maintained by Penn State University. Language itself is often problematic when discussing slavery, race, and related issues. Foreman and colleagues have created a useful guide, "Writing about Slavery / Teaching about Slavery: This Might Help." Other resources available online include the collections of the Library of Congress, the New York Public Library's Schomburg Center, Cornell University's Samuel J. May Anti-Slavery Collection, and the Newberry Library's Homefront and Civil War in Art exhibits.

Visual artists have also responded to Jacobs: Ellen Driscoll's *The Loophole of Retreat* was exhibited at the New York Historical Society. It featured a wooden structure designed to represent Jacobs's attic space in order to convey its nearly inevitable claustrophobic sense. Images of other objects were projected onto the structure's inner walls. Kara Elizabeth Walker's *The Emancipation*

Approximation uses the traditional art of paper cutting to evoke responses to slavery.[1] The twenty-seven pieces in Walker's exhibit stylistically evoked Victorian life while commenting ironically on the idea of abolition and on racism in contemporary America.

Electronic resources will undoubtedly continue to expand as new materials are discovered and as new tools are developed, particularly those that are interactive.

NOTE

1. A brief description of Driscoll's project is available on *YouTube* ("Legacies"). For more information on Walker's exhibition, see "Kara Walker."

Part Two

APPROACHES

Introduction

Lynn Domina

Incidents in the Life of a Slave Girl, by Harriet Jacobs, is one of the most frequently taught slave narratives in the United States and beyond. Significantly longer than Frederick Douglass's *Narrative*, the other most frequently taught memoir composed by a formerly enslaved person, *Incidents* explores several concerns central to women, especially the sexual abuse suffered at the hands of the men who enslaved them and of other men as well. Men were also sexually abused, of course, but enslaved women experienced these assaults alongside cultural pressure to remain "pure" and were then condemned for their lack of purity. Jacobs describes her internal conflict in leaving her children in the care of others, another topic often of greater concern for women narrators than for men. The corpus of slave narratives published in the United States reveals a multitude of methods individuals used to escape slavery, and Jacobs's is among the most memorable, for she didn't actually leave her enslaver's community until several years after she escaped.

The details of her escape are so astonishing that readers and critics resisted *Incidents*'s authenticity and classified it as a novel. Both Jean Fagan Yellin and Henry Louis Gates, Jr., cite, for example, John W. Blassingame's unequivocal pronouncement that the narrative is a novel written in the form of a slave narrative (Yellin, *Harriet Jacobs: A Life* xvi; Gates, *Classic Slave Narratives* xvi). Only through the tireless work of Yellin, well known to scholars of Jacobs, was *Incidents* proven to be unequivocally autobiographical. I describe Yellin's process in more detail in the introduction to part 1 of this volume. Scholars, including many of the contributors to this book, owe much gratitude to Yellin. Her work will surely influence interpretations of *Incidents* for many more generations. Today, Jacobs's story has secured a firm position in the canon of slave narratives and autobiographical writing.

Analogous to the verification of *Incidents* as factual is the continuing rediscovery of additional texts written about or authored or coauthored by formerly enslaved people and free African Americans. Some of these are complete books; others, such as *A True Tale of Slavery*, by John S. Jacobs, Harriet Jacobs's brother, were originally serialized. Still others existed only in manuscript form until recently, including Austin Reed's *Life and Adventures of a Haunted Convict*, which describes Reed's experience in a Northern prison. As scholars gain greater access to archives, especially through the digitization of archival material, the rediscovery of additional texts is almost certain and will continue to influence how instructors situate *Incidents*.

Incidents is taught in a variety of courses, including those in women's studies, Africana studies, and history departments as well as in English departments. It is taught as African American literature, as women's literature, and as American literature. It is taught in nineteenth-century history and literature surveys and in courses focused on genre, particularly autobiography. These multiple perspectives held by scholars and students with different backgrounds and training facilitate a broader range of insights than occurs with many other texts. Many of these scholars completed a survey through the MLA about the materials they rely on in teaching Jacobs, as well as the themes they foreground and the challenges they experience with this text. The results of these surveys have significantly influenced the contents of this book.

Part 2, "Approaches," is divided into four sections. Each essay participates in conversations with other essays in its section and also occasionally with essays in other sections. For the convenience of readers, I have organized the sections based on the most prominent concerns of the authors. The first section, "Thematic Approaches," includes essays that address themes instructors and students find most prominent, especially gender, sexuality, and violence, as well as several other themes that contribute to the fullness of *Incidents*. Marilyn Judith Atlas, Jolene Hubbs, and Ashley Burge explore many of the most troubling events in the book, those focused on sexual trauma and gendered and racialized stereotypes, though each author finds different theoretical entry points. Next, Chereka Dickerson also foregrounds gender in her analysis, though by relying on W. E. B. Du Bois's idea of double consciousness to compare Jacobs with Douglass. Corrie Catlett Merricks extends this discussion of gender to consider the influence of a presumed audience of women on Jacobs's authorial choices, analyzing the interplay of audience and author through theories of rhetoric. Amy Schmidt considers the question of genre, not of the slave narrative specifically but by importing characteristics from fiction, particularly the genre of southern gothic. Given the history of reception of *Incidents*, with readers and critics alike assuming the book was fictional, analysis of Jacobs's reliance on techniques frequently associated with fiction can be especially useful. The final two essays in this section examine themes of the book discussed less often and in doing so illustrate how much more there might be in it to discuss. Josh Doty describes the representation of medical treatment both by and for characters. Clark Moreland and Abbey Whigham analyze the theological assumptions that provide much of the tension in the book and in its surrounding culture.

The essays in the second section, "Intertextual Approaches," address the many ways of situating *Incidents* among other texts. Depending on the course, instructors frequently compare Jacobs's work with memoirs by other enslaved people, with other types of nineteenth-century American texts, and with several of the neo–slave narratives published during the last few decades. Eric Sterling pairs *Incidents* with the *Narrative of William W. Brown, a Fugitive Slave, Written by Himself*, relying on material from both books to both support and subvert the common argument that enslaved females experienced greater trauma than enslaved males did. John Hay discusses three dramatically different texts, *Our Nig*, *Typee*, and *Ruth Hall*, in order to dismantle the boundaries between fiction and nonfiction without irresponsibly ignoring them. Carl Ostrowski similarly relies on this comparative approach to examine generic expectations, this time by discussing the early antislavery novel *The Slave*, later republished as *Archie Moore*. Jericho Williams places *Incidents* in conversation with Mark Twain's *Pudd'nhead Wilson*, focusing on representations of childhood. The next several essays consider Jacobs within the context of contemporary neo–slave narratives. Amina Gautier connects *Incidents* with Toni Morrison's *Beloved*, connecting the two protagonists through their experiences of motherhood. Jennifer L. Hayes also considers the significance of the enslaved mother, this time by relying on a male-authored novel, Colson Whitehead's *The Underground Railroad*. Then, Colleen O'Brien places *Incidents* in dialogue with Dolen Perkins-Valdez's novel *Wench*, foregrounding legal questions around sex, love, and self-defense. The final two essays in this section turn to more political texts. Ingrid Diran provides a Marxist reading inflected with critical race theory in order to reposition *Incidents* within political thought. Kimberly Southwick-Thompson provides a comparison with another memoir, *Assata: An Autobiography*, by the Black Panther member Assata Shakur.

The third section, "Teaching Strategies," includes essays that describe several specific ways of teaching *Incidents*. Molly Ball describes how *Incidents* can be used to debate history and the tropes related to history as repetitious, as oriented toward progress, and so on. Susanna Hoeness-Krupsaw describes a group project assignment that links this nineteenth-century text with that most familiar form of twenty-first-century revelation, the talk show. Alex W. Black positions *Incidents* within the tradition of melodrama and focuses on several moments when music or references to music enter the text; he plays a recording of "Home, Sweet Home" to illustrate how evocative this music can be. Barbara Eckstein describes how she incorporated virtual reality into her class through the creation of Jacobs's virtual attic. Carrie Johnston includes an assignment she created for archival work, in which students research primary source material. Maura D'Amore relies on Cornell University's *Freedom on the Move* database to show her students a variety of historical documents now available to them, after which she leads them to focus on an advertisement for the escaped Harriet Jacobs. Finally, Kristin Moriah illustrates how she incorporates digital humanities resources and assignments, especially *Google Maps*, into her courses. This last group of essays demonstrates how much the tools for teaching have changed over the last generation, even as we consider older texts whose authors could not have imagined these options.

The final section, "Contextual Approaches," focuses primarily on the context of the student, that is, the course in which the text is taught. The first essay, by Heidi M. Hanrahan, describes the author's experience teaching *Incidents* in a gender and women's studies course, focusing on women as agents of change. Next, Melissa J. Lingle-Martin describes how her approach varies when she teaches *Incidents* in three different courses. The last essay in this section, by Lorraine Dubuisson, discusses teaching Jacobs with the excerpt included in *The Norton Anthology of Literature by Women*. Teaching an excerpt rather than an entire book is always a fraught decision, one faced by nearly everyone who teaches a survey course; Dubuisson illustrates how including Jacobs within the context of multiple other texts can help satisfy instructors' desires for both breadth and depth.

Because the essays in each section often also address thematic issues that overlap among sections, I have prepared a list of themes and essays to assist instructors as they explore themes as well as teaching methods. Nearly every essay discusses gender and sexuality, often as those ideas relate to motherhood and the cult of true womanhood. Also included are additional suggestions for exploring conversations among the essays, beyond those that emerge within the specific sections.

Theme	**Essay**
Individual autonomy and agency	Atlas, Ball, Burge, Dubuisson, Eckstein, Gautier, Merricks, Ostrowski
Genre	Atlas, Ball, Black, D'Amore, Hay, Lingle-Martin, Merricks, Ostrowski, Schmidt, Southwick-Thompson, Williams
Sentimentalism	Black, D'Amore, Hanrahan, Merricks, Williams
Christianity	Dubuisson, Moreland and Whigham

Given developments in contemporary technology as well as other national and international circumstances, many instructors have begun teaching online or developing units in their courses that are enhanced with virtual materials. Nearly all of the activities described in the following essays could easily be adapted for synchronous online learning. With a little more work and creativity, they could also be adapted for entirely asynchronous online courses. Indeed, some of the activities will be enhanced if students have access to digital as well as more traditional tools.

Many additional scholars have contributed to this volume through their completion of the MLA's survey about teaching *Incidents*. I hope that the number and range of essays included here will provide instructors with new ideas for presenting this text and will help students understand the significance of such a text within our historical and literary canon.

All essays cite the Norton Critical Edition of *Incidents* edited by Frances Smith Foster and Richard Yarborough.

Peeping through the Loopholes of Shame and Silence toward Freedom and Wholeness while Teaching *Incidents in the Life of a Slave Girl*

Marilyn Judith Atlas

When I teach *Incidents in the Life of a Slave Girl*, whether it is part of a course in women's studies, African American literature, or American literature (graduate or undergraduate) or an introduction to fiction and nonfiction or women and memoir class, I remind my students that while this slave narrative is definitely about gender troubles, it is also about the art of storytelling, negotiating the marketplace, interrogating individual and cultural values, outfoxing one's nemesis, accepting oneself, self-actualizing, and becoming a hero.

In this slave narrative, the prize for questing, taking the journey, slaying the dragon, is not inheriting the kingdom, but being free—independent, autonomous, self-respecting—so that one can be a person rather than a property and, in Linda Brent's case, also a good mother. This narrator breaks cultural rules, outwits her foes, and consistently refuses to be erased and silenced. Ultimately, with the help of nature, reading, writing, and analyzing, Linda Brent is guided (no one does everything alone) toward freedom and figuring out how to both understand and tell her story. As the narrative progresses, Brent finds strength in the natural world and faces and slays her demons, becoming increasingly able to inhabit her rightful place in the world as a person, not an object to be owned.

I also teach this narrative as a call-to-action document and as an explanation of why enslaved women should not be judged by the same standards as free women. In spite of her trauma and alleged missteps, Linda Brent does her best to maintain agency and is hopeful, resilient, and determined. Early in her life, she realizes that she prefers death to slavery, and throughout the narrative she does her best to avoid being forced. If the goddess Daphne can resist Apollo by turning into a laurel tree, then Linda Brent can escape her tormentor, the demonic Dr. Flint, by remembering and reconsidering what decency is and what human beings are meant to be, and readers can help the healing process, Linda Brent's and their own, by listening, speaking, and changing the laws and perceptions forced upon them (us) by a toxic, patriarchal, and aristocratic culture.

In the first section of Annis Pratt's *Archetypal Patterns in Women's Fiction*, "The Roots of Self," Pratt quotes an excerpt from Mary Daly's *Beyond God the Father*. It concerns a new space, a loophole, magically invisible to most unenlightened people, but to those who have need of it and who have entered it, who are in the process of attempting to become whole humans and require a space, a loophole, to work out the details of insight and redemption, that loophole is essential, priceless, and available, if not physically, then spiritually. Daly writes:

> The new space, then, has a kind of invisibility to those who have not entered it. It is therefore inviolable. At the same time, it communicates power which, paradoxically, is experienced both as power of presence, and power of absence. It is not political power in the usual sense but rather a flow of healing energy which is participation in the power of being. . . . Instead of settling for being a warped half of a person, which is the equivalent to a self-destructive non person, the emerging woman is casting off role definitions and moving toward androgynous being. (2)

This slave narrative, written in a certain time and place where African Americans and women had their forces minimized, aims to describe one woman's determined, complex, and secretive journey toward freedom, Harriet Jacobs's version of becoming the hero, and to call on all who are free and decent, asking them (us) to put an end to a legal, evil enterprise and to find or create, with a gimlet if needed, the physical and psychological space, or loophole, to do it.

Jacobs's narrative is a historical document, and it is structured to ensure that the reader knows that the author is honest, worthy of being heard, and although she is still in hiding during most of these dangerous pre–Civil War days and must protect those still in danger, the narrator requests that the reader pay attention to Brent's true, figurative, and literal story. Jacobs's narrative embeds not only documents, cultural history, prices paid for enslaved labor, sewing (Penelope is evoked here), and symbols (so many snakes) but also intertextuality (*Robinson Crusoe*, *Jane Eyre*, and slave songs) and archetypes such as demons and monsters. Recurrently Brent speaks directly to the reader, and repeatedly she demonstrates that she can read people and texts and write with power, complexity, insight, and nuance (65, 141). Recurrently she demonstrates her wit and cunning and alludes to and quotes literature—prose and poetry—and despite the constraints she faces, which prevent her from conceiving children within socially sanctioned wedlock, Linda Brent demonstrates that she is a good mother, family member, and friend, one who is perceptive, honest, and worth hearing and taking seriously. At the beginning and end of her narrative and throughout it, important contemporary cultural figures approve her qualifications as a respectable, bright, and clever woman.

Jacobs understands there is a connection between fictional stories and her "true" autobiography, and this slave narrative serves as a radical and realistic addition to women's hero stories. At the end of her narrative, and in many of its chapters, Linda Brent frequently addresses the reader directly. Jacobs-Brent reminds the reader, who she assumes is an ethical, practical, intelligent, and progressive human being and a reader of fiction, that her true story ends with freedom rather than marriage. She possibly alludes to Charlotte Brontë's popular 1847 novel, *Jane Eyre*, and reminds the reader that the trajectory of her life is different and perhaps more realistic: "Reader my story ends with freedom, not in the usual way with marriage" (167). Marriage is on her mind, but it is poignantly missing from her story: it is not a choice available to her. By sharing her past, by explaining an enslaved girl and woman's plight and limited choices as well as a culture's mean-spirited, mercenary, misguided, and evil missteps, as writer, victim, and witness, Linda Brent is not just freeing herself but furthering the emancipation of others. Linda Brent uses whatever methods she can—mixing law, logic, myth, intertextuality, and emotional appeal to further this righteous cause of freedom. By turns, she rushes forward in her angry telling and then backs away so as not to offend her reader: "Tell all the Truth but tell it slant— / Success in Circuit lies," Emily Dickinson's persona suggests, and Harriet Jacobs–Linda Brent takes Dickinson's persona's advice. The success of Jacobs's *Incidents in the Life of a Slave Girl* may be due to its complex style, its sophisticated framing and telling, and its powerful, memorable characters and anthropological, cultural, and geographic details, silences, and ambiguities, but significantly, it may also be due to this narrative's circuitous and compelling aesthetic and political routes.

Incidents in the Life of a Slave Girl aims to tell as much of the truth as possible within the confines of a text written by a woman who was still vulnerable as a formerly enslaved African American before the Civil War. In this narrative, Jacobs-Brent comes to terms with the cult of true womanhood, makes peace with her choices, and attempts to explain them. I remind my students that to understand this narrative one must read it slowly and well and also understand its context: historical, political, literary, mythological, and psychological. I refer my students to other books that can help them figure out the feminist and archetypal context of this story, not just its literal but also its symbolic truth as I remind them that the issues presented here may have changed for women and minorities, but they have not disappeared. Maria Tatar's *The Heroine with 1,001 Faces* dismantles the cult of warrior heroes and explores heroes more like Linda Brent, demonstrating how domestic crafts and words—sewn, written, and oral—can be and have been successfully weaponized.

This slave narrative is not simply an addition to hero myths but a good example of how close reading helps the reader to understand this text's subtleties. I also recommend that my students read Carolyn Heilbrun's *Hamlet's Mother and Other Women*, because it eloquently argues and demonstrates through example that even good readers often need to take another look and recheck the implications of words spoken, silences, and empty spaces so that a reader can be less influenced by how something has been seen in the past and more accurately perceive characters like Gertrude, Queen of Denmark, Hamlet's mother. Readers may think they understand Gertrude, but Heilbrun demonstrates that they do not and shows them why. When readers study Heilbrun's chapter on Hamlet and slowly reexplore the details within the text, they find a quite different mother of Hamlet than the one they thought they knew. By looking at women's hero myths, at female characters who have been dismissed and allowed to remain minor foils to heroes, by rethinking their understanding of characters and situations, readers can more accurately note and acknowledge what Linda Brent might be afraid to tell the reader—or herself; the reader might and should take a second look at absences, silences, and repetition. I remind my students that we are neither postracial nor postmisogynist in America or in the world, and so the problems of Linda Brent and what she may or may not say are not simply about the past but also about the present.

I also remind my students that American marriages and other relationships are not only the ones examined by Edith Wharton in *The Age of Innocence* or by William Faulkner in *As I Lay Dying* but also those examined by writers such as Tayari Jones in *An American Marriage*, where the author demonstrates through her characters' journeys that it is still dangerous to be Black, female, or both in America. We must read carefully and diversely, and we must not generalize so much that we distort what is happening to so many of our fellow human beings because of their race, religion, class, or sexual orientation. This slave narrative can lead the way toward those discussions.

In this slave narrative, Jacobs, through her pseudonym, Linda Brent, needs to figure out how to convince her reader that she, a woman who has given birth to two children out of wedlock, is not to be written off regardless of her unorthodox choices. The rule of law has betrayed her—because she feels she has a right to own herself, body and soul. Democracy has not called her "citizen," and capitalism has not compensated her for her labor. Linda Brent does not even have the right to teach a fellow enslaved person to read (65). Because she knows she is more than her dwarfed positionality, she does not drown in guilt or shame, though she recurrently feels and responds to both. Other emotions drive her forward toward freedom and wholeness: her righteousness, self-respect, and love for her children. She rises because of her nature and her nurture. For her first six years, Jacobs-Brent is allowed a gentle upbringing by decent people (9). She has a healthy connection to nature, flowers, and the world's beauty (72), and even in the worst of times she has a community that respects her and pushes her forward toward self-actualization, that guides her and helps her—and her children—to love and respect themselves, and eventually they become free, legally and, hopefully, emotionally. She has many guides, some well intentioned if dangerous, like her precious grandmother who sometimes pushes her away from freedom and toward safety, but also some who do the opposite, such as Aunt Nancy and a nearby enslaved neighbor, Aggie (113). And then there are the liars and manipulators, deceitful and dangerous "false" guides who are unsuccessful, outsmarted tricksters and simply wish to do her harm. Linda Brent must figure out her own values and the best paths to take to get what she deserves, and she does.

There are demons to be conquered in *Incidents in the Life of a Slave Girl*. For an enslaved woman such as Harriet Jacobs–Linda Brent, it is impossible not to experience sexual shaming: a "good girl" in 1827 must say "no" to sexual advances, and an enslaved girl in 1827, as property, does not have the authority for that "no" to stick. I encourage my students to be resistant readers, to explore the "loophole" of impossibility, to read, as Judith Fetterley in her paradigm-shifting book, *The Resistant Reader*, suggests we read—with a good dose of resistance and the right set of questions, noting that what is repeated, invisible, mirrored, and symbolically placed within a text tells its own simultaneous and sometimes contradictory story. Readers should never ignore a text's contradictions; rather readers should interrogate them. For instance, I ask my students, what are the chances that Linda Brent–Harriet Jacobs was actually never touched or raped by Dr. Flint, who, according to this narrative, fathered eleven children with various other enslaved women (33)? Why does Linda Brent tell the reader, repeatedly, that she was not raped and yet suggest that these others, many others, were?

In the Librivox audio recording of this slave narrative, an explanation is given that although *Incidents in the Life of a Slave Girl*, before it became a book, was partially serialized in the *New York Tribune*, publication was discontinued because of Jacobs's depiction of the sexual abuse of enslaved women. That might at least partially explain why she chooses not to reveal more details about how far Dr. Flint pushed her sexually. She explains that Dr. Flint does not force her to have sex; he merely torments her through whispers (27) and notes (36), intermittent violence (68), and threats (37). Her explanation of why she sleeps with Mr. Sands is also never fully or satisfactorily made clear. The reasons for her choice to have two children with him is a story the reader will never know. She, aware of her grandmother's values, asks her for "forgiveness" after her first pregnancy (52), feeling guilt and shame (53, 67, 104, 109, 155), but nevertheless believes she deserves support from both her righteous community and the righteous reader, and she gets that support, if not immediately, then eventually. Linda Brent explains her pregnancy with Ben, her first child, but not with Ellen, her second. For many chapters she does not even tell the reader Ellen's name.

The reader, with the guidance of the narrator, must rethink what it means to be silent on an issue and what it means to be "good" in a culture where girls have no choice or few choices around their sexuality and yet must remain virgins. In 1908, when Gertrude Stein creates her character Anna in the first section of her fictional study of immigrant women, "The Good Anna" in *Three Lives*, Stein interrogates what it means for a complicated, gay, Christian, immigrant servant like Anna to be good. As the narrative of "The Good Anna" progresses, so does the reader's understanding of what "good" means. Here, in this slave narrative written over fifty years earlier, Jacobs is questioning what it means for an enslaved woman or girl to be good, and she must do so in a way that is realistic but also does not offend her readers, and her readers must reevaluate their thinking concerning the obstacles that stand in the way of a women's self-esteem.

In Christina Rossetti's poem "Goblin Market" (1862), Rossetti is also exploring the nature of goodness, sin, forgiveness, community, and redemption—in this case, through romance or fantasy rather than realism. Jacobs's style and purpose are vastly different from Rossetti's, whose narrative, tellingly, does end in marriage. But Jacobs-Brent is also creating a powerful and memorable, if vastly different, archetypal narrative as she examines the life of one enslaved girl, shedding light on how the enslaved and the enslavers cope with guilt, sin, agency, friendship, risk, and redemption and asking whether enslaved women and girls should be forgiven or, more radically, whether some of their supposed missteps, such as getting pregnant out of wedlock, should be considered as such.

I encourage my students to understand that it is Jacobs's resistance to Dr. Flint's sexual propositions that advances the story, that makes her—a female adolescent and woman who refuses to be bribed, seduced, or bullied by Dr. Flint and who becomes his nightmare—a woman who chooses, says "no," and speaks truth to power. In this slave narrative, Jacobs-Brent allegedly becomes the one enslaved woman whose permission Dr. Flint needs before he dares to have intercourse with her. Is this realistic? Does it shed light on Linda Brent's declaration, "I resolved never to be conquered" (20)? And does "being conquered" change meanings as the narrative progresses? Can one be raped and not conquered?

While there is little enough shame in this white Southern community where white men act with impunity, there is some, and that shame (and sometimes subterfuge) is explored and interrogated by Linda Brent as she attempts to slay her dragons. Linda Brent explains that white enslavers and their wives desire to appear moral while behaving outrageously. Their behavior is often enraging, destructive, and pathetic, a transparently manipulative performance that can be and is used by Linda Brent to benefit both her and her children. Brent repeatedly slays the inner demons of guilt and shame and outwits and outlives the major outer demons, such as Dr. Flint. She has earned the kingdom, her freedom, but unfortunately, she still needs to be rescued: the law defines her as inheritable property, and she must still be purchased in order to be legally free. Both reality and myth contain painful contradictions, and Linda Brent can and must once again be compromised, but she is no less a hero for that compromise, which showcases this narrative as a modern feminist text of resilience.

Just like this slave narrative's complex images and values, Linda Brent's style changes from chapter to chapter. Some chapters are historical, others further the plot; some are theatrical or explore symbols, or the theme of outfoxing the fox, or silence. Names and specific "rule-breaking" incidents help guide readers through various points in the narrative. For example, mostly or at least partially to defy "Flint," "Brent" chooses "Mr. Sands"—who proves to be as reliable as "sand" and "lacking" integrity, if not as heartless and "hard" as Flint (hard with a flinty, obdurate heart that damages bodies and souls)—to father her children. Brent is an old English surname. It might be Celtic, meaning "holy one" and possibly referring to the river Brent or to a "high place," literally "from a steep hill" if it refers to the villages of Somerset and Devon, and it ties our hero, Linda Brent, to nature and to water, the giver of all life, as well. I encourage my students to stop and take another look, to interrogate the pseudonyms of major characters and their complex embedded implications, and to examine how the reader comes to understand the setting's sometimes contradictory ethics, the reality of twisted cultures, and the existence of unfair laws. In chapter 40, "The Fugitive Slave Law," the reader meets an enslaved man, Luke (or "light"), who escapes from the dark pit of an enslaver who abuses him. Early in the chapter, Jacobs showed the depth of that sadistic abuse. When Linda Brent meets Luke on the street later in that chapter, his cruel enslaver has died, Luke has escaped from a speculator who would have sold him, and he has enough money to get to Canada because of his "questionable" actions. Luke stuffs his enslaver's old trousers with "bills" and then asks those arranging the funeral and estate dispersal for those tattered pants. No one checks; the pants become Luke's—much-needed money (Luke plans on going to Canada) left in their pockets. Remorseless, with overt pride and glee, Luke tells his story to Linda Brent, and she responds with a modicum of mainstream, culturally imposed guilt but mostly with pleasure, seeing the "light" here. Linda Brent lets Luke explain, and then she further delineates how his story affects her:

> With a low chuckling laugh he added, "You see I didn't *steal* it; day *gub* it to me. I tell you, I had a mighty hard time to keep de speculator from findin it; but he didn't get it."
>
> This is a fair specimen of how the moral sense is educated by slavery. When a man has his wages stolen from him, year after year, and the laws sanction and enforce the theft, how can he be expected to have more regard to honesty than has the man who robs him? I have become somewhat enlightened, but I confess that I agree with poor, ignorant, much-abused Luke, in thinking he had a *right* to that money, as a portion of his unpaid wages. (159–60)

Linda Brent records Luke's story and then continues the argument and offers readers insights and her perspective. Soon after this incident, Brent directly references her own participation in breaking the law: Mrs. Bruce helps her, a fugitive from slavery, by law someone's property, and Bruce's very wealthy and benevolent male relative questions Mrs. Bruce's choices. This relative, Linda

Brent lets the reader know, is "benevolent" in "many respects" but "aristocratic" and "proslavery." On a formal level, Linda Brent places this anecdote near Luke's remarks. When this wealthy relative remonstrates with Mrs. Bruce, the British woman who hires Linda Brent to be her daughter's nurse and keeps her in that position with impunity even after she knows that Linda Brent is a fugitive from slavery—this relative makes sure that Mrs. Bruce is aware of the penalty of violating the Fugitive Slave Act. Mrs. Bruce defends her stance with a reply that admits knowledge and justifies behavior: "'I am very well aware of it. It is imprisonment and one thousand dollars fine. Shame on my country that it *is* so! I am ready to incur the penalty. I will go to the state's prison, rather than have any poor victim torn from *my* house to be carried back to slavery'" (160). By enjambing these incidents—Luke's and Mrs. Bruce's—Brent demonstrates her evolution as a person who empathizes first ambivalently with Luke's ethics and then definitely with Mrs. Bruce's choice: Mrs. Bruce is kind and right to keep Linda Brent safe in the country for a month and hidden from her obsessed, bestial pursuer, Dr. Flint. Signs, pseudonyms, and narrative object lessons matter, and they need to be studied in this slave narrative, as do laws. Narrator and reader together explore what one can and should do—or take—when a decent and "fair" road is nowhere in sight. Luke and Mrs. Bruce can be seen as different types of conscious and subliminal guides for Linda Brent as she makes her way toward slaying many of the demons, inside and outside, that prevent her attaining freedom. In this memoir, through art and analysis, Harriet Jacobs–Linda Brent attempts to explain—and reconsider—who she is and how she came to be that person.

And so, I teach that Linda Brent is an evolving and complex narrator telling a multilayered and symbolic as well as moral and true story, one conscious of the role of money in her culture and her life. Jacobs-Brent "costs" her friend, the second Mrs. Bruce (a name that means "from the brushwood thicket," a name that also ties this guide to nature), $300, and Jacobs-Brent is immediately freed by her, but Brent is also humiliated because at this point of her journey, she does not wish to be purchased, as she is not a property—nor does she wish to be complicit in a system that monetarily rewards demons (the progeny of Dr. Flint) and enslaves and tortures innocent humans like herself. Reality (compromise), the subconscious (symbolism, archetypes, fairy tales, and myth), and the market economy hold hands.

I instruct my students to read carefully what Linda Brent writes and to read between the lines—to understand that Jacobs is writing her story to explain how she, one girl and woman, representing many, finds the strength to fight back against an evil system, and while she does not always win, she wins enough so that at the end of this narrative she is a free woman. Linda Brent acts, has agency, but also leaves the reader with spaces and silences and the acceptance of compromise, so the reader can go infinitely further in understanding the writer and the telling.

The "Loophole of Retreat," the central chapter of the narrative, gives the reader a major, brilliant symbol of her complexity, drive, intelligence, and willingness to plot and to play the roles of observer, contemplator, analyzer, and trickster. Jacobs—using her uncle Phillip's gimlet, a tool available to her because it has been accidentally left in the garret—digs for light, and even in hiding finds ways to manipulate Dr. Flint, her double, her evil oppressive twin who, wishing to conquer her, is conquered instead and is dead by the end of the narrative. She writes letters and has them delivered from various ports to confuse him as to her actual location; she does this not to inherit a kingdom, as heroes in traditional quest stories do, but so that she can find a way to feel enabled, human, and viable in a world insistent on crippling her body, her spirit, and her soul. The more Dr. Flint is confused as to Linda Brent's location, the safer Linda Brent feels. It is in this loophole of retreat that Linda Brent makes many of her most important decisions. She is a role model for girls, women, and humans who persist and think outside of the box—she encourages readers to use what we have, to make our own our choices and errors, and to do what we can.

Jacobs, during various periods of her life, had many diverse doubles, mirrors, and helpers, among them her parents, uncles, friends, neighbors, and employers as well as her grandmother, her father's best friend, and her beloved aunt. They all help her on her nontraditional quest to become a new kind of hero, someone who can survive as a free woman, a writer, a person with integrity, intelligence, and skills; who can sew (Penelope, Ariadne), nurture, hide, deceive, and call others to action during a time of national and international crisis; who does not steal and who also does not want to pay for what she owns: her body, her time, her labor.

I also encourage my students to think deeply about the role of family and community in this slave narrative. Each kind gesture gives Jacobs-Brent her hope: where there is one star, one loophole, there are two, and more—and so Brent hints at what she cannot say. This is the story of a free, lonely, angry, increasingly disabled woman, imprisoned and cramped, silent, and hidden, bitten, rained upon, frozen, and frightened for years, but capable of perspective, irony, and mirth. She is never conquered. At the narrative's end, her aunt Nancy dies, satisfied that her sister's daughter and children are free; her uncle Phillip dies, finally called a citizen after his death (166); and her grandmother dies a free woman, knowing that she helped save her precious granddaughter, her great-grandchildren, and her son from a life of slavery. Linda Brent is left with two beloved children, including her daughter, Ellen, also sexually abused, learning the lessons of silence and also the power of education, patience, questing, independence, forgiveness, and self-love. The future is still possible for this formerly enslaved mother and her beautiful, worthy, though traumatized, children.

I ask my students to appreciate the fairy-tale ogre imagery associated with Dr. Flint (99); the damp, biting brutality of nature; and the well-crafted images, often doubled, of architecture and space (protection and entrapment) and to listen where and when Linda Brent recurrently tells the reader how little she thinks of herself, how guilty she is (105), how her freedom "costs" so many people she loves so very much. But one can be a hero without being perfect or consistent; one can be persistent even though one has moments of passivity and doubt.

Sidonie Smith, in *A Poetics of Women's Autobiography: Marginality and the Fictions of Self-Representation*, explores warring forces in autobiography, as I do in my classes. Some of these warring forces are overt, and others remain underground, such as shame and lack of self-respect. An article I often use when teaching this text, one by Ann Taves, explores Jacobs's use of conflicting messages and emotions: "Spiritual Purity and Sexual Shame: Religious Themes in the Writings of Harriet Jacobs," reprinted in the first Norton Critical Edition of *Incidents in the Life of a Slave Girl*. Church, God, ministers, organized religion, community attitudes toward feminine sexual purity, and conforming to the cult of true womanhood are what matter in this slave narrative. Jacobs-Brent is more comfortable exploring the hypocrisies of religion; she is less comfortable exploring themes related to women's pubescent bodies and female desire.

I ask my students to look at Linda Brent–Harriet Jacobs in light of what we know about other survivors of trauma, such as Holocaust survivors or war veterans. Many traumatized humans can articulate only robotic renditions of their traumatic stories. Survivors do not tell all—no one will or can listen to, let alone comprehend, the horror, and they themselves don't want to say, hear, or remember more than they must. Survivors have guilt because they are alive: no one makes it out of hell without intentionally looking past evil at least some of the time. Cynthia Ozick writes about survivor's guilt and silences in *The Shawl*, a novella I encourage my students to read to help them better understand the relationship between silence and trauma, a novella that might help them think about the relationship between Jewish and African American history.

Harriet Jacobs–Linda Brent tells a remarkable and complex story of a hero who quested and won the prize: freedom. She has the requirements to become an archetypal hero: (1) she is the requisite orphan; (2) she is a quester who first must find a tangible representation from the natural world to take along on her journey, and she does: nature itself; (3) she then manages to find many fine guides to help her along her journey; (4) with their guidance, she figures out how to slay her many dragons, emotional and real; (5) she ends up with the boon for which she searches, self-respect, which she brings to the reader; and (6) she is rewarded with freedom, her inherited kingdom. In my classes, we read this narrative as a unique American hero myth and as a historical artifact, a narrative that one must pass on; in this narrative, we read the telling of one enslaved girl and woman's guilt and anger enjambed with her desire to be good, a source of anxiety and pride to her grandmother. Law sometimes trumps ethics in this memoir, but not always; righteousness sometimes trumps expediency, but not always: Linda Brent, in order to be free, is "bought" by the second Mrs. Bruce and then legally freed—and that is not what Linda Brent wants, but it is what she settles for. That compromise is the best Linda Brent can manage in this pre–Civil

War, Fugitive Slave Act world. Perhaps most importantly, this is a narrative where we readers, like Jacobs-Brent, have and make imperfect choices, where we actively create a loophole so that we can better see what Linda Brent sees through her loophole. Linda Brent–Harriet Jacobs, a formerly enslaved person who becomes a role model of practicality, decency, reevaluation, and love, allows all of us to move with her toward freedom, wholeness, and the possibility of being more decent and more fully human.

Teaching *Incidents in the Life of a Slave Girl* in Historical Context

Jolene Hubbs

How can we provide students with an illuminating historical context for their study of *Incidents in the Life of a Slave Girl*? What historical concepts and terms might inform classroom discussions and support assignments that focus on Harriet Jacobs's text? Introducing specific nineteenth-century ideologies—in my teaching, I concentrate on the cult of true womanhood and the Jezebel and Mammy archetypes—can help move students beyond making ungrounded generalizations like "Back then women were X" or "In the past, people thought Y." Teaching about historical constructions of gender and race and their complex interactions can also assist students in analyzing Jacobs's rhetorical strategies for engaging with these constructs. Additionally, reading *Incidents* alongside polemical texts written by her contemporaries and scholarly studies published by our contemporaries can bring to light how Jacobs participated in mid-nineteenth-century debates about enslavement and exposed "the all-pervading corruption produced by slavery" (*Incidents* 47).

Understanding the cult of true womanhood and its four cardinal virtues—piety, purity, submission, and domesticity—can help students recognize how Jacobs strove to make common cause with her readership. To explain why Jacobs might have endeavored to express admiration for these qualities in her autobiography, I let the upper-level undergraduate students in my Women in the South course know that Jacobs's target audience—white middle-class women in the North—was also true womanhood's core demographic. From there, in discussion or during small-group work, students might be asked to identify passages in which Jacobs established not simply that she set store by the cult of true womanhood's central principles but also, and more importantly, that she believed the ideology's devotees should take an active role in abolitionist efforts. I kick off this two-pronged analysis by drawing students' attention to Jacobs's second epigraph, from the Book of Isaiah, which exhorts "careless daughters" to "rise up." After talking about how this epigraph serves both to demonstrate Jacobs's devoutness (by displaying her knowledge of the Bible) and to call readers who share her faith to begin working on behalf of the oppressed, I ask students to identify other passages that pay tribute to piety, purity, submission, or domesticity. Analyzing a few of these examples reveals some of the complexity of Jacobs's text by focusing students' attention on the narrative's rhetorical aims and argumentative strategies.

A working knowledge of the cult of true womanhood can also assist students in identifying the ways that Jacobs bolstered her claim that "slavery is a curse to the whites as well as to the blacks" (48). If tasked with analyzing how slavery harms domesticity, for instance, students might explore how enslavement made a mockery of any domestic ambitions Jacobs may have had by breaking up the nuclear family: the slavery system not only encouraged her children's father to feel proprietorship over, not paternal responsibility toward, his son and daughter but also tore Jacobs away from her youngsters when, trying to escape sexual violence, she sought refuge in the garret of her grandmother's storeroom. Jacobs also directly addressed white women's self-interest by representing how enslavers' sexual violence against enslaved women wrecked white domestic tranquility. Jacobs's sixth chapter, called "The Jealous Mistress," describes the disillusionment that awaits Northern women who marry Southern enslavers. Having envisioned a "happy home" in a "sunny clime," the "young wife" finds instead that, because her husband "pays no regard to his marriage vows," as Jacobs put it, "jealousy and hatred enter the flowery home, and it is ravaged of its loveliness" (34). And, lest her readers in the North think of slavery as a regional rather than national scourge, Jacobs's narrative spotlights how legislation like the Fugitive Slave Act compelled Northerners to act as "human bloodhounds" working in the service of the Southern plantocracy (41). Divorcing Northern women from the emotional and physical delicacy and docility characteristic of true women by depicting them as beasts in relentless pursuit, this powerful imagery reveals slavery's wide, pernicious reach.

Exploring how Jacobs reworked figures and scenes from proslavery fiction, a genre that mushroomed in the decade in which she penned *Incidents*, also enhances students' knowledge of how the writer addressed the politics of her moment. In response to Harriet Beecher Stowe's antislavery novel *Uncle Tom's Cabin* (1852), which was a runaway bestseller, dozens of writers published proslavery novels. My students read an excerpt from *The Planter's Northern Bride* (1854), by Caroline Lee Hentz, a text accessible on *DocSouth*, *HathiTrust*, and other repositories of digitized content. I assign just the first chapter of Hentz's novel—a little proslavery propaganda goes a long way in illustrating the racism and falsehoods that buttress this genre. In Hentz's opening chapter, enslaver Mr. Moreland travels to the North and crosses paths with a gravely ill young white woman who can no longer work to support herself and her mother. The woman's plight prompts Moreland to reflect on what he sees as the differences between free workers in the North and enslaved laborers in the South. Hentz's text recapitulates the proslavery party line, familiar from antebellum works like hers and from postbellum plantation fiction, which peddled the idea that old and ill enslaved people were "kindly nursed and ministered unto, with no sad, anxious lookings forward into the morrow for the supply of nature's wants" (27). By contrast, Hentz's Moreland is moved to pity for "the starving sons of Ireland, the squalid operatives of England . . . [and] the free hirelings of the North, who, as a *class*, travail in discontent and repining" (31–32) because they are subjugated to "the bondage of poverty" (27). To launch a classroom conversation about how Jacobs's text counters the claims circulating in the works of apologists for slavery like Hentz, I ask students to look at the opening sentence of chapter 6, which sounds like a direct rebuttal of *The Planter's Northern Bride*: "I would ten thousand times rather that my children should be the half-starved paupers of Ireland than to be the most pampered among the slaves of America" (29). At this point, students might be asked to point out and discuss other passages in *Incidents* that refute Hentz's claims.

To study how Jacobs's narrative challenges stereotypical constructions of Black women's identities, I assign students an excerpt from Deborah Gray White's field-changing book *Ar'n't I a Woman? Female Slaves in the Plantation South*, first published in 1985. White's first chapter, called "Jezebel and Mammy: The Mythology of Female Slavery," limns "a complicated set of myths about black womanhood" (28). In my course, I open the discussion of this reading assignment by spending some time underscoring that by describing ideologies, not identities, White's work offers insights into fallacious ideas circulating in mid-nineteenth-century America (and beyond) that Jacobs worked to oppugn. To reinforce this idea, I draw students' attention to White's assertion that "[t]he Mammy image is fully as misleading as that of the Jezebel" and ask them how studying these misleading images helps us understand Jacobs's text (49). Students often astutely discuss how white people in Jacobs's orbit—both the individuals Jacobs describes in *Incidents* and the readership she strove to reach via *Incidents*—might have bought into these stereotypes. Yet some undergraduates may struggle with how to bring the knowledge gleaned from White's chapter to bear on particular passages in Jacobs's text. I've taken to trying to concretize these ideologies by suggesting that students think of each as a vision-warping monocle forged by American cultural forces that people like the Flints looked through every time a Black woman came into their line of sight despite the fact that it distorted rather than improved their eyesight. Because they peered through the distorting Jezebel lens each time they gazed at Jacobs, and looked through the distorting Mammy lens whenever Jacobs's Aunt Nancy came into their field of vision, the Flints grossly misperceived these women's actions, emotions, motivations, and aspirations. Working through an example—perhaps the account of Nancy's funeral in chapter 28, which contrasts white onlookers' perceptions of the scene with what "*we* could have told them" (123)—can model how to bring White's analysis into conversation with Jacobs's narrative.

To set up a historical framework for considering Jacobs's representation of how white women not only actively engaged in abusing and exploiting enslaved people but also played pivotal roles in the economic structures of slavery, I assign a chapter from Stephanie E. Jones-Rogers's award-winning book *They Were Her Property: White Women as Slave Owners in the American South*. Jones-Rogers's study of female enslavers speaks to Jacobs's experience of being enslaved by—and later sold by—Emily Dodge, née Flint. Chapter 3 of *They Were Her Property*, entitled "Missus Done Her Own Bossing," can inform discussions about brutal female enslavers like Mrs. Wade, who "lashed the slaves with the might of a man" (*Incidents* 44).

Like other authors of antebellum slave narratives, Jacobs wrote about her own experiences as an enslaved person in an effort to convince her readers that slavery should be abolished. Teaching students about nineteenth-century gender and racial ideologies that Jacobs strategically addressed as well as polemical literary genres that she powerfully repudiated can aid in illustrating how Jacobs crafted her narrative to speak to her mid-nineteenth-century readership. Pairing *Incidents* with scholarship by historians can help students identify and analyze some of the myriad ways Jacobs's narrative lays bare the "wrongs, and sufferings, and mortifications" inflicted on enslaved women (*Incidents* 68).

Reanimating the Unsexed: Using *Incidents in the Life of a Slave Girl* to Recast the Black Body and Redesign Black Female Sexuality

Ashley Burge

My experience exploring African American literature through the discourse of Black womanhood in predominately white academic spaces often illuminates inauthentic and demoralizing monolithic ideologies projected onto Black women and Black women's sexuality. Many of these monoliths are as antiquated as the dehumanizing systems that engendered them, but they are deeply entrenched in the American psyche and continue to dictate constructs of Black womanhood. This is my literary entry point into Harriet Jacobs's harrowing and empowering autobiographical slave narrative, *Incidents in the Life of a Slave Girl*. When I dissect this text with predominately middle- to upper-middle-class white students in the midwestern classroom, I am sympathetic to the indoctrination of patriarchal, white ideologies that have engulfed them since adolescence; however, I am vigilant in puncturing these discourses in order to encourage new pathways of thinking as they pertain to gender, sexuality, and Black womanhood. Jacobs's text is ideal for this endeavor, because her work presents ruptures in the patriarchal, white supremacist construct of Black womanhood through her characterization of Linda Brent, the cunning, passionate heroine whose triumphant journey from enslavement to freedom mirrors Jacobs's own pathway to liberation from her Southern hometown in Edenton, North Carolina, to her Northern haven in New York. Presenting these disruptions to my African American literature students is paramount, because many of them enter the classroom with well-established notions of Black womanhood that have been tainted by dehumanizing constructs that oppress Black women in American culture. Even if students are not fully invested in the oppressive anti-Black images of mainstream popular media and literature, such as the Mammy figure or the trope of the angry Black woman, they are still often entranced by the masculine, white-centered narratives that dictate value and power in American society. And at these intersections of power and value in American culture, Black women are disenfranchised.

Many of my students have been indoctrinated, often unknowingly, by the damaging dominant narrative that Chimamanda Ngozi Adichie calls the "single story." Adichie posits that the detrimental power of the single story is that the storyteller has "the ability not just to tell the story of another person, but to make it the definitive story of that person." I use Jacobs's *Incidents* to liberate the text from these detrimental, one-dimensional narratives by positioning Jacobs's narrative as the preeminent origin story of Black womanhood and Black female sexuality in American letters. *Incidents* should be interpreted as a nascent exploration of Black womanhood and Black female sexuality, because Jacobs presents one of the first subjective portrayals of a woman's journey to liberate herself from enslavement and define her sexuality and gendered identity apart from the patriarchal trappings of early American discourse. In her portrayal of Linda Brent, Jacobs creates a protagonist that appeals to the sympathies of Northern white women on behalf of Jacobs's subjugated sisters in the South. In doing so, Jacobs elevates the Black female voice while defining sexual agency and gendered identity apart from the male gaze. She creates a space of rebirth for Black womanhood that is not mired by patriarchal "ideal" tropes of womanhood that limit subjectivity. I have found that students in my African American literature courses are intrigued and invigorated by Jacobs's origin story and are often encouraged to interpret her narrative in ways that work to dismantle oppressive structures in contemporary American society and create safe spaces for Black women and other marginalized populations.

The narrative's sentimental undertones allow Jacobs to interweave her sexual awareness and sexual vulnerability in ways that appeal to the sympathetic humanity of her primarily white female audience while also creating vitally important discourse on the sexual and identity politics enslaved Black women had to navigate during the antebellum era. Even as late as the mid-eighties, the scant scholarship on the sexual politics of Black women posed a problem for Black intellectuals. Hortense Spillers adequately articulates the detriments to this void as she asserts, "[B]lack women are the beached whales of the sexual universe, unvoiced, misseen, not doing, awaiting their verb. Their sexual experiences are depicted, but not often by them" ("Interstices" 197). Though she wrote in the late nineteenth century, Jacobs attempts to remedy the dearth of discourse on Black women's sexuality by authenticating the Black female voice of her protagonist, Linda Brent. Jacobs begins *Incidents* at the precipice of Linda's innocence and naivete as an enslaved child who does not know the realities of chattel slavery until the age of six, when her mother dies. Prior to her knowledge of bondage, Linda notes that she "was so fondly shielded that I never dreamed I was a piece of merchandise, trusted to them [her parents] for safe keeping, and liable to be demanded of them at any moment" (9). Linda's close-knit family shields her not only from the realities of her commodified existence but also from the intrinsically predatory nature of white male enslavers, who were legally permitted to prey on enslaved Black girls and women. Linda remains unscathed while she is with her first enslaver, a woman who teaches her how to read and sew and whom she loves with the same fervor as her own mother. However, her contentment is short-lived, since the woman dies when Linda is twelve years old. The realities of the injustices of slavery soon begin to impress themselves on Linda as the woman reneges on her promise to Linda's mother to emancipate her children. Linda feels betrayed and, in grief, laments, "My mistress had taught me the precepts of God's Word: 'Thou shalt love thy neighbor as thyself.' . . . But I was her slave, and I suppose she did not recognize me as her neighbor. I would give much to blot from my memory that one great wrong" (12). Linda is inherited as property by the woman's niece, who is also the daughter of Dr. Flint, a tyrant who preys on Linda with threats of rape and concubinage that he intends to carry out at a house that he begins to build on the outskirts of town, out of the public view and away from his family and Linda's grandmother. Because Linda is Dr. Flint's property and is therefore afforded no protection by the law to challenge his possession of her body, Linda engages in an illicit affair with a wealthy lawyer named Mr. Sands in order to control the paternity of her children and challenge Dr. Flint's authority over her body. She then outwits Dr. Flint by hiding in her grandmother's garret for seven years while she strategizes to have her children bought by their father so they will all be able to escape to the North to freedom. Jacobs does not adhere to the standard tropes of seduction typical for the sentimental novel genre; however, students are intrigued by the sensual conventions that Jacobs uses to appeal to her primarily white female readership. This is an ideal intersection to explore the innate humanity of sexuality while also critiquing sexual exploitation in patriarchal societies.

Scholars rightly interpret Jacobs's industriousness and ingenuity as strategies to shift power dynamics and challenge systems of oppression. For instance, Melissa Daniels-Rauterkus notes that "it is important to underscore how black women may have used these relationships as strategies to claim agency and move beyond the binaries of enslaver/enslaved and oppressor/oppressed" (505). These observations are apt in fully understanding the horrific conundrums that enslaved Black women experienced in slavery and in celebrating the triumphs that they wrested from such a draconian system as American slavery. When engaging with this text in any college course, I foreground discussions of sexuality by centering the vulnerable status of Black girls and women during the antebellum era and beyond. The theme of sexual autonomy and resistance against the lawless system of white enslavers is a prominent concern when interrogating the text. Indeed, I believe these constructs should be interlaced in the development of Black women's identity politics in America. I motivate students to focus on the sensual conventions of the text in order to isolate Jacobs's burgeoning sexual identity as a Black woman, particularly in her interactions with her first love, a free Black man. Jacobs uses this romantic relationship to identify with her white female readership and their affinity for the erotic overtones of the sentimental novel; however, in isolating the passion and longing of Linda Brent toward her paramour, Jacobs also affirms Linda's humanity in a way that dismantles white supremacist constructs of Black womanhood. Jacobs quips, "Why does the slave ever love?" and she continues, stating: "I loved him with all the ardor of a young girl's first love" (35). In these confessionals, Linda confirms that "the slave" has the capacity for one of the strongest human emotions: romantic love. And with this emotion comes the capacity to connect with another person on a level that surpasses social and cultural constructs often used to create oppressive hierarchies. An emphasis on the humanity inherent in Jacobs's romantic relationships is a necessity when interrogating these texts, because mainstream racist and sexist discourse is often used to dehumanize Black women.

Prior to Jacobs's text, the identity and sexual politics of Black women had been primarily dictated by white males under the auspices of racist, sexist discourses that interrogated the perceived differences of the Black body in comparison to white bodies. I position Jacobs's narrative as evolving commentary on Black womanhood and sexuality that had not been authenticated before *Incidents* was published in 1861. In this instance, Jacobs's text becomes a counternarrative to foundational discourse connected to human sexuality. An influential text that would go on to impact various theories of human sexuality and their intersection with race and class is Sander Gilman's "Black Bodies, White Bodies: Toward an Iconography of Female Sexuality in Late Nineteenth-Century Art, Medicine, and Literature," which postulates that "[t]he antithesis of European sexual mores and beauty is embodied in the black, and the essential black, the lowest rung on the great chain of being is the Hottentot" (231). Gilman mentions the Hottentot to refer to Sarah Baartman, a South African woman who was exploited in traveling freak shows across Europe; Europeans characterized her bodily characteristics as "primitive" or "distorted," which led to discourses that connected Black body types to "savages" or animals. These white supremacist notions about race and sexuality circulated in the early Americas as well. bell hooks notes:

> At the onset of their arrival in the American colonies, black women and men faced a society that was eager to impose upon the displaced African the identity of "sexual savage." As white colonizers adopted a self-righteous sexual morality for themselves, they even more eagerly labeled black people sexual heathens. Since woman was designated as the originator of sexual sin, black women were naturally seen as the embodiment of female evil and sexual lust. (33)

These projections, though manufactured, would greatly influence gender dynamics used to justify the enslavement of Black women under the American institution of slavery and oppress middle- and upper-class white women to the domestic cult, which espoused rigid adherence to purity, piety, domesticity, and submission. More importantly, and more nefariously, for centuries these projections would also stagnate identity formations of Black womanhood in literature, media, visual imagery, and art. I contextualize these European and colonial American discourses as distorted narratives that work to further oppress women in general and Black women specifically. In this context, Jacobs's narrative works to demythologize the stigmas around Black women and Black sexuality.

Other prominent slave narratives authored by formerly enslaved Black women vehemently shied away from sexuality and sexual exploitation because of these stigmas, which is a testament to the progressiveness of *Incidents*. Margaret Washington notes, for instance, the "ostensible silences" about sexuality in Sojourner

Truth's slave narrative, reflecting the high stakes that Truth would have faced for sexual impropriety (58). Although it has also been noted by Washington and other scholars that Louisa Picquet's slave narrative, titled *Louisa Picquet, the Octoroon; or, Inside Views of Domestic Life*, which dates to the same year as Jacobs's narrative, discusses a forced sexual relationship with a white enslaver, Jacobs's narrative has been deemed by audiences and later scholars of literature and history as the more exceptional work in terms of its exploration of sexual identity and politics in accordance with the cult of true womanhood and American slavery. Jacobs presents an authentic counternarrative to denigrating portrayals of Black womanhood, and she also fills gaps of discourse that female Black authors felt were too "delicate," as Lydia Maria Child asserts in the introduction to *Incidents*, to reveal to the public ("Introduction" 6). By disregarding social conventions of the antebellum era and creating a literary and rhetorical infrastructure for Black female empowerment in the midst of racism and sexism in American culture, Jacobs almost single-handedly redesigns constructs of Black womanhood in ways that affirm Black female identity. Jean Fagan Yellin notes that *Incidents*

> defied the taboos prohibiting women from discussing their sexuality—much less their sexual exploitation—in print. Within its pages, a well-known woman writer presented to the public the writing of a pseudonymous "impure woman" on a "forbidden subject." Here a black American woman, defying barriers of caste and class, defying rules of sexual propriety, was joined by a white American woman to make her history known in an attempt to effect social change. ("Written" [H. Jacobs] 219)

In my African American literature courses, we explore the wealth of Jacobs's portrayal of this "forbidden subject" in order to expand the scope of students' understanding of Black female sexuality and identity in ways that affirm Black women's experiences in contemporary culture.

One of the primary, and most accessible, ways for students to explore the redesign of Black womanhood and sexuality is through Jacobs's ingenious use of language in *Incidents*. Interrogating the use of language as a mode of resistance in a text such as *Incidents* is always ironic, because the foundations of language itself in American culture are based on conventions that oppress people who are "othered." Historically, Standard American English has been used in legal discourse and sacred American documents to elevate white supremacy while subjugating marginalized communities. Language then becomes an extension of the bondage that the Black community has had to navigate in order to authenticate their Black identity in American discourse. As Martha J. Cutter argues in reference to Audre Lorde's comparison of the English language to the "master's tools," "One cannot overcome oppression by using the master's tools, and if language is an instrument of oppression, simply taking of it will not lead to liberation, nor will it lead to a dismantling of the master's house" (209). The dilemma for students is, then, to theorize how Jacobs can manipulate a language that belongs to the oppressor in order to liberate herself. Indeed, *Incidents* is deliberate in showing that the tyrant, Dr. Flint, owns language and uses it to demean and exploit Linda. In several instances, Jacobs reveals that Dr. Flint's words are his chief mode of exploitation. Jacobs illustrates this as Linda is on the cusp of adolescence:

> But I now entered on my fifteenth year—a sad epoch in the life of a slave girl. My master began to whisper foul words in my ear. Young as I was, I could not remain ignorant of their import. . . . He tried his utmost to corrupt the pure principles my grandmother had instilled. He peopled my young mind with unclean images, such as only a vile monster could think of. I turned from him with disgust and hatred. But he was my master. I was compelled to live under the same roof with him—where I saw a man forty years my senior daily violating the most sacred commandments. (27)

Here Dr. Flint divests Linda of her innocence and virtue, which, in the context of the tropes of ideal womanhood to which she subscribes, are moral and spiritual crimes that would incense Northern white women. It is telling that Jacobs emphasizes the "foul words" that "peopled [her] young mind with unclean images," because she is demonstrating a type of psychological bondage connected to the sexual depravity of Dr. Flint's words. And initially, Linda has no recourse to challenge these words, because Dr. Flint threatens to kill her if she is not "silent as the grave" (28).

In the crux of Dr. Flint's superfluous words and Linda's oppressive silence, I introduce students to the antics of trickster figures and trickster traits in order to reconcile the power imbalances of language in oppressive systems. Specifically, I introduce students to the literary maneuvers of signifyin(g), language strategies used by trickster figures in African American folklore tales to outsmart and outwit their adversaries. In the context of folklore tales, these adversaries primarily symbolize white enslavers. In his *The Signifying Monkey*, named after the popular folklore ballad of the same name, Henry Louis Gates, Jr., argues that signifyin(g) is the ultimate Black cultural form of creative expression (51). Signifyin(g) is grounded in the ambiguity of language, especially as it concerns language in Black spaces. Gates posits, "[T]he Signifyin(g) Monkey, he who dwells at the margins of discourse, ever punning, ever troping, ever embodying the ambiguities of language, is our trope for repetition and revision . . . repeating and reversing simultaneously as he does one deft discursive act" (52). Jacobs summons the antics of the trickster and his cunning manipulation of language in her deliberate calculations against Dr. Flint. This is evident during her voluntary imprisonment in the undisclosed garret of her grandmother's house. While she awaits an opportune time to buy her children from Dr. Flint through a trader in enslaved persons and escape with them to the North, she begins writing letters from her North Carolina confinement under the guise of residing in various cities in the state of New York. Her plan is simple but clever:

> I resolved to match my cunning against his cunning. In order to make him believe that I was in New York, I resolved to write him a letter dated from that place. I sent for my friend Peter, and asked him if he knew any trustworthy seafaring person, who would carry such a letter to New York, and put it in the post office there. He said he knew one that he would trust with his own life to the ends of the world. (*Incidents* 108)

The genius and empowerment in this trickery are such that Linda successfully dupes Dr. Flint through the letters, thereby subverting the oppressive power of the English language and creating a space for Linda to reclaim her agency in the text. Further, as Valerie Smith argues, "she 'clearly delights' in the letter writing maneuvers enacted from her grandmother's garret" (qtd. in Foreman, "Politics" 334). Yellin seconds this stance as she speculates about the motives of the real Harriet Jacobs, stating, "It was delicious to realize that she could play mind games with the man who for years had tried to control her consciousness" (*Harriet Jacobs: A Life* 57). Her white female readers might also read this deliciousness as titillation, alluding to Linda's sexual control, which subverts the power dynamics that exist between enslaved and enslaver. The same can be said of Linda's initial confession to Dr. Flint, when she tells him she is with child. When Dr. Flint threatens Linda with the prospect of moving her to a secluded house outside of town, she directly states: "I had a feeling of satisfaction and triumph in the thought of telling *him*. . . . I replied, 'I will never go there. In a few months I shall be a mother'" (51). Dr. Flint leaves her presence astonished and defeated. Linda's empowerment is in the telling. She breaks her oppressive silence and the gratifying result is the sexual control that she exerts apart from Dr. Flint's exploitation. In essence, she recasts her sexual identity and sexual autonomy outside of the dehumanizing constructs of American slavery, and she does this by using the "master's tools" against him.

Perhaps one of the most profound ways that Jacobs uses language to redesign Black womanhood and sexuality is through her manipulation of the slave narrative genre itself. The nascent beginnings of authentic Black womanhood commence with Jacobs's transmutation of Black women in slave narratives from victims of sexual exploitation to triumphant purveyors and sovereigns of their own bodies and sexual identities. The slave narrative genre in itself is a product of empowerment and affirmation of humanity, because it began with Black male authors such as Olaudah Equiano and Frederick Douglass who challenged white supremacist ideologies that purported that West Africans and African Americans were intellectually inferior to white people and, therefore, could not master the supreme measure of one's humanity: literacy. Though these narratives successfully appealed to the abolitionist cause and forced its white readers to reckon with their complicity in enslavement, they did so at the expense of

Black women, who were often portrayed as victims with no agency to resist white enslavers or the horrific institution of slavery. Many scholars attest to Frederick Douglass's *Narrative* and its usage of the graphic beatings of Black women as plot devices to enhance Douglass's hero status. Jacobs is, by far, the first slave-narrative writer to challenge this construction, and she does so through her awareness of the complexities of power and sex in the antebellum era. While Douglass grounds his freedom and agency in his capacity to exert his manhood over white enslavers and white supremacist structures, Jacobs uses her reclamation of Black female sexuality and choice to liberate herself from enslavement.

The power of this strategy is evident in Linda's illicit but gratifying relationship with Mr. Sands. As Jacobs states in *Incidents*, Dr. Flint had "blighted the prospects of [her] youth" (49), and she found herself "entirely unprotected by law or custom" (49), "reduce[d] to the condition of chattel, entirely subject to the will of another" (50). The tyrannical Dr. Flint had dispossessed Linda of the agency to choose her lover as a young girl, and there were no laws in place to protect her from his threats of rape as a young woman, because he legally owned her body under the statutes of American slavery. In this space of powerlessness, Jacobs makes the choice to define her sexuality in terms that affirm her identity as a Black woman independent of oppressive patriarchal constructs. She accomplishes this by accepting the advances of Mr. Sands, a wealthy white lawyer. Jacobs paints this engagement as a necessary evil that lends itself to sexual autonomy, a form of freedom that symbolizes subjectivity and self-actualization. Jacobs writes of Linda's tryst: "So much attention from a superior person was, of course, flattering: for human nature is the same in all. . . . It seems less degrading to give one's self, than to submit to compulsion. There is something akin to freedom in having a lover who has no control over you, except that which he gains by kindness and attachment" (49–50). Jacobs grounds Linda's humanity in the passionate affair that she has with Mr. Sands when she states that "human nature is the same in all," but she also emphasizes how the basic human right to choose her sexual partner and, consequently, the father of her children can be likened to freedom. In this instance, her victimhood is dissolved, because she chooses to give herself to a man of a higher social status than Dr. Flint in order to challenge his possession of her body and his authority over her sexuality. As bell hooks argues, "Those black women who resisted sexual exploitation directly challenged the system; their refusal to submit passively to rape was a denouncement of the slaveowner's right to their person" (27). Jacobs's transmutation of Linda Brent from powerless victim to sexually autonomous victor transcends the patriarchal confines of the slave narrative genre while it simultaneously creates space for Jacobs to redesign womanhood and sexuality in ways that affirm Black women's identity politics.

Jacobs's *Incidents* is rightly celebrated for its progressive and distinctive appeals to dismantle the dehumanizing system of American slavery. However, instructors and students will also find a plethora of themes that can inform their understanding of constructs of Black identity, gender, sexuality, and power when they approach this text as a foundational discourse that elucidates Black womanhood in America. I believe interpreting *Incidents* from this perspective will allow a more empathetic stance toward the struggles of Black women in American culture and a more informed understanding of how historical and contemporary systems of oppression work to disenfranchise those who are othered. Further, I believe interpreting Jacobs's progressive text as an early foundation for Black female agency through subjective identity and sexuality formations provides a template for Black women and other marginalized populations to create their own pathways to empowerment.

Exploring the Double Consciousness of Harriet Jacobs through Incidents in Her Life

Chereka Dickerson

Harriet Jacobs's *Incidents in the Life of a Slave Girl* importantly situates the study of African American literature. Using W. E. B. Du Bois's double consciousness as a lens for analysis of the text and as a theoretical framework for a junior-level undergraduate African American literature course enables a better understanding of the work accomplished by the text and how it can be used as a pedagogical tool for studying African American literature. *Incidents* is an exemplary text for studying the way that slavery shaped the social perception of enslaved Black Americans. *Incidents* can be used to understand the extent to which Black people recognize their agency as it informs their understanding of both personhood and freedom. Most specifically, through an inspection of Harriet Jacobs's characterized self, Linda Brent, we can better understand themes as they emerge in both *Incidents* and African American literature more generally.

Du Bois's theory of double consciousness calls attention to performance as a survival tactic. According to Du Bois's theory, oppressed individuals can never realize a true self-consciousness, because they must filter their understanding of their self through the perception and interpretation of others, most notably those in oppressing classes. As Du Bois articulates, "[T]he negro is a sort of seventh son, born with a veil, and gifted with second-sight in this American world,—a world which yields him no true self-consciousness, but only lets him see himself through the revelation of the other world" (7). Though at the turn of the twentieth century, Du Bois was specifically writing about the plight of Black American men, this ideology can be applied to anyone who is faced with performing in the face of contradiction. For Du Bois:

> It is a peculiar sensation, this double-consciousness, this sense of always looking at one's self through the eyes of others, of measuring one's soul by the tape of a world that looks on in amused contempt and pity. One ever feels his twoness,—an American, a negro; two souls, two thoughts, two unreconciled strivings; two warring ideals in one dark body, whose dogged strength alone keeps it from being torn asunder. (7)

In other words, it is not only that individuals cannot exist in the world without first reconciling and confronting the perceptions that have long preceded them but also that the preceding perceptions are in direct contradiction to how they recognize and understand themselves. Brent had to reconcile the perceptions of her enslavers in order to navigate her world.

In a junior-level African American literature course, students grapple with Brent's daily reality as an enslaved girl and consider her actions, thoughts, and behaviors both from her perspective and from the outside perspective of her contemporaries. From there, students recognize the different ways that Brent reconciled her perception of herself through the eyes of her enslavers, and even other enslaved people, as she navigated her world. Below, I apply the theory and framework as explained above to a typical conceptualization of a junior-level African American literature course, where we unpack Brent's agency as it lends itself to the emergent themes of personhood, motherhood, and freedom.

In the course, we begin the semester by reading chapter 1 of Du Bois's *Souls of Black Folk*, "Of Our Spiritual Strivings," to immediately delve into a discussion about double consciousness. The purpose of this discussion is to get students to understand that double consciousness is largely characterized by performance and contradiction. The "two warring ideals" of which Du Bois speaks shape how and the extent to which one feels compelled to perform (7). Students' understanding of the theory is crucial to the application of the theory.

Once the framework for the semester is set, we dive into the literature. I use slave narratives as the foundation of the course to unpack course themes and as reference points throughout the term. To begin, I pair Jacobs's *Incidents* with Frederick Douglass's *Narrative* to mostly compare gender dynamics in relation to the three interconnected themes of agency, personhood, and performance of "slave." A person's performance of the role of "slave" is directly tied to their need to acquire or claim agency given that their double consciousness soberingly reminds them that their personhood does not exist. Douglass calls direct attention to the enslaved person's performance as he critiques one enslaver's expectations. He says, "When he spoke, a slave must stand, listen, and tremble," even if the enslaved person was not really terrified (Douglass, *Narrative* 352). For an enslaved person to refuse to perform such deference would result in punishment, thereby instilling the fear that was not previously performed. With this, we see contradicting performance operate as a survival tactic. On the one hand, the enslaved person attempts to recognize or assert their humanity; on the other hand, their owners and overseers refuse to acknowledge them as persons.

In *Incidents*, we see this fraught contradiction as well. Early in the text we are introduced to Brent's uncle Benjamin, "who dared feel like a man" and fought his enslaver after committing a minor offense (18). The consequence of his raising his hand to his enslaver was a public whipping (21). As a teenage boy growing into adulthood, he recognized whippings as tools to instill obedience in children and not men. But as an enslaved person, he could never realize the status of manhood, so he resolved to run away: "I implored him not to go, but he paid no heed to my words. He said he was no longer a boy, and every day made his yoke more galling. . . . He grew vexed, and asked if poverty and hardships with freedom, were not preferable to our treatment in slavery" (21). Through double consciousness, we understand why running away was Benjamin's only option. For Benjamin, manhood is supposed to represent status, power, and authority in society. Though he feels like a man, his enslavers do not perceive him to be. For him, the requisite of performing boyhood to appease his enslavers is akin to death. He says, "Linda . . . we are dogs here; foot-balls, cattle, everything that's mean. No, I will not stay. Let them bring me back. We don't die but once" (21–22). In other words, as an enslaved person, his manhood was denied, and as a result, the prospect of death was negligible.

Juxtaposing these two slave narratives makes plain that violent actions by enslavers were not anomalous and that enslaved people were more inclined to resist such actions than to concede. Though students may already understand and accept that such violence was commonplace during the slavery era, they might not understand why the enslaved did not all just run away or revolt. The double consciousness lens elucidates that enslaved people were humans with human needs and human thoughts and that one's decision to run away was not always effective. Through double consciousness, we can track how the remnants of slavery appear in contemporary African American literature.

To continue the discussion of the personhood theme, we focus on unpacking the ways in which Black men, most specifically, seek affirmation for or try to assert their personhood. A good text to explore for this theme is Richard Wright's *Native Son*. Double consciousness helps us unpack Bigger Thomas's search for a validated manhood. Additionally, we interrogate Bigger's fear as it manifests on the South Side of Chicago in contrast to his fear as it manifests in the Daltons' house, which illuminates his performance of "Black boy" prior to his flight as he reconciles the perception of his personhood once his fate is determined.

Incidents broaches the subject of Black women's personhood differently. Even though "Black women were hardly 'women' in the accepted sense" (Davis, *Women* 7), Jacobs still made it apparent to use the idea of womanhood to appeal to the sentimentality of her largely white woman readership (Stover 134). Through Linda Brent's actions regarding sex and motherhood, the reader delves into Brent's double consciousness as she grapples with her status as an enslaved individual, her personhood, and her claim to motherhood. Altogether, an enslaved Black woman's status rendered moot her bodily agency and nullified her claim to motherhood. Furthermore, she was subjected to sexual violence in a way that her male counterparts were not. Indeed, "[a]s females, slaves were inherently vulnerable to all forms of sexual coercion. . . . Rape, in fact, was an uncamouflaged expression of the slaveholder's economic mastery and the overseer's control over Black women as workers" (Davis, *Women* 7). This is evidenced in *Incidents* through Brent. She recounts, "For years, my master had done his utmost to pollute my mind with foul images, and to destroy the pure principles inculcated by my grandmother, and the good mistress of my childhood. The influences of slavery had had the same effect on me that they had on other young girls; they had made me prematurely knowing, concerning the evil ways of the world" (49). This rhetorical move where Jacobs talks directly to her audience through Brent represents the extent to which double consciousness shaped the way that she recounted her narrative. As a Black woman, Jacobs is hyperaware of the narratives that depict

Black women as morally lose and as disavowing virtue (Collins 72). In stark contrast to these narratives, Jacobs foregrounds enslaved Black women's inability to consent to the violence inflicted on their bodies.

To further the discussion of Black women's autonomy, a great follow-up to *Incidents* is Toni Morrison's *Beloved*. For Morrison, choosing motherhood, a choice not afforded to enslaved Black women, was the ultimate freedom. In an essay, "On *Beloved*," Morrison notes:

> One area of principal debate was control of one's own body. . . . [M]any women were convinced that such rights extended to choosing to be a mother, suggesting that not being a mother was not a deficit and choosing motherlessness (for however long) could be added to a list of freedoms; that is, one could choose to live a life free from childbearing and no negative value or judgment need apply. (418–19)

During the slavery era, Black women had no say over their bodies. Yet, for Morrison, the choice of motherhood represents so much more than bodily agency. For Morrison, "having children, being called a mother, was the supreme act of freedom" (419). This was an act of freedom because enslaved women had no right to their own children given how their personhood remained in question: "Since slave women were classified as 'breeders' as opposed to 'mothers,' their infant children could be sold away from them like calves from cows. . . . [F]emale slaves had no legal claims whatever on their children. . . . [C]hildren could be sold away from their mothers at any age because 'the young slaves . . . stand on the same footing as other animals'" (Davis, *Women* 7). In other words, enslaved children's personhood was an even bigger question. Under US slavery, a Black woman's claim to her children "was not only unacceptable, it was illegal, anarchic. . . . It was freedom" (Morrison, "On *Beloved*" 419). Because enslaved women were property, and likewise were their children, enslaved women were not able to claim possession over that which they did not own. In Jacobs's narrative, Brent's motivation for surviving those seven years in the attic was for her children. Not only did she not want to see them enslaved, the prospect of catching a glimpse of them or hearing their voices also gave her life. Brent nearly came to her demise because she chose motherhood—and because she dared to love her children.

Choosing motherhood was an act of anarchy, and daring to love one's own children was even more so. *Beloved* provides commentary on this bold act of rebellion by challenging the idea that a mother's love is inherent. For the Black women in *Beloved*, choosing to love one's own children was foolish given that there were no guarantees that one could or would keep their children. In *Beloved*, the choice of motherhood is illuminated through commentary on Black women's lack of bodily agency and maternal autonomy. In the scene where we learn about Sethe's journey to freedom, Sethe's concerns about her baby's potentially not surviving prompt another Black woman to respond, "If anybody was to ask me I'd say, 'Don't love nothing'" (Morrison, *Beloved* 108). This challenge to the choice of motherhood is further illuminated by Paul D when he criticizes the love that Sethe gives her children. He says, "Your love is too thick," to which Sethe responds, "Too thick? . . . Love is or it ain't. Thin love ain't love at all" (193–94). In both instances, Sethe is discouraged from loving her children; Sethe is discouraged from realizing her freedom. Through her double consciousness, Sethe's love is evidence of her personhood. Everything else about her existence denies that personhood. Her daring to love her children, in contrast, affirms it.

We see a similar instance in *Incidents* when Brent witnesses the aftermath of a woman's last child being sold away from her. The scene unfolds with the woman striking her chest in sorrow, saying, "I can't tell you what's in here! They've got all my children. Last week they took the last one. God only knows where they've sold her. They let me have her sixteen years, and then—O! O! . . . I've got nothing to live for now. God make my time short!" (63). This experience is telling, because it calls attention to the reality that all enslaved women faced. They were powerless to determine if or when they got pregnant, they were powerless to protect their children from bondage, and they were powerless in determining whether or not they would get to raise them. For this woman, and Sethe alike, death would have been a welcomed respite for both mother and child. These women's fatal resignation echoes Benjamin's decision to run away.

Seeing her children grow up free from bondage was Brent's end goal and motivation for running north. Beyond motherhood as a choice for enslaved women, the discussion on the choice of motherhood could be carried forward in other texts that deal with Black women's agency as free women. In other texts we see free Black women both choose and reject motherhood. Many of Morrison's other texts include discussions of motherhood, either directly or indirectly. Motherhood as a choice is most prominent in *Sula*, where Sula chooses to make herself over making somebody else (92). In *Tar Baby*, Jadine Childs refuses to parent her aunt and uncle upon her return to the island. And in *Jazz*, Violet so desperately seeks motherhood that she steals a baby. By reading these texts through a lens of double consciousness, we recognize the extent to which these discussions of motherhood as a choice are directly tied to the agency that these characters possess.

To provide a wider scope for this discussion of motherhood as a choice, instructors might consider texts like Alice Walker's *The Color Purple*, where Celie's children are stolen from her arms and sold, Shug Avery is estranged from her children, and Sofia is jailed away from her children. Zora Neale Hurston's *Their Eyes Were Watching God* completely challenges this notion of motherhood as a choice, through childless Janie. Hurston brushes over this discussion in the text and all but dismisses it. This dismissal shows us that motherhood does not make Janie; instead, Janie makes Janie.

Brent's action to secure her freedom is the final emergent theme from *Incidents* that shapes discussion of other course texts. Brent longs to be free, yet she refuses the idea of purchasing her freedom. She notes, "The more my mind had become enlightened, the more difficult it was for me to consider myself an article of property" (165). Brent grapples with her personhood through her double consciousness. Brent sees herself as a human, as a person, but the idea that she could be purchased as a piece of property directly contradicts the idea of herself that she had come to accept once she had lived "free" for many years. Moreover, as Brent notes, "to pay money to those who had so grievously oppressed me seemed like taking from my sufferings the glory of triumph" (165). After suffering seven years in that attic and steadfastly outwitting her enslaver, resigning herself to *pay* for her freedom would have wholly defeated the personhood that she had cultivated for so long. Even as her freedom was purchased, the relief she felt for no longer having to run was outweighed by the damage to the concept of herself that it created. Brent says, "So I was *sold* at last! A human being *sold* in the free city of New York! The bill of sale is on record, and future generations will learn from it that women were articles of traffic in New York, late in the nineteenth century" (165). For her freedom to come at a literal price was in direct contradiction to what she had come to believe about the North. And though she had known that the streets would not be paved with gold, she had expected a greater disregard for the practice of slavery. However, as she notes early in the narrative, "the Free States sustain a law which hurls fugitives back into slavery," so she was already leery of the "freedom" that was supposed to be attained by running north (40). Even outside the chains of slavery, double consciousness continued to shape her life.

That Brent had to settle for her freedom being purchased makes clear her position as a Black person in America, free or not. So, it is unsurprising that her securing of her freedom is anticlimactic in the text, as it was in her real life. Her hyperawareness of her Blackness prohibits her from realizing what she sees as true freedom given how her agency is constrained by her race, and gender to a lesser extent, and how her Blackness perpetually undermines her personhood. Though her quest to secure her freedom is successful, her disappointment at how she secures her freedom has a resounding echo in African American literature written in the late nineteenth century through today.

In African American literature, the promised land of the North was not so promising as the emancipated had been led to believe. Black authors make clear that the divide between the North and South was not as great as hoped. Richard Wright's *Native Son* illuminates the continued struggle of Black people on the South Side of Chicago. Claude Brown's *Manchild in the Promised Land* highlights the stagnant mindset of Black people as they migrated north. Ralph Ellison's *Invisible Man* and James Baldwin's *Go Tell It on the Mountain* make clear that opportunities in the North were limited without the right connections. Zora Neale Hurston's *Their Eyes Were Watching God* contrasts the promise of the North with her characters moving farther south to find a respite from the hostilities of white Southerners. This promised land exists against a backdrop of white society that did not include Black people in its vision.

To bookend the term with a nonfiction narrative, Ta-Nehisi Coates's *Between the World and Me* calls attention to the great divide between the world that he knows and the white world that is promised. Playing on the same themes of agency, personhood, and freedom, Coates's text illuminates what Du Bois means by "the veil." The veil, or the perception of the white world, exists between the world and him. For Jacobs and Douglass, the veil is the institution of slavery that exists between the free world and them. For the other characters in the other texts mentioned, the veil is the legacy of slavery that exists between the world and them. Regardless of which veil exists in a text, its presence shapes the double consciousness of the characters and is a force that acts within and upon the text.

Taken together, *Incidents* is a pedagogical tool that foregrounds discussions of agency, personhood, and freedom in an African American literature course where Du Bois's double consciousness provides the theoretical framework. Slave narratives in general provide an historical point of reference for the oppression and maltreatment of Black people. And Black women's slave narratives, like *Incidents*, provide a point of reference for nuanced discussions about agency in relation to one's personhood and one's desire for freedom.

"Reader, Be Assured This Narrative Is No Fiction": *Incidents in the Life of a Slave Girl* as Rhetorical Theory

Corrie Catlett Merricks

Harriet Jacobs's *Incidents in the Life of a Slave Girl* is a captivity narrative, a sentimental novel, and an argument against the evils of slavery itself. Additionally, it is an argument about rhetorical theory and the means of communication available to enslaved and formerly enslaved women in the American South during the mid–nineteenth century. *Incidents* can be used as a teaching tool to introduce students to a variety of rhetorical concepts and theories while also engaging with the text itself in a meaningful way. I required students in Rhetoric for Writers, a 300-level English class, to read *Incidents* together with several critical texts, and my students and I had a productive month learning rhetorical theory. I argue that portions of the text can also be used in introductory-level writing classes.

I have chosen to use Jacobs's famous opening line in her "Preface by the Author" as the title of my essay, because in this opening Jacobs takes control of the rhetorical situation. She creates an audience, and she names her "reader" (5). Teaching this text gives instructors a chance to dive into rhetorical theory from the first day, and the preface is short enough to be read out loud together in class along with the book's title page. Jacobs also articulates who her reader is in her preface: "I do earnestly desire to arouse the women of the North to a realizing sense of the condition of two millions of women at the South, still in bondage, suffering what I suffered, and most of them far worse" (5). In his article "The Rhetorical Situation," Lloyd Bitzer argues that a rhetorical audience "consists of only those persons who are capable of being influenced by discourse and of being mediators for change" (8). Additionally, each rhetorical situation presents a complex arrangement of individuals, events, objects, and relationships that can influence the rhetor's choices. Jacobs's choice to directly address her "reader" and engage her in conversation indicates Jacobs's skill as a rhetor. She is "altering reality" as described by Bitzer: "The rhetor alters reality by bringing into existence a discourse of such a character that the audience, in thought and action, is so engaged that it becomes a mediator of change. In this sense rhetoric is always persuasive" (4). Jacobs's choice to directly address her audience, her decision to emphasize her own "deficiencies," and her knowledge of her readers' tastes and fascinations allow her to connect with her audience quickly and create a discourse that activates change like Bitzer describes.

In *Engaging Ideas*, John Bean asserts that students have trouble reading "difficult texts" for a variety of reasons, including "failure to adjust reading strategies for different purposes," "difficulty in adjusting reading strategies to different genres," and "difficulty in reconstructing the text's original rhetorical context" (165–66). Bean argues that "inexperienced readers often do not see what conversation a text belongs to. . . . [T]hey have difficulty perceiving a real author writing for a real reason out of a real historical moment" (165). Jacobs's narrative gives instructors the chance to practice these strategies in the classroom in real time: *Incidents* joins a significant historical conversation, and students are often familiar with at least the basics of the abolitionist movement, although *Incidents* may be the first female-authored slave narrative with which they have engaged. Careful consideration of the rhetorical situation Jacobs faced helps students adjust reading strategies to different genres and consider the text's original rhetorical context. Because students are reading a book that requires them to step outside of their own historical and cultural contexts, it is easier for them to perceive "a real author writing for a real reason out of a real historical moment" like Bean describes (165). In my classroom, we discussed the rhetorical context of slave narratives and considered historical background to help us understand the original purpose and argument of Jacobs's text. I assert that once students have practiced understanding and articulating the rhetorical situation of a historic text, this skill can transfer to contemporary texts, especially when the instructor encourages conversation about metacognition and transfer.[1]

Doug Downs moves beyond the concept of "rhetorical situation" and advocates for the concept of "rhetorical ecology" in his article "Rhetoric: Making Sense of Human Interaction and Meaning-Making."[2] Downs explains that rhetorical ecology "invokes a sense of a place defined by a network of myriad interconnecting and almost inseparable elements that all shape the rhetorical interaction and meaning that emerges from them" (378). My class read Downs's article, and we practiced mapping *Incidents*'s rhetorical ecology on the board. I have included an image of our partial map here (fig. 1). I think that in future classes, it would be helpful to create an electronic version of our map (possibly on *Google Docs* or a similar file-sharing platform) and add to it over a few weeks as we read the entire text. My students acknowledged some key pieces regarding the interconnecting elements that Jacobs was presented with: her own position as a Black woman and formerly enslaved person created a kind of double jeopardy regarding her own credibility; the Fugitive Slave Act was an important piece of political knowledge that her readers would have been aware of; Jacobs had to accommodate white stakeholders who were part of the abolitionist movement in order to tell her story; she crafted a story that focused on motherhood in order to connect to her primary audience; and her narrative is specifically written in the context of nineteenth-century Christianity. The process of creating a rhetorical ecology guided us and helps students continue building their reading skills after completing the class. This can be practiced in both lower- and upper-level classes—the map may look different, but students' ability to articulate the idea of rhetorical ecology always grows as a result of the exercise.

Downs asserts that considering a text's rhetorical ecology allows us as readers to see a text as a piece of a web or network and to understand the multiple roles

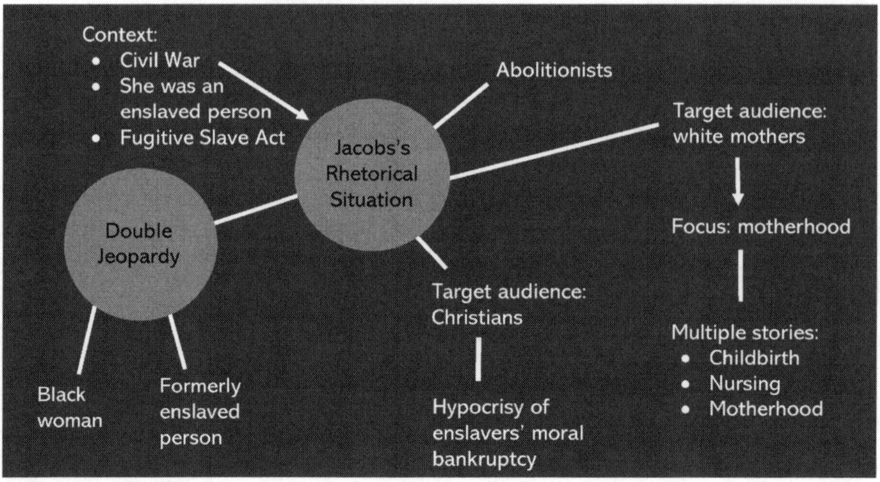

Figure 1. Recreation of the rhetorical ecology of *Incidents* created by Corrie Catlett Merricks and her students.

speaker and audience might play as they are interacting. He writes: "what emerges in any rhetorical ecology, then, is a network of rhetors, many people with a variety of connections to each other" (379). Considering this idea of "a variety of connections" allowed my class to examine the ways Jacobs is placed within a network of rhetors herself. My class began with Lydia Maria Child's introduction. In this introduction, Child validates Jacobs's story so readers can believe that Jacobs actually wrote it and that she is telling the truth ("Introduction"). The inclusion of the introduction written by Child is a good place to begin: reading Child's introduction and considering the definition and history of authenticating texts allows us the chance to consider several questions: How is the abolitionist movement itself a network of rhetors? What role did Child play in the creation of the text? How did Jacobs craft her story in order to accommodate her audience? This discussion enables us to understand the idea that Downs presents when he argues that "rhetorical interaction is therefore inevitably collaborative and shared" (380).

Reading Child's authenticating documents and the early chapters of Jacobs's text works well in a lower-level class focused on writing and rhetoric, as an introduction and a chance to practice understanding the ideas of rhetorical situation and ecology.[3] In a higher-level class, a few of the essays included in the Norton Critical Edition were also helpful. Frances Smith Foster's essay "Resisting *Incidents*" was helpful in understanding and digging into the concept of stance: How does Jacobs approach her subject when she can assume that her reader will be resistant to her? As Foster asserts, "African Americans inevitably encounter a significant number of obstinate readers. . . . [T]he mimetic details, social relevance, and political implications of their texts have been particularly challenged" (256). Jacobs's text provides an example of this, because white university students at a predominantly white institution can often immediately empathize with an audience who might be resistant to the ideas Jacobs presents; however, the text also evokes their empathy for Jacobs and her experience. My students were quickly able to see some of the ways the authenticating texts, the introduction, and even the direct address to the reader are designed to break down the immediate resistance a white reader might maintain as they enter into the text. Students provided some excellent examples, including the way Jacobs shared the story of Linda Brent's pregnancy with her audience: "But, O, ye happy women, whose purity has been sheltered from childhood, who have been free to choose the objects of your affection, whose homes are protected by law, do not judge the poor desolate slave girl too severely!" (49). Jacobs's choice to directly address her audience and call out their privilege was inspiring to my students, who readily understood this as one way to combat resistance in her readers, with the concept of calling out privilege so relevant in contemporary popular culture. Another student was very interested in Jacobs's desire to expose a false version of Christianity and to undermine the myth of the "kind, Christian slaveholder" as she exposed the character of Dr. Flint: "When I was told that Dr. Flint had joined the Episcopal church, I was much surprised. I supposed that religion had a purifying effect on the character of men; but the worst persecutions I endured from him were after he was a communicant" (67). He wrote an excellent rhetorical analysis of several passages that specifically question the Christianity of Southern enslavers.

Incidents also allows for an opportunity to argue that Jacobs's rhetorical choices involve what she leaves out of her story; her narrative is a "rhetorical performance," as described by Jacqueline Jones Royster and Gesa E. Kirsch in their book, *Feminist Rhetorical Practices*. Royster and Kirsch contend that "the symbolic move to name, describe, and assess more thoroughly what we observe and interrogate as rhetorical action encourages us to set aside our disbeliefs about who rhetors are and what constitutes, with meaning and consequence, rhetorical action" (16). Jacobs says in her introduction that she has "not exaggerated the wrongs inflicted by Slavery; on the contrary, my descriptions fall far short of the facts" (5). Her claim is engaging and titillating; she draws in her audience, for whom literature was often censored or modified for propriety's sake. This example shows students that what Jacobs doesn't say is just as important as what she does say and that her choice to keep part of her story quiet is also "rhetorical action," as described by Royster and Kirsch. Because Jacobs's chosen audience was very concerned about propriety, she could only hint at the sexual advances and graphic language used by Dr. Flint. As Valerie Smith writes in her article "Form and Ideology in Three Slave Narratives," "[I]f slave narrators in general were restricted by the antislavery agenda, she was doubly bound by the form in which she wrote" (222–23). Smith adds that this doubly bound writer opened up space for her audience to look into the text for what is unspoken or implied, by utilizing "the rhetoric of the sentimental novel . . . at least in part because it provided her with a way of talking about her vulnerability to the constant threat of rape" (223). Looking for what is not there allowed my students and me to understand that Jacobs's choice to utilize the rhetoric of the sentimental novel was a prudent rhetorical move.

Smith's article also helped us think about the way *Incidents* integrates multiple genres into the text. James E. Porter's definition of *intertextuality* helped us understand why Jacobs utilized multiple genres: "Not infrequently, and perhaps ever and always, texts refer to other texts and in fact rely on them for their meaning. All texts are interdependent: We understand a text only insofar as we understand its precursors" (418). My students and I looked at some examples of sentimental novels, examined the definition of a sentimental novel, and considered the ways this particular genre is a part of the texts that formed the text we were studying. Considering the inclusion of the authenticating text by Child allowed us to see the multiple layers of complexity of the rhetorical situation Jacobs faced. Jacobs not only had to work "through the ordering intelligence of a white amanuensis or editor," but she had to work with an audience that would have been highly skeptical of her truthfulness (V. Smith, "Form" 222). My students and I discussed the concept of intertextuality—does this blending of genres mean that Jacobs didn't create a new text? Smith asserts that she did: "Some narratives . . . elude the domination of received generic structures and conventions. Such narratives test the limits of the formula [and] tell us most about what those conventions signify" (222). Reading through and carefully considering *Incidents* gives students a living example of intertextuality and helps them connect with Smith's assertion that "[s]ome narratives . . . test the limits of the formula."

As my students and I discussed the multiple players in the publishing of Jacobs's text, the fact that she had to establish credibility (ethos) by developing and maintaining a seventeen-year relationship with a "distinguished family in New York," and the ways she included multiple genres in her own story, the concept of rhetorical ecology came to life for us. *Incidents* is an example of the works Cheryl Glenn describes when she argues that "feminist research has also worked to resist the Western paternal narrative of rhetoric . . . by recovering and recuperating women's contributions in the broad history of culture making (292). Inviting students into a conversation about feminist rhetorics and the recovery of women's contributions opens the door to the idea that Jacobs's text is a collaborative work in which the reader can begin to see "the interconnectedness and blurred boundaries among various rhetorical agents, showing us how an interaction is shaped not by a single rhetor but by many, and the shape of the resulting text or discourse depends on (is contingent on) the exact interplay among those agents" (Downs 380).

Pairing conversations about rhetorical theory and *Incidents* grows students' understanding of the text in a significant way: because of our conversation about rhetorical ecology, students can see moves that Jacobs makes throughout the text in order to connect with or engage her audience. Exploring Jacobs's choices together with students allows for engaging conversations about rhetorical power. Jacobs "reads" her audience and creates a dynamic text that will help her readers view her with compassion in spite of her unorthodox choices while also arguing that the same readers should become involved in ending "that pit of abominations" that is slavery (5). She frequently discloses to her reader her intentions to expose some truths while hiding others, therefore making her narrative an argument about how to communicate complex and difficult stories. Teaching *Incidents in the Life of a Slave Girl* through the lens of rhetorical theory allows instructors to engage with the text and explore it in its great complexity while also introducing students to important concepts in rhetoric that they can apply to other texts.

NOTES

1. In "Tutoring for Transfer," Heather Hill writes that "metacognition, the idea of having an awareness and understanding of one's own learning and thought processes, is often associated with the ability to transfer knowledge successfully. Research shows that if students are able to reflect on their learning, they will be more likely to remember and draw on that learning when they get into new situations" (81).

2. Downs acknowledges that this term was pioneered by a number of scholars, including Marilyn Cooper and Jenny Edbauer.

3. I have had success with chapter 7, "The Lover," in first-year writing classes. From the opening question of "Why does the slave ever love?" to the layered challenges Jacobs presents as her character, Linda Brent, argues to her enslaver that she should be allowed to marry, this passage provides an excellent example of "a network of myriad interconnecting and almost inseparable elements that all shape the rhetorical interaction" as described by Downs (378). I have required this chapter in several versions of Freshman Composition, and I have had success using it to put the concept of rhetorical situation or rhetorical ecology into practice in the classroom.

Teaching *Incidents in the Life of a Slave Girl* as a Southern Gothic Text

Amy Schmidt

Typically taught as a female slave narrative in literature surveys, Harriet Jacobs's *Incidents in the Life of a Slave Girl* can also be taught as a southern gothic text in freshman composition courses. Teaching Jacobs's *Incidents* as a southern gothic text highlights the historical context of slavery and its continued impact on the socioeconomic present; moreover, this approach to teaching *Incidents* does not discount but rather reinforces the more conventional reading of the text as a portrayal of the gendered specificity of slavery's trauma and violence. Ultimately, this approach highlights the cultural constructions and material consequences of the institution of slavery while exposing students to multiple literary genres and historical contexts.

While this approach to the second half of freshman composition may not be the most effective one for teaching students to do research, it is productive for teaching Jacobs's text. Though the course framework asks students to do too much in too little time, using the Norton Critical Edition of Jacobs mitigates this by providing secondary sources. Additionally, while the framework may be less engaging for students who are not majoring or minoring in English, Jacobs's text, as nonfiction, elicits more engagement than works of fiction do.

Most of my students identify as southerners, so they find the southern gothic more familiar and, thus, more engaging than the British gothic. Worth noting is that I teach at a Christian liberal arts institution in the US South, so class meetings elsewhere may not produce such lively discussion about themes such as faith in relation to race.

Southern literature, in general, and the southern gothic, in particular, have historically been viewed as implicitly "white"—including slave narratives, which are seen as fundamental to the definition of the canon—and scholarship on the genre has shifted over the past several decades to correct this misrepresentation.

Students begin the semester reading British gothic texts by Horace Walpole and Ann Radcliffe. They then read gothic texts from the US South, beginning with Jacobs's narrative, and the unit on Jacobs focuses on how the genre of southern gothic literature is significantly impacted by the American experience of slavery. The essay assignment for this unit asks students to respond directly to this impact; to provide students with a manageable focus, the assignment asks them to explore the text through literary devices. This requirement encourages students to develop close reading skills alongside historical awareness. Because one of the course's student learning outcomes is engaging in academic research, the assignment requires them to find three to five secondary sources to integrate into their argument. Since this assignment can be a daunting one for first-year college writers, class discussions focus on how the literary devices in Jacobs's text apply gothic conventions from the classic British model to the American experience of slavery.

While most class meetings are discussion-based, an initial lecture on contexts (slavery) and frameworks (the southern gothic) for the text is helpful for facilitating participation later on. Reminding students of significant dates for slavery in the United States helps them situate Jacobs's narrative in a concrete way. Additionally, giving them a more nuanced understanding of the realities of slavery enables them to see the dynamic of control and resistance that Jacobs frequently invokes.[1] For example, Jacobs's resistance directly counters Dr. Flint's attempts to control her with surveillance, sex, and literacy (27–28, 87). Furthermore, most white students conceive of slavery's violence as public whippings, not as private sexual assaults such as those Jacobs endures.[2] Because Jacobs directly addresses it, the gendered reality of slavery's violence necessitates an explanation of the cult of true womanhood and how it was denied to Black women (35). Recognizing that the cult's ideal characteristics simply build upon what earlier texts present as desirable in female characters, students can engage in discussions of how audience shapes Jacobs's narrative. Discussions of audience can contextualize how *Incidents* employs the ideal's characteristics to elicit sympathy from her Northern white female readers within a larger framework of slave narratives as a genre; typically, students need an explanation of how slave narratives function as deliberately crafted rhetoric for a largely racist (even when abolitionist) audience.[3] Briefly explaining the context and tropes of slave narratives helps students understand Jacobs's rhetorical choices.

An overview of southern gothic literature's characteristics is the most important background information to give students. Having read several examples of the British gothic, they follow this explanation rather easily—simply transferring what they already know to a different geographic context, one with which they are more familiar. Correlating the characteristics of the southern gothic with literary devices helps student understanding. They can focus on the setting of the antebellum US South as historically situated in a plantation economy; the characters in relation to power, for example as tyrants (a recurring staple character in gothic fiction) or as survivors of others' abuses of power; the plot as driven by grotesque instances of violence, trauma, and abuse; the symbol of hauntings as a consequence of traumatic events; and the ironies of slavery as a perverted socioeconomic system.[4]

Asking students to list examples of each of these devices encourages them to engage in discussions. Some examples need more explanation than others, and some devices require more prompting than others; however, having students provide the lists ensures they have completed the reading, engages them in discussion, and empowers them as they take ownership of what we do in class.

Students begin by listing the concrete realities of the setting, which supports their engagement early in the unit. They typically focus on how Jacobs depicts the North and the South, highlighting the differences and similarities;

significantly, the main similarity is the gothic presence of tyranny in both regions. Jacobs disrupts regional distinctions and boundaries with her disillusioned depictions of the North and its complicity with the exploitative plantation economy of the South. Students employ the background information about slavery to contextualize Jacobs's examples of federal and state legislation that categorically denied enslaved people's human rights. For example, Jacobs describes how the Fugitive Slave Act reveals the United States' collusion with slavery's tyranny (160). This historical reality is personalized by Jacobs when she describes her and her children's experiences of living in the North—the humiliation of riding on a segregated train through the "Free States," the racism she encounters at Northern hotels, and the discrimination Benny faces at his apprenticeship. These examples of Northern racism and Southern slavery illustrate how tyranny is portrayed in gothic texts.

After identifying these regions as locations where abuses of power occur, students identify more specific spaces in the text as gothic in a particularly southern way. The hidden passage, rather than existing underneath a castle and leading to where a ghost is hiding, becomes the attic where Jacobs hides to escape enslavement and from which she haunts Flint; moreover, the attic's coffin-like quality and the indirect violence done to Jacobs's body while she hides there exemplify the grotesque consequences of slavery (106–07). The secrecy surrounding her hiding place, who knows about it and how that puts them in danger, is much more terrifying to students than a ghost living in an abandoned castle.

As with the features of the setting, students can simply list the characters; then, they can discuss what they know about each character, what each does in the reading for that day, what adjectives best describe each, and, most importantly, how each fits into a gothic framework. They, of course, spend more time discussing Jacobs (Linda) than any other character in the text. After the introductory lecture, they are able to discuss how the cult of true womanhood is denied to Jacobs. Central to this discussion is the sexual abuse Jacobs survives. Though unaccustomed to thinking about sexual assault in terms of power and control, students identify Dr. Flint as a gothic tyrant, enabling them to expand their conceptions of sexual violence. Indeed, they easily recognize Dr. Flint as a power-hungry tyrant bent on revenge (91). Additionally, emphasizing Flint's attempts to isolate Jacobs by putting her in a house of her own reveals their unequal power dynamics (48). Contextualizing Flint's abuse within the exploitation of slavery further illustrates the relationships between power and sexuality: Jacobs illustrates the tyranny of a system that denies women the privilege of picking their partners (or of legally marrying them) (49–51). In other words, Jacobs's objectification as an enslaved woman not only illustrates double jeopardy—the intersection of multiple forms of exploitation, in this case, Jacobs's exploitation as a Black person and as a woman—but also exemplifies the grotesque abuses of power in the southern gothic.

When using a gothic framework, some of the text's secondary characters tend to garner more attention than others. For instance, students, particularly white ones, are eager to discuss Mrs. Flint's cruelty because it surprises them; they find her neglect and emotional abuse of Jacobs horrifying as they grapple with the idea that white women can be tyrants, much as white men can. These students' interest in Mrs. Flint encourages close reading, demonstrating for them how less obviously gothic examples can contribute to their analyses. For similar reasons, the character that students are most anxious to talk about is Aunt Nancy. With a little prompting, they connect Nancy back to earlier discussions of the cult's ideals being categorically denied to enslaved Black women. Moreover, framing the extreme abuse Nancy endured as grotesque provides an opportunity to illustrate why Jacobs employs gothic tropes: the grotesque works to grab readers' attention even today. The violence in Jacobs's narrative reveals how the grotesque works in a way that British gothic texts do not and perhaps cannot. The traumatic violence of slavery is easily recognizable to students as something that exposes the extent of systemic exploitation. Moreover, the abuses of power under the system of slavery are more horrifying to them than those in British texts, because students see them as "real" and as "ours."

When helping students identify symbols, instructors may want to ask specific questions; however, using a southern gothic framework easily engages them in the discussion. For instance, students describe the text's "ghosts" before identifying them as symbols of slavery's trauma. As consequences of a painful past, the hauntings in slave narratives (and in southern literature, generally) tend to be historical rather than supernatural.[5] Underscoring the economic dimensions of slavery, Jacobs describes how the grave of a particularly violent enslaver is repeatedly opened up and plundered (43). The soil refuses to contain this wealthy tyrant's remains, demonstrating in a concrete way how traumas refuse to be repressed and, instead, return to haunt survivors. Significantly, Jacobs describes her personal traumas as "great shadows from the mournful past" that regularly return to her (135). One of the most intense hauntings Jacobs experiences is her guilt about having sex with Sands (51); she feels guilty for failing her grandmother's (and the cult of true womanhood's) expectation of chastity, but her feelings also highlight how sexual harassment and assault are traumatic experiences with long-term effects. Because she has sex with Sands to avoid being raped by Flint, the experience haunts her. Similarly, Jacobs expresses guilt for not spending enough time with her children—or failing to meet the expectation of maternity (80); however, her time with her children is limited because she is in hiding, trying to escape in order to free them, too. Thus, Jacobs ties both hauntings to the exploitation of slavery; she fails to meet the expectations of chastity and maternity because of her active resistance to Flint, in particular, and to her enslavement, in general. Students can contextualize these hauntings not only with the cult's ideals but also with slave codes' material realities. Systemic exploitation allows the trauma because the legal system offers Jacobs no protection from sexual assault, denies her the ability to marry, and prevents her from protecting her own children. The most conventional haunting in the text also demands to be historically contextualized; Jacobs hears her dead father's voice urging her to escape, combining historical and supernatural hauntings and highlighting for students that our nation continues to be haunted by its painful past (79).

Jacobs often portrays this painful past with irony; as with symbols, students may struggle with this device and need prompting with specific questions. The examples they tend to be most eager to discuss are Jacobs's portrayals of Christmas, death, and Christianity; significantly, her ironic portrayals illustrate how slavery's grotesque realities pervert the meaning of each. For the enslaved, Christmas signifies an impending sale of family members and thus a tearing apart of family units (100–01), while for many Christian students, the holiday entails celebrating with family and strengthening those bonds. Inverting their expectations, Jacobs impacts students by exemplifying the grotesqueness of the system. Similarly, Jacobs's presentation of death as preferable to slavery garners student attention; they are outraged by the circumstances leading to Jacobs's wish not only for her own death but also for that of her children (56, 70). Framing this sentiment with the southern gothic reminds students that the attitude is a product of an exploitative system rather than mental illness. Moreover, Jacobs's death wish illustrates how slavery grotesquely perverts even the most basic of human impulses. Finally, students easily identify Christian justifications for slavery as problematic; while they may not initially recognize Jacobs's use of religion in the narrative as irony, they see it as an abuse of power, which, because of the gothic framework, they are already looking for. They are eager to discuss the reverend who, hired by enslavers, admonishes the enslaved to obey their "earthly masters" as they do their "heavenly Master" (62). With such examples, Jacobs depicts how even religious institutions become perverted by the grotesque system of slavery. This situation prompts Jacobs's assertion to Flint that he doesn't allow her to live like a true Christian (67). Some students are troubled by this claim, as they may have difficulties distinguishing their faith from the institutions that oversee it, but reminding them that it illustrates Jacobs's struggle to live as a Christian in an un-Christian system further highlights slavery's tyranny. These examples also suggest a parallel between Jacobs's lack of access to Christian values and her lack of access to the cult of true womanhood's ideals; making this comparison enables students to connect multiple approaches to the text in a focused way.

Approaching *Incidents* as a southern gothic text is productive for both instructors and students. The gothic framework enriches the variety of ways the narrative can be interpreted and engages readers concretely and abstractly. Perhaps most importantly, the framework expands Jacobs's place in the American literary canon; while her text significantly portrays a gendered experience of slavery, it also demonstrates how African American women's voices impact and shape southern US literature in meaningful ways that are far too often overlooked.

NOTES

1. Many race theorists discuss resistance in this regard. Henry Louis Gates, Jr. (*Signifying Monkey*), bell hooks (*Ain't I a Woman*), and Patricia Hill Collins (*Black Feminist Thought*) contextualize the racial dynamic of control and resistance in US literature and history. Nell Irvin Painter (*Southern History*) and Lucinda MacKethan (*Daughters of Time*) analyze instances of resistance in Jacobs's text specifically; additionally, Frances Smith Foster's essay included in the Norton Critical Edition, "Resisting *Incidents*," discusses Jacobs's resistance.

2. Angela Davis (*Women, Race, and Class*) and bell hooks (*Ain't I a Woman*) describe this power dynamic and how it is impacted by both gender and race. Also, Deborah Gray White (*Ar'n't I a Woman?*) and Nell Irvin Painter (*Southern History*) detail the reality of sexual exploitation for enslaved women.

3. William Andrews (*To Tell a Free Story*), Houston Baker, and Henry Louis Gates, Jr. (*Signifying Monkey*) provide helpful frameworks for critically reading slave narratives as a genre. While the Norton Critical Edition includes an essay by Andrews, it approaches *Incidents* with a different, though equally helpful, focus (*Incidents* 365–80).

4. Though Jacobs's text is only briefly mentioned in them, *Approaches to Teaching Gothic Fiction* and *The Cambridge Companion to American Gothic* outline the characteristics of the overall genre (Hoeveler and Heller; Weinstock). Each also contains an essay relating the genre to slavery and race; see Jerrold E. Hogle's in the former (Hoeveler and Heller 215–22) and Ellen Weinauer's in the latter (Weinstock 85–98).

5. Several of the essays in *Haunted Bodies* express this sentiment; essays by Anne Goodwyn Jones and Anne Bradford Warner focus on Jacobs in particular (Jones and Donaldson 185–200, 201–19). While she applies the concept to twentieth-century southern women's literature, Patricia Yaegar's *Dirt and Desire* also employs a similar argument.

Health and Illness in *Incidents in the Life of a Slave Girl*

Josh Doty

In my experience, teachers and readers of Harriet Jacobs's *Incidents in the Life of a Slave Girl* are conversant with the racial, sexual, and political contexts of the narrative, but they are less aware of its medical contexts. I think this is a missed opportunity to explore topics central to the text—race, power, motherhood, bodily autonomy, and more—in ways that speak powerfully to current-day issues at the crux of race, gender, and medicine. These issues resonate with most students, but I have found that the students I teach at a Catholic liberal arts university with a strong social justice emphasis are especially eager for the chance to tie nineteenth-century literature to twenty-first-century social issues.

It is important for teachers to take the medical contexts of *Incidents* into consideration for at least two reasons, one having to do with the past and one having to do with the present. First, as scholars such as Paul Starr and Charles Rosenberg have shown, the middle decades of the nineteenth century were host to a stunning proliferation of medical concepts and practices, including homeopathy, hydrotherapy, the abstentious dietetics of health reformer Sylvester Graham, and the botanic medicine of herbalist Samuel Thomson. Practitioners of these forms of healing often disagreed with one another about how to conceptualize and treat illness, but they generally agreed in their opposition to the theories and practices of what they variously called allopathic or simply "regular" physicians. Today, medical historians describe allopathic methods as "heroic" medicine, not because they were heroically efficacious but because they involved rigorous treatments such as bloodletting, purging, and cupping to shock the body into health. At several points in *Incidents*, Jacobs narrates both herself and others practicing modes of healing alternative to allopathy and, in so doing, creates a powerful site for resistance against her enslaver, James Norcom, who was an allopathic physician. Teachers familiar with antebellum medical history will be able to connect Jacobs's depictions of health and illness to more commonly discussed themes such as sexual violence and the ideology of slavery.

Second, the connections among medicine, race, and gender are as relevant today as they have ever been. Teachers who wish to surface the powerful connections between *Incidents* and the Black Lives Matter movement can walk students through the historical links between racial health disparities in Jacobs's time and today. According to a 2019 report by the Centers for Disease Control and Prevention, African American women die of complications related to pregnancy at a rate three times that of white women (Petersen et al. 423). They are also roughly forty percent more likely to die of breast cancer than white women (Richardson et al. 1095). These stunning disparities, among many others, can be traced in part to nineteenth-century medical attitudes toward African American women, upon whose bodies the foundation of modern women's health was built. For instance, the Alabama physician James Marion Sims, widely considered the father of modern gynecology, developed surgical techniques for repairing vesicovaginal fistulas by performing surgical experiments on enslaved women. As Harriet A. Washington notes in her groundbreaking book *Medical Apartheid*, the subjects of these torturous experiments did not receive anesthesia, partly based on Sims's belief that they did not feel as much pain as white women; Sims's white patients received anesthesia (65). Similar beliefs persist today: according to recent research, African American women are still widely believed by physicians to be less sensitive to pain than are white women, resulting in significant racial disparities in pain management specifically and medical care generally. Understanding Jacobs's medical context and the ways she navigated that context allows teachers to draw resonant connections between the challenges she faced and those confronting African American women today.

In *Incidents*, Jacobs describes a continual struggle to gain control of her body, a challenge compounded by her identity as an enslaved African American woman and also because her enslaver was a physician notorious for the intensity of his medical treatments. Prevailing scholarship on Jacobs's depictions of medicine focuses on Norcom's immense cruelty, for good reason. As Mary Titus writes, the relationship between Jacobs and Norcom is of not only an enslaved person and an enslaver but also a patient and a doctor. Norcom therefore exercises two forms of power over Jacobs's body: that of legal ownership and that of medical expertise (199). Sarah L. Berry likewise points up the cruelty of Norcom's medical practices. Drawing on archival research, Berry uncovers how even by comparison with his allopathic colleagues in Edenton, North Carolina, Norcom administered unusually severe bleedings and purgings to his patients, including white women and children (6). He extended that severity to the people he enslaved, particularly Jacobs.

In one harrowing passage, Norcom visits Jacobs as she struggles through a difficult first pregnancy:

> For some weeks I was unable to leave my bed. I could not have any doctor but my master, and I would not have him sent for. At last, alarmed by my increasing illness, they [Jacobs's family] sent for him. I was very weak and nervous; and as soon as he entered the room, I began to scream. They told him my state was very critical. He had no wish to hasten me out of the world, and he withdrew. (55)

Berry draws our attention to Jacobs's statement that she "could not have any doctor but my master"; in other words, she is unable to exercise any degree of bodily autonomy and must, if she wishes to have medical care, suffer through Norcom's "extremely vigorous, non-palliative treatments" (12). She avoids seeing him by refusing to send for him, but he is her only choice for medical care. Berry also notes that Jacobs's family, by informing Norcom of her precarious state and instigating his departure, "affirmed their intimate knowledge of her condition over his professional knowledge" (12). However, this moment of resistance is short-lived. When Jacobs gives birth, her son, Joseph, whom she calls "Benjamin" in the narrative, is premature and weighs only four pounds. Jacobs's recovery is difficult—she "was a mere wreck of my former self," afflicted with "chills and fever" for a year—and Joseph himself "also was sickly" (55). Norcom continues to visit them, to "look after" their health, so he says, but he does not, Jacobs writes, "fail to remind me that my child was an addition to his stock of slaves" (55). By combining his medical visits with reminders of the enslaved status of those nominally under his care, Norcom makes explicit the connections between his medical mastery of the human body and his legal mastery of the bodies of enslaved persons.

After Jacobs continues to refuse Norcom's sexual advances, he and his wife, Mary, punish her by separating her from her children and sending her to a nearby plantation; she escapes and takes refuge in the home of a friend. When a search party looking for her draws near the house where she is hiding, the following scene ensues, which I quote at length to preserve its effect:

> I flew out of the house, and concealed myself in a thicket of bushes. There I remained in an agony of fear for two hours. Suddenly, a reptile of some kind seized my leg. In my fright, I struck a blow which loosened its hold, but I could not tell whether I had killed it; it was so dark, I could not see what it was; I only knew it was something cold and slimy. The pain I felt soon indicated that the bite was poisonous. I was compelled to leave my place of concealment, and I groped my way back into the house. The pain had become intense, and my friend was startled by my look of anguish. I asked her to prepare a poultice of warm ashes and vinegar, and I applied it to my leg, which was already much swollen. (85)

When I bring up this passage in class, students tend to focus on Jacobs's suffering and express their sadness that she does not receive what they consider to be effective medical care. I suggest that there might be another point to take away, and I work to highlight Jacobs's active role in her medical treatment. After she is bitten, she herself quickly determines that the bite is poisonous. And after retreating to her friend's house, Jacobs herself gives directions to "prepare a poultice of warm ashes and vinegar" (85). This passage conveys suffering, but it also conveys self-determination and agency.

Unfortunately, the poultice does not decrease the swelling in her leg even though it relieves her pain, so her friend "asked an old woman, who doctored among the slaves, what was good for the bite of a snake or a lizard. She told her to steep a dozen coppers in vinegar, over night, and apply the cankered vinegar to the inflamed part" (85). A footnote to these passages, written by Lydia Maria Child, editor of *Incidents*, claims that snake venom is "a powerful acid, and is counteracted by powerful alkalies, such as potash, ammonia, &c" (85). "The

Indians," she continues, "are accustomed to apply wet ashes, or plunge the limb into strong lye. White men, employed to lay out railroads in snaky places, often carry ammonia with them as an antidote" (85). This footnote offers many possibilities for discussion. I ask students what they think about how Child's footnote brings up the treatment first as a Native American practice and then as a white practice but not as an African American practice. We discuss how Jacobs's use of vinegar mixed with warm ashes complicates what Child writes about alkaline materials. And indeed, the cure prescribed by the old woman "who doctored among the slaves" isn't alkaline; because it also uses vinegar, it is acidic. The "cankered vinegar" may be a type of "vinegar nail," a general-purpose remedy used by many plantation owners, as the historian Herbert C. Covey notes, to treat both white and Black patients (35). Jacobs's self-treatment may easily be overlooked in the classroom, yet it seems significant that she sustains and treats this wound in the course of fleeing from men who seek to return her to slavery. In flight, poised between freedom and enslavement, Jacobs's medical choices affirm her self-determination.

After Jacobs's successful escape from Norcom's household, she hides in her grandmother's attic for seven years. Only a thin roof protects her from exposure to North Carolina's humid summers and bracing winters, and during her second winter in hiding, the cold lays her low: "My limbs were benumbed by inaction, and the cold filled them with cramp. I had a very painful sensation of coldness in my head; even my face and tongue stiffened, and I lost the power of speech. Of course it was impossible, under the circumstances, to summon any physician. My brother William came and did all he could for me" (103–04). Despite William's efforts, Jacobs loses consciousness, experiences delirium, and lies in bed "six weeks, weary in body and sick at heart" (104). Earlier in *Incidents*, she relates that Norcom taught William the basic repertoire of heroic medicine: "William was a bright lad, and of much use to the doctor. He had learned to put up medicines, to leech, cup, and bleed" (55). That he "did all he could for me" to no avail illustrates the failure of Norcom's methods to heal her. She experiences some relief after "William finally went to a Thompsonian doctor, and described himself as having all my pains and aches" (104).[1] The Thomsonian remedy "did me some good," she writes, although her recovery was "very slow" (104). Covey notes that Thomsonian medicine, named after the health reformer Samuel Thomson, was an eminent system of popular medicine in the antebellum South (20). Thomsonian medicine posits too-low internal body temperature as the source of all disease; its methods therefore seek to raise the body temperature, usually through the consumption of *Lobelia inflata*, an herb also known as "puke weed" for its emetic effects, but also through steam baths and the consumption of chili powder steeped into a tea.

Giving students even a small amount of information about Thomsonian medicine allows for a discussion of how Jacobs's description of her illness and her frank assessment of her treatment's efficacy suggests her knowledge of Thomsonian medical principles. That Jacobs frames her affliction as one brought about by the frigid North Carolina winter—"My limbs were benumbed by inaction, and the cold filled them with cramp"—situates her not only as the passive recipient of Thomsonian treatment but as a knowledgeable patient able to discern the principles behind the medicine she takes. In class, I often note that she exemplifies the advice Thomson gives in his medical treatise *New Guide to Health; or, Botanic Family Physician*, many editions of which were published throughout the antebellum decades: "Pray for your own soul, if you know what it is, doctor your own body, and make your own will" (145). By doctoring her own body, Jacobs gives expression to her will. Ultimately, her narrative not only critiques Norcom's methods but also affirms alternate medical systems predicated upon her ability to know her body and participate in its care.

After a century of neglect and Jean Fagan Yellin's recovery of *Incidents*, Jacobs's narrative is now a staple in courses on American literature and African American literature, as it should be. But the narrative would be just as at-home in medical humanities courses—it offers lessons on race, gender, and medicine that are as timely as they are haunting. Crucially, *Incidents* also gives teachers an opportunity to discuss the means by which Jacobs asserted medical control over her own body. To facilitate this important discussion, an appendix to this essay compiles a list of sources on antebellum-era medicine and medicine as it is depicted in *Incidents*. Too often, classroom discussions focus on Jacobs's suffering in ways that risk overlooking her agency and occluding her intelligence and resourcefulness: foregrounding key moments of medical resistance in the narrative centers her personhood.

NOTE

1. Referring to Thomsonian medicine, Jacobs used the spelling "Thompsonian."

APPENDIX: SOURCES FOR FURTHER READING

There are many sources that would be useful to anyone who wishes to address the medical aspects of *Incidents in the Life of a Slave Girl* in the classroom. Each of the sources below addresses medicine as practiced by enslaved people or medicine as represented in *Incidents in the Life of a Slave Girl.*

Altschuler, Sari. *The Medical Imagination: Literature and Health in the Early United States.* U of Pennsylvania P, 2018.

Berry, Sarah L. "'[No] Doctor but My Master': Health Reform and Antislavery Rhetoric in Harriet Jacobs's *Incidents in the Life of a Slave Girl.*" *Journal of Medical Humanities*, vol. 35, no. 1, 2014, pp. 1–18.

Covey, Herbert C. *African American Slave Medicine: Herbal and Non-herbal Treatments.* Lexington Books, 2007.

Fett, Sharla. *Working Cures: Healing, Health, and Power on Southern Slave Plantations.* U of North Carolina P, 2000.

Mitchem, Stephanie Y. *African American Folk Healing.* New York UP, 2007.

Rosenberg, Charles. *The Cholera Years: The United States in 1832, 1849, and 1866.* U of Chicago P, 1962.

Rusert, Britt. *Fugitive Science: Empiricism and Freedom in Early African American Culture.* New York UP, 2017.

Schiebinger, Londa L. *Secret Cures of Slaves: People, Plants, and Medicine in the Eighteenth-Century Atlantic World.* Stanford UP, 2017.

Schuller, Kyla. *The Biopolitics of Feeling: Race, Sex, and Science in the Nineteenth Century.* Duke UP, 2017.

Starr, Paul. *The Social Transformation of American Medicine: The Rise of a Sovereign Profession and the Making of a Vast Industry.* Basic Books, 2008.

Stone, Andrea. *Black Well-Being: Health and Selfhood in Antebellum Black Literature.* U of Florida P, 2016.

Titus, Mary. "'This Poisonous System': Social Ills, Bodily Ills, and *Incidents in the Life of a Slave Girl.*" *Harriet Jacobs and* Incidents in the Life of a Slave Girl*: New Critical Essays,* edited by Deborah M. Garfield and Rafia Zafar, Cambridge UP, 1996, pp. 199–215.

Washington, Harriet A. *Medical Apartheid: The Dark History of Medical Experimentation on Black Americans from Colonial Times to the Present.* Doubleday, 2007.

Blind Doctors of Divinity: Theological Concepts in *Incidents in the Life of a Slave Girl*

Clark Moreland and Abbey Whigham

In the eulogy delivered for his friend Harriet Jacobs, the Reverend Francis J. Grimké offered conventional praise for a woman of the Victorian age: she was a "wonderfully sympathetic" and generous woman who "never hesitated to share what she had with others, to deny herself for the sake of helping a suffering fellow creature." Yet he also hints at a side of Jacobs's character that hardly befits an Angel in the House: "She did her own thinking," Grimké reflected, "had opinions of her own, and held to them with great tenacity." He wryly observed that Jacobs "had great will power" and "knew how to say, No, when it was necessary." Nevertheless, he summed up her character by paraphrasing a familiar scriptural passage: "The very Spirit of the Lord was upon her, that Spirit to which the prophet referred when he said: 'The spirit of the Lord God is upon me, because he hath sent me to bind up the broken hearted; to comfort all that mourn; to give unto them beauty for ashes, the oil of joy for mourning, the garment of praise for the spirit of heaviness'" (Yellin, *Harriet Jacobs Family Papers* 2: 898). Grimké's parishioners at the Fifteenth Street Presbyterian Church would likely have recognized his allusion to Isaiah 61 (King James Version). They may have also remembered Jesus's quotation of the passage at the beginning of his Galilean ministry in Luke 4, where he identified himself as the fulfillment of Isaiah's messianic prophecy. Yet those who were not closely attending to Grimké's eulogy may have missed a striking omission from the first verse of Isaiah 61: "The Spirit of the Lord God is upon me; because the Lord hath *anointed me to preach* good tidings unto the meek" (*Holy Bible*; our emphasis). Perhaps the minister known as the "Black Puritan" of Washington, DC (Smyth 35), felt that it was inappropriate to quote that portion of the text in reference to a woman, even his friend whom he had known and ministered to for nearly thirty years.

Yet Grimké is not alone. Despite the fact that Harriet Jacobs had a deep and persistent interest in theology and spirituality, most readers today focus on other facets of her masterpiece, *Incidents in the Life of a Slave Girl*. Ever since Jean Fagan Yellin's groundbreaking demonstration of the authorial authenticity of Jacobs's slave narrative in the 1980s, scholars have often focused on the ways in which *Incidents* departs from the conventional parameters of the slave narrative genre, its "emphasis on family and collective action" as opposed to individualism (Zafar 7), and, most commonly, its unflinching portrayal of the systemic and intersectional violence inflicted on Black women's bodies in America. Deborah M. Garfield and Rafia Zafar's collection of essays on *Incidents*, published in 1996, set out to "contextualize both the historical figure of Harriet Jacobs and her autobiography as a created work of art" (Zafar 7), but the volume makes only a few passing mentions of how Jacobs's religious views inform her narrative. The scholarly criticism included in Frances Smith Foster and Richard Yarborough's Norton Critical Edition of *Incidents* is even less observant of Jacobs's theological perspectives, even as the narrative itself includes, in almost every chapter, existential musings about God, sin, religious hypocrisy, the existence of evil, the ultimate meaning of suffering, and forgiveness. Chapter 13 in particular—"The Church and Slavery"—boldly asks, "Are doctors of divinity blind" to the horrors of slavery and institutional racism, "or are they hypocrites?" (66). In her blistering indictment of religious hypocrisy, she spares neither Southern ministers like "the sanctimonious Mr. Pike" (62), the rector of St. Paul's Episcopal Church, who at the behest of enslavers like Dr. James Norcom (Dr. Flint) rebuked enslaved people for their rebelliousness, nor Northern clergy who blithely claimed that enslaved people were content to "have hallelujah meetings, and other religious privileges," ignoring the cries of mothers whose children were torn from their arms or of "young girls dragged down into moral filth" (66). This chapter tracks closely to the indictments against the "Christianity of the Land" found in the celebrated appendix to the *Narrative of the Life of Frederick Douglass.*

Yet instructors are often disheartened to find that while collegiate literary anthologies include the entirety of Douglass's book, Jacobs's work is often anthologized piecemeal, and chapters such as "The Church and Slavery" are hardly ever included. The six or seven chapters typically selected by editors tend to focus more explicitly on the psychosexual abuse that Jacobs and other women in bondage faced but do not allow students to see how Jacobs's deep interest in religion and theology are informed by these experiences. But enterprising teachers and readers of her entire autobiography may discover that Jacobs was fascinated by theological concepts such as hamartiology (the study of sin, whether at an individual, social, or systemic level), theodicy (the study of why sin and evil exist, especially in theologies where God is assumed to be omnipotent and omnibenevolent), and forgiveness (the theological study of forgiveness and repentance of sin). Students in American literature courses are often exposed to the religious writings of the Puritans, the evangelical preachers of the Great Awakening, and abolitionist preachers such as Douglass, yet we fear students are largely unaware that women writers, particularly women of color such as Jacobs, also engaged profoundly with religious themes in ways that remain relevant today.

In *Approaches to Teaching* Narrative of the Life of Frederick Douglass, John Ernest describes how he couples Jacobs's *Incidents* with Douglass in order to decenter conventional frameworks and student responses to slave narratives. Likewise, the teaching strategies described below not only help students gain expertise on theological concepts but also challenge their preconceived notions of what theology is and who a theologian can be. The purpose of these workshops is not to indoctrinate students but rather to broaden their understanding of the theological concepts that inform and shape our understanding of Jacobs's work while also decentering theology itself as the magisterium exclusively regulated by white men. Simply put, we seek to help students see Harriet Jacobs as a theologian, a doctor of divinity whose prophetic preaching, long denied, deserves to be heard.

Though there are numerous passages in *Incidents in the Life of a Slave Girl* that touch upon theological and spiritual issues, we focus on five chapters where Jacobs extensively discusses theological concepts. In chapter 1 ("Childhood"), Jacobs mourns Margaret Horniblow's decision not to free her in her will, which Jacobs argues was the result of Horniblow's disobedience of Jesus's Great Commandment to "love thy neighbor as thyself" (11). Chapter 10 ("A Perilous Passage in the Slave Girl's Life"), which describes her relationship with Mr. Sands and the "sorrow and shame" she felt as a result, is one of the more talked about chapters of *Incidents* and contains interesting meditations on the nature of structural or systemic sin. Next we assign two chapters not anthologized in our course textbook (*The Norton Anthology of American Literature*): chapter 13 ("The Church and Slavery"), described above, and chapter 23 ("Still in Prison"), a powerful passage from Jacobs's second year of hiding in her grandmother's attic, where, under extreme physical duress, she entertains "dark thoughts" about divine justice and the meaning of her suffering (104). Finally, we ask students to closely read chapter 41 ("Free at Last"), where Jacobs not only wrestles with whether she can forgive Dr. Norcom, as her grandmother had seemingly done (161–62), but also confesses to thinking "black and bitter thoughts" on a Sabbath day about the cowardice and hypocrisy of Northern ministers who failed to preach against the injustices of the Fugitive Slave Act.

For the purposes of the workshop we describe below, which was originally designed for an introductory survey course of American literature at a public, regional comprehensive, Hispanic-serving institution, we typically use an active learning strategy called a jigsaw group discussion, an independent learning activity developed by Elliot Aronson that helps students develop expertise in a particular field and then share it with classmates (www.jigsaw.org). As Deborah Shapiro and Joseph Cuseo note, jigsaw groups allow students to become educational resources for their classmates and decenter the instructor as the sole authority and source of information (115). In this case, we ask students to develop expertise in a particular branch of theology and then bring that expertise to bear as they explain to classmates how Jacobs's theological views conform to, undermine, or otherwise compare to various theological viewpoints. Initially, all students are asked to read the five chapters from *Incidents* noted above. Next, a few days prior to the workshop, students are individually assigned one or two short theological readings (less than two thousand words) that address subjects that Jacobs was interested in: hamartiology, theodicy, and forgiveness. These readings were selected for their relevance to Jacobs's own exploration of these theological concepts as well as their suitability for a sophomore literature survey course; readings can be expanded or varied depending on students' reading level and familiarity with theology. We include a wide variety of readings from the ancient to the modern world, including readings that postdate Jacobs's book. We also assign a few readings from outside the Christian tradition (such as those from Hindu, Islamic, and Jewish theologies). Nevertheless, the readings below are merely a starting point and can easily be traded out for other texts more suitable to the reading level, academic discipline, or size of the class.

Hamartiology Readings

Thomas Aquinas, *Summa Theologiæ* (II-II, q. 79, a. 4)
Kenneth Himes, "Social Sin and the Role of the Individual"
Old Testament, Amos 5–6 and Isaiah 58
New Testament, John 8, 1 Corinthians 6, and James 2
Walter Rauschenbusch, "The Social Gospel and the Atonement" (from *A Theology for the Social Gospel*)
Upanishads, Taittiriya-Upanishad (Third Brahmana, 1–10 [*Upanishads* 78–80])

Theodicy Readings

Augustine, *Enchiridion* (9–10, 12, 23, and 26–27)
Zachary Braiterman, "Three Theodicies in Modern Jewish Thought" (from *(God) after Auschwitz*)
Martin Luther King, Jr., "Love in Action" (from *Strength to Love*)
C. S. Lewis, "Human Pain" (from *The Problem of Pain*)
Old Testament, Job 3
Frances E. Wood, "Take My Yoke upon You" (from *A Troubling in My Soul*)

Forgiveness Readings

Stacey Floyd-Thomas and Juan Floyd-Thomas, "Patchwork Redemption: Suffering and Joy in Racial Perspective" (podcast)
Mohandas Gandhi, "The Gita and Satyagraha"
New Testament, Luke 6.27–38
Qur'an 42.29–43
David Remnick, "Blood at the Root" (*The New Yorker*)
Howard Thurman, *Jesus and the Disinherited* (chapter 5)

The day of the workshop, we begin by gathering students into "home groups," where they summarize the chapters and identify specific passages where theological concepts (i.e., hamartiology, theodicy, and forgiveness) are addressed by Jacobs. Then we redistribute the class into "expert groups," where they share about the theology texts they selected, compare notes, and ask questions about how the readings compare to each other. This may seem a daunting task, considering that most students have never encountered theological readings in an academic setting, at least outside their communities' traditions or values. However, we find that students pick up quickly on the similarities and differences and need minimal contextualization beyond an occasional footnote to support students who are unfamiliar with philosophical terminology (for instance, when

Aquinas makes an Aristotelian distinction between contradiction and contrariety). To conclude the workshop, students are reassembled into their home groups, and the group answers questions on how Jacobs's statements on certain theological subjects compare to others across time and culture.

Often, students are quick to pick up on how closely Jacobs aligns with hamartiologies that emphasize the social as well as the individual nature of sin. "I knew what I did, and I did it with deliberate calculation," Jacobs says of her relationship with Mr. Sands, but she is quick to remind Northern white women that they were "free to choose the objects of [their] affection" and therefore should not judge her too harshly (49). "I wanted to keep myself pure," she says mournfully, but "the condition of a slave confuses all principles of morality, and, in fact, renders the practice of them impossible" (50). She also is careful to inform Dr. Flint that though she feels she has "sinned against God and myself," she has not sinned against *him* (53). Jacobs's simultaneous recognition of her individual culpability and the social and systemic conditions that prevented her from making moral choices compares to Aquinas's distinction between sins of commission and those of omission, to Rauschenbusch's conception of the "kingdom of evil" (256), or to Langdon Gilkey's argument that any explanation of sin that "ignores or explains away either side—the fateful and the tragic or the free and responsible side—will in the end prove both unempirical and inconsistent" (124). Likewise, Jacobs's justification for running away from Dr. Flint prefigures the arguments of Howard Thurman, who says that there are "times when to tell the truth is to be false to the truth that is in you" (52). And of course, Jacobs draws upon the prophetic judgments of Amos, Isaiah, and James when she condemns the hypocrisy of Southern religious institutions (67) as well as the cowardly failure of Northern churches to protect fugitives from slavery from the Fugitive Slave Act (164). "No wonder," Jacobs concludes, "the slaves sing,—'Ole Satan's church is here below; Up to God's free church I hope to go" (67).

However, Jacobs also wrestled with questions of divine justice and human pain. In a letter to Amy Post in March 1857, she writes, "When I see the evil that is spreading throughout the land my whole soul sickens. . . . I am almost ready to exclaim—where dwells that just Father—whom I love and in whom I believe . . . is his arm shortened—is his power Weakened" (Yellin, *Harriet Jacobs Family Papers* 1: 232–33). In one particularly moving section of chapter 23 that is not often anthologized, Jacobs recalls her second winter in hiding, where she suffered debilitating numbness in her limbs, lost the power to speak, and eventually became so delirious with fever that her family worried she might die. Since she was unable to seek medical treatment on her own, her brother returned with herbal remedies and ointments, which helped her slowly recover, but meanwhile,

> [d]ark thoughts passed through my mind as I lay there day after day. I tried to be thankful for my little cell, dismal as it was, and even to love it, as

> part of the price I had paid for the redemption of my children. Sometimes I thought God was a compassionate Father, who would forgive my sins for the sake of my sufferings. At other times, it seemed to me there was no justice or mercy in the divine government. I asked why the curse of slavery was permitted to exist, and why I had been so persecuted and wronged from youth upward. These things took the shape of mystery, which is to this day not so clear to my soul as I trust it will be hereafter. (104)

Jacobs's theodicean crisis resonates deeply with students who have similarly asked why an omnibenevolent and omnipotent deity could allow the evils and suffering that occurred under slavery, or during the Holocaust, or more recently in the era of the coronavirus pandemic. The more conventional explanations provided by Augustine and Lewis, which tend to take a Western and abstract view of the "problem of pain," also tend to fall flat when set against Jacobs's lament. Instead, students see her adhering more closely to King's humble confession in *Strength to Love*: "I do not pretend to understand all of the ways of God and his particular timetable in grappling with evil" (83). Similarly, they are excited to read womanist theologians like Francis E. Wood and M. Shawn Copeland who critique theological idealizations of suffering, positing instead a theology of suffering that "is rooted in and draws on black women's accounts of pain and anguish, of their individual and collective struggle to grasp and manage, rather than be managed by their suffering" (Copeland 39).

Critically, it is important for students not to miss the final lines of this passage: though, like King, Jacobs confesses that her suffering has taken "the shape of mystery," which "is to this day not so clear to my soul," she hopes and trusts that it will be made clear later (104). Just as King says that "the Kingdom of God as a universal reality is *not yet*" and as Job remains convinced that even through intense suffering, "I know that my redeemer liveth . . . yet in my flesh shall I see God" (*Holy Bible*, Job 19.25–26), so Jacobs retains hope that she will one day understand why she had to endure suffering. Hers is not an anti-theodicy, a term coined by the Jewish theologian Zachary Braiterman, as much as it is a *not-yet-theodicy*. Jacobs confirms elsewhere in the book her abiding belief in God's providence (25, 89, 131) even as she resists any "ersatz spiritualization of evil and suffering, of pain and oppression" (Copeland 44). "The dream of my life is not yet realized," she plaintively concludes, "but God so orders circumstances" as to provide her with friends like Mrs. Bruce to help her continue her struggle (167). Like another dreamer who wished to "hew out of the mountain of despair a stone of hope" (King, "I" 186), Jacobs ultimately waives aside the question of why God allows suffering, choosing instead to believe that "as we struggle to defeat the forces of evil, the God of the universe struggles with us" (King, *Strength* 83).

Struggle and resistance are also key to understanding Jacobs's theology of forgiveness. Students who read the divine injunctions found in the New Testament and the Qur'an to forgive one's enemies look to Jacobs's grandmother Molly Horniblow (aka Aunt Martha) as an example of loving and forgiving one's enemies

(Luke 6.27). Jacobs herself often stands in awe of her grandmother's piety and sympathy for even someone as deplorable as Dr. Flint. When she delivers the news of his death, she calls him a "poor old man," hoping that he had "made his peace with God" (162). But where her grandmother offers pity for Dr. Flint, Jacobs says she cannot "entirely forgive him. . . . There are wrongs which even the grave does not bury. The man was odious to me while he lived, and his memory is odious now" (162). At this point, it is understandable for some students to jump to the conclusion that Jacobs has rejected forgiveness as a virtue or has contradicted the Christian faith she had confessed a few pages before (153).

Here we direct students back to chapter 10, where Jacobs confesses her sexual liaison with Mr. Sands to her grandmother. After Aunt Martha's initial reproach of Jacobs (which was based on misinformation supplied by Mrs. Flint), she returns to Jacobs and

> listened in silence. I told her I would bear anything and do anything, if in time I had hopes of obtaining her forgiveness. I begged of her to pity me, for my dead mother's sake. And she did pity me. She did not say, "I forgive you;" but she looked at me lovingly, with her eyes full of tears. She laid her old hand gently on my head, and murmured, "Poor child! Poor child!" (52)

There are several ways to read the grandmother's words: Does she merely mean to pity her granddaughter in the same way that she pitied Dr. Flint upon his death? Does she offer forgiveness? Or does she realize the truth of what her son Joseph (Benjamin) said, that slavery makes people forget there is a God (23), or what Jacobs herself said about how it "confuses all principles of morality" (50)? In the case of Joseph, Aunt Martha says in response to his request for forgiveness for running away from bondage that "she had nothing to forgive; she could not blame his desire for freedom" (23); was she saying something similar to her granddaughter? It is unclear, but Jacobs does occasionally problematize her grandmother's appeals to Joseph and Harriet to forgive their white enslavers, who have so deeply traumatized and wronged them. Joseph in particular expresses rage at Martha's suggestion of humbling himself before his enslaver and requesting his forgiveness: "Forgive me for *what*, mother? For not letting him treat me like a dog? No!" (23).

Yet we remind students at this point in the workshop that Jacobs does not reject forgiveness as much as aspire to it. Benjamin and Harriet both view the grandmother as a hero and a paragon of goodness. Likewise, Jacobs admires the sweet spirit of Uncle Fred, the old Black man whom she teaches to read the New Testament and "whose piety and childlike trust in God were beautiful to witness" (65). Having noted that after only six months of instruction he had read the entire New Testament, she delivers a prophetic message for those who would seek to exploit the gospel message to keep Black people in bondage: "Tell them that they are answerable to God for sealing up the Fountain of Life from souls that are thirsting for it" (66). This is reminiscent of Thurman's argument that forgiveness is not only a work of grace and humility but also a demonstration of one's belief that ultimately "the evildoer does not go unpunished," for "[v]engeance is mine; and I will repay saith the Lord" (98). Forgiveness, seen in this light, is less about carrying a burden than it is about letting that burden go. As James Cone, a founder of Black liberation theology, eloquently described in the aftermath of the shooting at the Emanuel African Methodist Episcopal Church in 2015, forgiveness is a key doctrine in the Black church: "it is a form of resistance, a kind of resilience. It is not bowing down." In a culture that actively seeks to destroy both the bodies and the souls of Black people, Jacobs's grandmother not only outlived Dr. Norcom but also retained her spiritual purity, Jacobs writes, and was rewarded at her death with being able to go "where the wicked cease from troubling, and the weary are at rest" (166). Her resistance and resilience grew out of her forgiving spirit.

The previous time we offered this workshop, we concluded by asking students to watch a video of Brandt Jean offering forgiveness to the white Dallas police officer who murdered his brother, Botham. At the sentencing hearing for the officer, who received ten years in prison for the crime, Botham says from the witness stand, "If you truly are sorry, I can speak for myself, I forgive, and I know if you go to God and ask him, he will forgive you." His words and subsequent request to hug his brother's murderer sparked conversation across the nation about the meaning of forgiveness. Some praised Jean for his stunning offer of forgiveness, but others such as Cornell Brooks argued that even though Jean was entitled to forgive as he saw fit, "using the willingness of Black people to forgive as an excuse to further victimize Black people is SINFUL" (Chappell and Gonzales). Likewise, after the Charleston shooting, some Black Lives Matter activists in that community were concerned that Black people's forgiveness for white supremacist violence amounted to "political masochism" that was more about "accommodating white feelings and white superiority" (Remnick). These perspectives were shared with students, who engaged in a thoughtful and stirring conversation, which continued into the hallway long after the class concluded.

Harriet Jacobs was front and center in that conversation, and that is where she belongs. Though scholars have only recently begun to recognize the theological depth and profundity of Jacobs's writings (Allen; Grendler et al.; Martin; Taves), students remain largely under the assumption that theology is predominantly the concern of ivory-towered men, "blind doctors of divinity" who are far removed from the realities they experience. But it is time that Jacobs is heard and seen for what she is: a theologian, squarely in the prophetic tradition of the Black church and a precursor to womanist theology in the twentieth century. The title page of *Incidents in the Life of a Slave Girl*, which famously omitted Jacobs's name, quotes from Isaiah 32.9: "Rise up, ye women that are at ease! Hear my voice, ye careless daughters! Give ear unto my speech." By giving ear to Jacobs's theological views, we are inviting students to heed the call of a long-neglected prophet whose time of anointing has finally come.

INTERTEXTUAL APPROACHES

An Interdisciplinary Approach to *Incidents in the Life of a Slave Girl*

Eric Sterling

I teach Harriet Jacobs's *Incidents in the Life of a Slave Girl* in two of my courses, a sophomore-level class titled Survey of American Literature and my graduate-level Tragedy, Horror, and Genocide class. Depending on the semester, I teach these courses in the classroom or online. In both courses, I pair Jacobs's poignant memoir with William Wells Brown's *Narrative of William W. Brown, a Fugitive Slave, Written by Himself* (1847). I bring together these two important slave narratives partly so that I may teach Jacobs's memoir in regard to gender and other issues that relate to slavery. One of my goals in the survey course and graduate class is to make the sections of the syllabus meaningful to my students. Over the past several years, more than half of the incoming freshman class at my university has consisted of African Americans. The reasons for the significant increase in African American students include a strong focus on the university's recruitment and retention of Black students, a public school system that is nearly eighty percent African American ("Montgomery Public Schools"), a city that is predominantly Black and that has seen the exodus of many white people, the recent election of the city's first Black mayor, a Black majority on the city council, and the creation of many civil rights memorials. In fact, Auburn University, Montgomery, is annually recognized by *US News and World Report* for having a diverse student body. Many of our African American students are interested in knowing more about their heritage, including such topics as Black Lives Matter, racism, and slavery. They see a connection between their present lives and the past, particularly in the lack they experience by comparison with the educational and socioeconomic opportunities afforded to white citizens because of race. The Montgomery County public schools are still racially segregated today—not legally segregated, of course, but the separation is unmistakable.

I used backward design when envisioning the classes, particularly the graduate course. Rather than creating my syllabus and then looking at learning objectives and assessment, I began by contemplating my desired results and class outcomes for the students and then decided what path would allow me to achieve these goals. I wanted the students to learn more than simply what the texts had to offer and to extend the learning boundaries far beyond literary interpretation. The graduate class is required to have an interdisciplinary approach, as stated in the university catalog. It is insufficient for my students to read *Incidents in the Life of a Slave Girl* and then discuss the memoir in the classroom or on the *Blackboard* discussion boards, because they would merely be reading the text in a vacuum, without knowledge of the historical and cultural context or an understanding of how the work pertains to current societal issues. I want them to do more than read as they learn background and cultural information pertaining to Jacobs's memoir. Students, for instance, listen to enslaved people's hymns such as Ed Lewis's "I Be So Glad . . . When the Sun Goes Down" ("I Be So Glad"). The hymns create a somber and empathetic mood in class, help students comprehend how music comforted and inspired enslaved people, and bring emotion to the forefront.

I show my students a photo of the "wanted" poster that James Norcom (Flint in the text) advertised ("Harriet Jacobs Wanted Poster"). After Jacobs escaped in 1835, he created a poster offering a $100 reward (equivalent to about $3,489 in 2023) for the "apprehension and delivery of my Servant Girl, HARRIET," which indicates how much her services and body were worth to him financially. Norcom's poster claimed that Harriet was an eloquent speaker and that since she often wore fine clothing, she might be "tricked out in gay and fashionable finery." This is an unusual description of an enslaved person. Norcom's poster states that Jacob escaped "without any known cause or provocation," suggesting that he did not consider his incessant sexual harassment, his physical and emotional abuse, or her desire as a human being to be free to be legitimate reasons to escape. However, another interpretation is that Norcom was fully cognizant of his sexual abuse and the emotional pain that he caused Jacobs but did not want to reveal to the public—his neighbors in particular—that his lechery might have incited her escape. The poster concludes with a threat against anyone who might aid her escape. Viewing the poster, which Norcom circulated throughout North Carolina, provides students with a sense of the terror she experienced. Because my university has many African American students, many of the students in my class can identify with the fear of being hurt or killed, having felt unsafe while walking the streets, particularly after a Montgomery policeman fatally shot Greg Gunn, an unarmed Black man, in 2016. Furthermore, students note, among other ideas, that the enslaver refers to Jacobs as "my Servant Girl," indicating that he considers her a mere possession, like a farm tool on the plantation. My students and I talk about why Norcom listed the reward for her capture at $100, such as the value of her labor and how much he could perhaps acquire if he sold her. This brings us to a discussion of slavery as an economic and capitalistic enterprise. I could simply mention the poster in class, but it would not provide my students with the same effect as their seeing it.

I show my students slavery art to provide them with visual representations of the human cruelty that the victims endured. For instance, combining visual images with psychology, the students and I discuss the art of the British painter Eyre Crowe, who attended a slave auction on 3 March 1853 in Richmond, Virginia (Crowe 130–36). Crowe created a painting he titled *Slaves Waiting for Sale: Richmond, Virginia*. Fifteen enslaved people were supposed to be auctioned, but when Crowe arrived and started drawing sketches of the sale of the human beings (he labeled it "the stifling atmosphere of human traffic"), the traders and prospective buyers, realizing that an artist was drawing their faces and that they could thereby be identified, became so embarrassed that they refused to purchase any enslaved people. The interruption of this sale of human beings and capitalistic enterprise infuriated the auctioneer and traders—one of whom offered to pay an enslaved person $25 to literally kick Crowe out of the area so that he could not draw pictures of the auction (136). I show my students the results of Crowe's art (wood engravings and oil paintings) but also expect them to tell me why people would consider it acceptable to purchase enslaved people except when being drawn by an artist. Students ponder why enslavers considered slavery acceptable in their society but were frightened by the notoriety they would have received had their portraits been made public: Is it possible that they did not justify slavery inwardly as they did publicly? Students explore this matter in class discussion, in groups, or in essays.

Gender is a crucial theme in Jacobs's work, and students can acquire greater insight into the text by comparing and contrasting it with a male narrative voice and perspective. My students agree with me that gender plays an integral role in the memoir, because Jacobs stresses that the hardships faced by enslaved women were intense and more difficult than tribulations encountered by enslaved men, for women were raped and aggressively coerced into having sex with male enslavers. Furthermore, enslaved women carried their babies for nine months during their pregnancies, creating a strong maternal bond that led to gut-wrenching heartbreak when their babies grew up and were considered the landowners' property rather than belonging to their own mother. The plantation owners often traded away the children to other enslavers, thus separating mothers from the children they gave birth to and raised, perhaps forever. In fact, Flint implies to Jacobs in chapter 15 that her children are not only enslaved but also hostages who will be freed only if she succumbs to his sexual advances. Students point out that although Brown escapes to Canada, he has no children, unlike Jacobs, who initially decides not to escape because of her responsibility to her children. My students devote significant time to discussing Jacobs as a loving mother who feels great pain for being prevented from bonding or communicating with her children, even when they live in the same house.

Part of Jacobs's purpose in writing and publishing her memoir was to draw attention to the often overlooked plight of enslaved women. To familiarize themselves with Jacobs's text, students locate passages that support her argument that enslaved women encountered more tribulations than enslaved men. They point to the passage in which she laments that Flint "peopled my young mind with unclean images, such as only a vile monster could think of. I turned from him with disgust and hatred. But he was my master. I was compelled to live under the same roof with him" (27). They also focus on the passage when Flint informs her that he intends to build a shack for her in Louisiana, far from the watchful eyes of his jealous wife, and that she cannot to refuse to go there (38). My students realize that he intends to force her to have sex with him, with her relatives too far away to learn about her plight and intervene on her behalf. Students find sections where Jacobs mentions the hardships she faces: for example, when Flint, out of sexual jealousy, prevents her from marrying the man she loves, and when she agonizes over the knowledge that the baby she carried for nine months and gave birth to did not legally belong to her because she was enslaved. The law was called *partus sequitur ventrem*, a Latin phrase meaning "what is brought forth follows the belly," that is, children born to enslaved women were themselves born into slavery and legally belong to the enslaver. Noticing parallels between the two slave narratives, students point out that Brown mentions a beautiful quadroon woman named Cynthia, who was forced into a sexual relationship with Mr. Walker and could not use the legal system to protect herself, but they find Jacobs's account more poignant because of its emotional intensity and first-person point of view as opposed to Brown's more detached, secondhand, male perspective. Through this exploration, students learn about gender issues in regard to slavery and narrative theory.

I show my students Keith Krawczynski's powerful and shocking video about the Middle Passage, the punishment of the enslaved, the correlation between slavery and capitalism, and the American South's refusal to allow enslaved people to have recourse to the law ("American Slavery" [parts 1–7]). Krawczynski is an accomplished African American history specialist who teaches at Auburn University, Montgomery. We collaborate, allowing my students to learn about Jacobs and slavery from both literary and historical perspectives. It is important to show students perspectives from different media, so I show the video of Wining Boy's story about berries in August Wilson's *The Piano Lesson* to demonstrate the legal disenfranchisement of African Americans ("*Piano Lesson*" 30:24). I also show Doaker's poignant recitation of Sutter's trading an enslaved woman and her young son in exchange for a piano, to allow students to conceptualize, as best they can, the pain and suffering caused by the separation of enslaved families that permeates Jacobs's narrative. Students observe the suffering in Wilson's play as the wife is separated forever from her husband and traded for an inanimate object, a visual example of how slavery dehumanized and objectified human beings, a point that Jacobs alludes to frequently in her memoir.

When I break the students into groups, we use a flipped classroom whether in the classroom or asynchronously in an online class. If the class is online, I create a video with instructions, which works better than a long, detailed description: "Both the task and the team roles should ensure a collaborative, interdependent approach in which the positive contributions of each team member impact the success of the whole" (Darby 167). The online courses are effective in general and increase access for many students who cannot come to the classroom because of work or because they live in rural areas in Alabama's Black Belt. Robert John Robertson and Shannon Riggs note that "historically underserved students comprise many of the same student populations that online providers of higher education are trying to serve by bringing higher education to where they are. . . . [Thus,] promoting collaborative activities online is becoming more essential" (72). One group focuses on slavery as capitalism, with other students concentrating on the following topics: gender issues as they pertain to Jacobs's memoir; Jacobs's narrative style and voice; her love of men, her children, and her family; Christianity and slavery; and connections between her memoir and Brown's.

The group focusing on slavery as capitalism talks about the economic issues that led to and perpetuated slavery. I help them by showing them visual rhetoric, such as the aforementioned "wanted" poster of Harriet Jacobs when she escaped from Flint. The students who focus on capitalism invariably link this poster to the price paid for Jacobs's freedom in New York: they remind the class that Flint's daughter and her husband, Dodge, received $300 in exchange for Jacobs's freedom. The students point out that Flint and Dodge attribute a price to her, and there is an exchange of money for her life, particularly in light of Congress's passage of the Fugitive Slave Act of 1850, which many students know about from their American history classes. Students ponder whether the lack of legal recourse indirectly led to slavery-based capitalism, with slavery being a profit-based enterprise. Enslavers controlled a powerful workforce and imposed long hours of labor upon those whom they enslaved. They did not have to treat the enslaved people well, because enslaved people could not seek justice from police or judges, file a lawsuit, or change to another workplace of their choice. Many students also raise an objection to the word *employer*, since the enslavers paid no salaries. Plantation owners amassed large fortunes partly because of huge profit margins derived from not paying salaries to those whom they enslaved. They paid meager amounts of money for food and shelter, only enough to keep those whom they enslaved alive.

After the students meet in their groups, they report their conclusions to the class. Following each group's presentation, I open up that topic to the class for feedback and further conversation from the students in the other groups. The group work encourages the shy and quiet students, who don't enjoy speaking in front of the entire class, to speak freely in their small units, verbalizing their ideas to just a few people before sharing their opinions with the larger class. The group work leads to the formulation of a thesis and ultimately a paper.

Learning in the classroom can take students only so far. Fortunately, our campus is located in Montgomery, rightfully known as the cradle of the civil rights movement. Martin Luther King, Jr., preached in his church on Dexter Avenue; his church and home are only a few miles from campus. Several miles from campus, Rosa Parks refused to give up her seat to a white passenger, initiating the Montgomery bus boycott. There is the National Civil Rights Museum; the Southern Poverty Law Center, which offers many videos and lesson plans; the National Memorial for Peace and Justice dedicated to victims of lynching; and the Legacy Museum: From Enslavement to Mass Incarceration, which covers the history of slavery, lynchings, and racial segregation—the last of which is arguably still prevalent in the Deep South. The civil rights activist Bryan Stevenson created the Legacy Museum, which my students visit for a profound learning experience that correlates with their reading of Jacobs's text.[1] After our field trip to the Legacy Museum, one American Literature I sophomore student wrote in a reflection piece, "Before the impactful experiences of visiting the Legacy Museum and reading Jacobs' memoir, I never understood the extent of the cruelty, heartbreak, and emotional damage that many women faced when losing or being separated from their child." Yet another significant civil rights landmark, the Edmund Pettus Bridge—where Bloody Sunday occurred on 7 March 1965 and which links Montgomery to Selma—is located nearby. In the past, I have had students meet at one of these sites and write papers on how their learning experience there relates to Jacobs's slave narrative.

Across the street from where Rosa Parks boarded the bus to begin the Montgomery bus boycott stands the Court Square Fountain, the location where slave auctions were held in the nineteenth century. On 19 June 2020, the anniversary of 19 June 1865 (Juneteenth, the holiday commemorating the emancipation of enslaved people in the United States), members of the Montgomery community painted a beautiful and colorful Black Lives Matter mural around the fountain, transforming a site with tragic memories into a positive and hopeful work of art. The mural made national news and was featured on many media outlets, including the *Today* show ("Black Lives Matter Mural"). Now that the pandemic has subsided and regular classes have resumed, this mural will serve as a powerful teaching moment for my students. The mural is new, but the site shows students that less than two hundred years before, slave auctions were held at that location.

To learn about the living conditions and everyday life of Jacobs and other enslaved individuals, the class looks at the work of the historic preservationist Jobie Hill and her Saving Slave Houses Project database (www.savingslavehouses.org), in which she explores the living quarters of those enslaved in the nineteenth-century South. Hill considers it "vital for our national self-worth to give a voice to enslaved individuals and to recognize and present authentic and truthful accounts of slavery. Stories of enslaved people, told in part by the houses they inhabited, have the capacity to facilitate our nation's efforts to collectively move forward from the legacy of slavery" ("Slave House Preservation"). Students can learn much about how enslaved people lived in the states that allowed slavery, judging by the houses Hill explores. Jacobs writes in her memoir about going to her grandmother's house as well as the houses of other enslaved people. Seeing examples of such houses enables my students to visualize and better understand what Jacobs's living conditions were like. I also share with my students the work performed by historical and applied archaeologist Jodi Skipper of the University of Mississippi. Skipper deals with historical preservation and historical archaeology involving slave quarters of the nineteenth century. She has uncovered the houses of enslaved people and preserved the artifacts that she has found for museums so that they can be studied, enabling people to learn how enslaved people such as Jacobs ate, dressed, and lived their lives in the nineteenth-century South.

Breaking into groups and employing an interdisciplinary approach examining Jacobs's situation from literary, historical, political, sociological, and women's studies perspectives enables students not only to examine Jacobs's poignant memoir, which provides them with a wealth of information about how many enslaved women lived and suffered, but also to learn more by comparing and contrasting it with a narrative written by an enslaved man. Taking advantage of the rich cultural history memorialized in our city allows students to further contextualize Jacobs's story.

NOTE

1. The field trips to the Legacy Museum were made possible through the support of Grant 62339 from the John Templeton Foundation.

Truth and Fiction: *Incidents in the Life of a Slave Girl* and the Question of Genre

John Hay

The story of how *Incidents in the Life of a Slave Girl* came to be a staple of the college classroom informs our understanding of the text itself. Jean Fagan Yellin's archival work revealed to scholars that a publication long suspected to be a fiction penned by a white abolitionist was in fact a genuine memoir by an African American woman. By insisting on the "authenticity" of Harriet Jacobs's book, Yellin removed it from the generic sphere of the novel, claiming that her research had decisively "transformed" *Incidents* "from a questionable slave narrative into a well-documented pseudonymous autobiography" (qtd. in *Incidents* 213). Through her recovery scholarship, Yellin achieved two important goals. First, she conclusively identified Jacobs (and not Lydia Maria Child, or any other white writer) as the author of *Incidents*, a finding now universally acknowledged. Second, Yellin classified *Incidents* as factual rather than fictional, establishing "Linda Brent" as the pseudonym of (not a character invented by) Jacobs. The story, in other words, is true; only the names have been changed. Jacobs was the author of a slave narrative, not an antislavery novel. "What she has written is not fiction," declared Yellin (*Harriet Jacobs: A Life* 135).

The insistence that we view *Incidents* as a "pseudonymous autobiography" rather than as a novel harks back to its nineteenth-century context, specifically the concern among abolitionist publishers that fictional elements in slave narratives would destroy their authority and credibility. Because enslavers and their descendants wanted to view slave narratives as mere fictions, twentieth-century scholars had to work hard to verify the facticity of these valuable documents. But today in the twenty-first century, while endorsing the authentication of slave narratives, we might also promote the genre of early African American fiction—without suggesting that fiction somehow diminishes or impeaches the historical record.[1] The decade leading up to the American Civil War was, as scholars are increasingly discovering, a rich era for the development of the African American novel. William Wells Brown's *Clotel* (1853) is hailed as the first in the genre, and Harriet E. Wilson's *Our Nig* (1859) is now considered the first published novel by an African American woman. *The Bondwoman's Narrative*, a novel written by Hannah Bond in the late 1850s under the pen name Hannah Crafts but not published until 2002, has been recognized as another significant title from the period.

Scholars of early African American fiction have argued that the genre is characterized by ambiguity regarding what is factual and what is fictional. "The African American novel was extraordinarily fluid and unstable," notes Robert Levine, "wrestling with generic hybridity and racial and national uncertainties"

(271). Wilson's and Bond's novels in particular have been analyzed scrupulously for their great degree of factual accuracy—and thus for the light they shed on the actual historical conditions of their authors and of their time. *The Bondwoman's Narrative* is essentially an "autobiographical novel," and *Our Nig* has been praised as "a sophisticated hybrid of autobiography and prose fiction" (Gates, Introduction xcvii; Foreman, Introduction xxvi).

But the same observations about generic hybridity—especially regarding the relationship between memoir, travel narrative, and fiction—could be made of the American novel generally in the antebellum period. The most famous novel of the era, Harriet Beecher Stowe's *Uncle Tom's Cabin* (1852), was promoted for its special fidelity to true accounts of slavery. "It is not a fiction," wrote Stowe, but rather "a close wrought mosaic of facts" (qtd. in Diller 636). To emphasize this point, Stowe next authored a work of nonfiction, *A Key to* Uncle Tom's Cabin (1853), which was a compendium of factual anecdotes meant to reveal that her novel, "more, perhaps, than any other work of fiction that ever was written, has been a collection and arrangement of real incidents" (5). We know that the tremendous success of Stowe's novel inspired Jacobs, who approached Stowe about coauthoring her own narrative and declined Stowe's request to use her work as part of *A Key to* Uncle Tom's Cabin (Yellin, *Harriet Jacobs: A Life* 119–25).

Such light fictionalization, rooted in the factuality of "real incidents," was characteristic of the antislavery literature of the period. As Frances Smith Foster observes, by the time Jacobs began writing up her story in the 1850s, "the generic and racial boundaries within anti-slavery literature had become so indistinct that readers could not rely upon subject matter, style, or structure to determine whether a writer were white or black or if a text were fiction or nonfiction" (*Written* 102). Yet just as Foster reads *Incidents* in the context of the nineteenth-century antislavery novel, we might consider the broader context of the "autobiographical novel," an enormously popular genre in the antebellum United States. Today, given our possession of Yellin's biographical scholarship, a hard distinction between fiction and nonfiction can be an obstacle for our students, many of whom (certainly many of the undergraduates I teach at the University of Nevada, Las Vegas) have a tendency to refer to *any* book—fiction or nonfiction—as a "novel." There is nothing to be gained by suggesting that aspects of fictionality (changed names, invented dialogue) somehow weaken Jacobs's text. Fictionality does not entail falsehood.[2] Jacobs's book might be appreciated not only as a factual slave narrative but also as an artful autobiographical novel.

Rather than aiming to cast doubt on the complete veracity of Jacobs's text, we might instead find new ways of appreciating her narrative by viewing Jacobs as a mature literary artist rather than as a guileless ingenue. While not always clearly recognized in our classroom anthologies, the mode of American literary realism was already under development well before the Civil War—a development that can be discerned from the era's distinction between "novels" (generally set in the present or near past and expected to be realistic) and "romances" (often more speculative or fantastic and frequently set in a deeper past).[3] Jacobs was particularly emphatic that her story "needed no romance," but her engagement with the level of fiction appropriate to the novel was more complicated (Yellin, *Harriet Jacobs Family Papers* 1: 195).[4]

Jacobs begins *Incidents* by declaring to the reader that "this narrative is no fiction" and that her adventures are "strictly true." But in the same breath she admits that she has "given persons fictitious names" and that her "descriptions fall far short of the facts" (5).[5] This is not a detrimental contradiction but rather an artful declaration of the ambiguity that elevates the literary arts above straightforward reportage. Following this observation, I suggest that a student's appreciation of *Incidents in the Life of a Slave Girl* can be enhanced by placing the text in proximity with three popular novels of the era: Charlotte Brontë's *Jane Eyre* (1847), Herman Melville's *Typee* (1846), and Fanny Fern's *Ruth Hall* (1854).

Charlotte Brontë's classic novel was first published as *Jane Eyre: An Autobiography, edited by Currer Bell*, and the first American edition appeared as such the following year. The subtitle was left off subsequent editions and is usually forgotten today. But its influence was considerable, and the fictional autobiography became quite popular over the next two decades. Many British novels took a similar cue, such as Frederick Marryat's *Valerie: An Autobiography* (1849), Charles Kingsley's *Alton Locke, Tailor and Poet: An Autobiography* (1850), and Margaret Oliphant's *The Days of My Life: An Autobiography* (1857). The trend was no less noticeable in America. Orestes Brownson's *The Spirit-Rapper: An Autobiography* (1854), for example, is a satire promoting the reality of Satan, told by an anguished mesmerist, rather than a candid self-account of the author. And yet, while Brownson admits in his preface that the book is "not a biography of a real individual," he nevertheless insists that "there is no fiction in it, save its machinery" (v, vi). Health reform advocate Mary Gove Nichols, meanwhile, adhered more closely to the details of her own life in her autobiographical novel *Mary Lyndon; or, Revelations of a Life: An Autobiography* (1855), in which she attempted "to write the real and actual Life of a Human Being" (14).

Brontë herself had been influenced by reading American slave narratives, and *Jane Eyre*, enormously popular in the United States, likewise influenced Jacobs.[6] More than a few readers have observed the parallel between Linda Brent's situation in her grandmother's garret and the nonwhite "madwoman in the attic" in Brontë's novel. Similarly, Jacobs echoes Brontë's direct addresses to the reader (while Brontë was by no means the only novelist to employ these, they are a signature element of her style)—most notably in her concluding statement, "Reader, my story ends with freedom; not in the usual way, with marriage" (167), a play upon Brontë's famous "Reader, I married him." Yet also notable is the very title of Jacobs's book. While the first page of the original 1861 edition displayed the title *Incidents in the Life of a Slave Girl* (the title featured on all modern reprintings), indicating what the book contained, the book cover's spine was marked with the name "LINDA," stamped in gold across the top (Otter 114).

And those who read the book in the 1860s generally referred to it as *Linda*. This very title, then—like the title *Jane Eyre*—would have drawn attention to the specific, fictitiously named autobiographical protagonist rather than to the series of incidents characterizing the life of an indefinite "slave girl."[7]

Herman Melville's *Typee* offers a similarly illuminating example by an American author. Melville's breakthrough novel was first marketed as a work of nonfiction when it appeared in 1846 in English publisher John Murray's Home and Colonial Library series. Many readers understood the author simply to be changing his name to "Tom" (or "Tommo") and relating an accurate account of his adventures, in the same vein as Richard Henry Dana's popular 1840 memoir, *Two Years before the Mast*. Melville opens the book by declaring his "anxious desire to speak the unvarnished truth" (2). But he had, at the very least, stretched this truth, extending his stay on the Marquesan island from an actual several weeks to a fictional several months.[8] We have never been entirely sure how seriously to take Melville's claims in the book. Some have considered it primarily a work of romantic invention; one British reviewer of his second novel even assumed that "Herman Melville" was a fake name.[9] But others have accepted *Typee* as nonfiction. "This book is not a novel," announces the Melville scholar John Bryant in his introduction to the Penguin paperback (xi). For the book's 1892 edition, Arthur Stedman, with the permission of Melville's widow, changed the subtitle of *Typee* to "A Real Romance of the South Seas," and the ambiguous descriptor "real romance" probably remains the most fitting classification. Jacobs's *Incidents* is more serious than a sailor's yarn, but her claims to the "plain truth" (34) echo Melville's adherence to the "unvarnished truth." Both authors offer narratives of escape from captivity, and the intensity and vividness of their descriptions are as valuable as the vetted accuracy of their personal histories.

Perhaps the most helpful contemporaneous American novel for situating Jacobs's work is Fanny Fern's *Ruth Hall*. "Fanny Fern" was the pen name of Sara Willis, sister-in-law of Jacobs's New York employer, Cornelia Willis. In fact, Jacobs's daughter, Louisa, worked briefly for Sara Willis, and Jacobs was certainly familiar with the woman who, chiefly as a newspaper columnist, had become one of the highest-paid writers in America (Chaney). *Ruth Hall*, a smash hit, was a narrative adventure of a woman's fall from domestic grace and subsequent rise into literary stardom that closely matched the details of Fern's own life. Fern introduced *Ruth Hall* as a "continuous story" rather than as a "novel" (3), and many have since characterized it as a roman à clef, a literary depiction of real people achieved by fictionalizing their names (Applegate). While Ruth Hall's story is conveyed through third-person narration, it nevertheless features direct addresses to the reader and contains examples of Ruth's fan mail (sent to "Floy," her own pen name within the novel) that readers would have understood as lightly fictionalized versions of Fern's own. *Ruth Hall* allows us to appreciate the artistic moves necessary for even the basic work of fictionalizing the names of characters in what may otherwise consist of a factual account. Fern's exercises in pseudonymity (from Willis to Fern and from Ruth to Floy) would have been illuminating for Jacobs in her own attempt to disguise the identities of the characters in her work. Just as Fern had to rewrite her own mail to apply to Ruth, Jacobs had to revise the published details of her own life to apply to Linda—modifying, for example, the real-life 1835 advertisement for her capture (Blackwood 60–62).

These examples of popular antebellum books operating in the nebulous space between fiction and nonfiction reveal how "*Linda*" could have been received as an autobiographical novel. They also remind us of the multiple ways in which we might appreciate Jacobs's literary artistry. As Saidiya Hartman has noted, Jacobs's narrative "illuminates the equivocations that surround agency," the complications of establishing a self on the page (102). Finally, we might also note that *Incidents* resonates quite well with today's literary genre of autofiction. Taking seriously Siddharth Srikanth's observation that "for authors of autofiction both autobiographies and novels are formally inadequate to register the truths about the modern self" (351), we can teach *Incidents* as more than just a memoir. It is a rich and various text that shines in several contexts and continues to engage and to challenge new readers.

NOTES

1. For an earlier critique of the notion that the value of Jacobs's text depends on its complete historical accuracy, see Goldsby.

2. Anxieties about fictionality are as old as the rise of the novel and are perhaps, as Catherine Gallagher suggests, coeval with "modern subjectivity" (346).

3. For an impressive argument that the slave narrative genre was key to the development of American literary realism, see Rohrbach.

4. For an alternative consideration of Jacobs's work as a romance, see C. Pratt.

5. Levy begins his essay by noting Jacobs's seemingly contradictory statements.

6. On the influence of American slave narratives upon the composition of *Jane Eyre*, see Lee 30.

7. Koenigs argues that, especially by using the title *Linda*, Jacobs was essentially employing the form of fiction to deliver nonfictional content (233–41). Similarly, Mansouri refers to Jacobs's narrative as a "novelized memoir" (360).

8. For an overview of Melville's fictionalizing, see Edwards.

9. "Herman Melville sounds to us vastly like the harmonious and carefully selected appellation of an imaginary hero of romance" (J. Wilson 755).

Incidents in the Life of Archy Moore: Harriet Jacobs and Richard Hildreth

Carl Ostrowski

In 1849, Harriet Jacobs worked with her brother John in the Rochester, New York, Antislavery Office and Reading Room. An advertisement in the 23 March edition of the *North Star* listed some of the reading room's holdings, which included "Despotism in America, and Archy Moore" (J. Jacobs). Neither of these titles is likely to appear on a syllabus for antebellum American literature, and some educators may be hard-pressed to identify their author as Boston editor, historian, and lawyer Richard Hildreth. Yet in his day, Hildreth achieved a notable reputation for his contributions to the antislavery cause, including a significant literary first. Hildreth's *The Slave* (1836), colloquially identified (as in the *North Star* ad) by the name of its protagonist, Archy Moore, was the first antislavery novel published in the United States. The book was popular within abolitionist circles, reaching a sixth edition by 1846 ("Review 1"). Long before agreeing to edit *Incidents in the Life of Slave Girl*, Lydia Maria Child had written enthusiastically of *The Slave*: "If I were a man, I would rather be the author of that work, than of anything ever published in America" ("Communications").

The presence of Hildreth's pioneering novel in the reading room Harriet Jacobs comanaged, along with strong endorsement of the novel on the part of her editor, Child, constitute compelling circumstantial evidence that Jacobs would have been familiar with the book. Because Jacobs and Hildreth moved within the same abolitionist circles during her residence in Boston in the mid-1840s, moreover, they may even have met. Jean Fagan Yellin believes that Jacobs "doubtless" attended a Faneuil Hall meeting in 1846, when a forty-member vigilance committee was formed to prevent the abduction from Massachusetts of fugitives from slavery (*Harriet Jacobs: A Life* 89). Hildreth was one of the members of this committee (Emerson 130). Given these links between the two antislavery authors, Hildreth's *The Slave* represents an illuminating intertext to teach alongside *Incidents*. Analysis of the character of Cassy in *The Slave* provides readers with a new angle from which to consider the question of Linda Brent's sexual agency within *Incidents*. A chapter from Hildreth's novel on the behavior of self-appointed vigilance committees during an insurrection panic may have provided a model for chapter 12 of *Incidents*, where Jacobs recalls the response in her hometown to Nat Turner's revolt. The reception histories of the two books invite pedagogically valuable discussion of matters of genre and authenticity pertinent to antislavery writing.

Because Hildreth's novel remains much less known than *Incidents*, a brief summary will be helpful. *The Slave* is narrated by its protagonist, Archy Moore, the illegitimate (and enslaved) son of an aristocratic Virginia planter known as Col. Moore. Archy falls in love with another enslaved person on the plantation—his half-sister, Cassy—and is sent away by their father, who has designs on Cassy himself. Sold in the slave market of Washington, DC, Archy experiences a variety of conditions of slavery under subsequent enslavers in the Carolinas. Fortune reunites him with Cassy, now living with a new owner; she and Archy marry and have a child before he is sold away from her a second time. Escaping from a South Carolina plantation, Archy joins a swamp community of maroons before moving north and passing as white. When the ship on which he serves as a merchant marine is commandeered by a privateer during the War of 1812, Archy joins the British Navy. A wealthy man living in England at novel's end, Archy vows to return to the United States to search for his long-lost wife and son. Following the success of *Uncle Tom's Cabin*, Hildreth reissued the novel in 1852 with additional chapters, in which Archy makes good on his vow, traveling across the South in the 1830s in search of Cassy and their son. Eventually he tracks them down and rescues them from the machinations of their would-be owners.

Perhaps the most provocative use a teacher could make of *The Slave* as an intertext for *Incidents* is in addressing the complicated matter of sexual consent. Linda Brent explains her decision to accept Mr. Sands's advances, as a calculated response to Dr. Flint's relentless sexual harassment. In Linda's telling, by choosing a lover for herself rather than submitting to Flint's coercion, she exercises something (in her carefully qualified phrasing) "akin to freedom" (50). Modern readers accustomed to viewing a woman's sexual choices in binary terms of coercion versus choice may view Linda's decision as an empowering expression of female sexual agency. P. Gabrielle Foreman provides a representative example of this line of opinion: "Indeed, through being a sexual actor, by understanding and choosing it knowingly, [Linda] attempts to assert the rights of African American female speech and being. It is not only Jacobs's victimization but also her sexual agency, then, that generates much of *Incidents*'s narrative energy" ("Manifest" 81).

Other readers have cautioned, however, that evaluating sexual agency under the conditions of slavery is far from straightforward. In her book *Scenes of Subjection*, Saidiya Hartman contextualizes Linda's relationship with Sands by way of antebellum legal codes, refusing "to pose the question of desire in terms of compulsion versus unhindered choice" (104). Under the laws of slavery, Hartman reminds us, it was impossible for an enslaved woman to be raped; willingness to engage sexually on the part of a Black woman was taken for granted. Where coercion has no legal meaning, neither does consent: "Outside the shadow of the law, compulsion eclipses choice, as neither right nor protection secures the line between consent and nonconsent. . . . [T]he line between something akin to choice and nonconsent is permeable and uncertain because an absolute distinction between them cannot be sustained in the context of slave relations" (109).

If Linda is unable to exercise consent in a meaningful way in her relationship with Sands, then readings exploring the liberating implications of her sexual choices need reassessment. In teaching *Incidents*, however, I find that students default toward interpreting Linda's relationship with Sands as just such an act of empowerment. A reading that carries such obvious appeal, giving us a protagonist whose control over her sexuality implies resistance to the dual oppressions of slavery and patriarchy, can be difficult to dislodge. While exposing students to the outlines of Hartman's careful explanation of the legal regime of slavery is one way to complicate their responses to this element of the book, examining the character of Cassy in Hildreth's novel is another, supplementing Hartman's intricate argument with a concrete, readily grasped comparison.

In *The Slave*, Cassy knows herself to be her enslaver's daughter; in one scene, she fends off Col. Moore's impending sexual advance by alluding verbally to their hitherto unspoken relationship. But she remains unaware of Archy's paternity. Archy claims that half-siblinghood poses no impediment to their union; a society that winks at Col. Moore's actions, refusing to acknowledge enslaved children's paternity, he self-servingly reasons, has no grounds to prevent their marriage on its basis. He chooses not to inform Cassy of their relationship, because he knows she would object to their marriage. Archy says, "I feared to put our mutual happiness in jeopardy; I was unwilling to harrass [sic] Cassy, with what I esteemed unnecessary scruples" (49). Archy never informs Cassy of their half-sibling relationship.

Students can be guided toward a more complicated view of Linda's union with Sands by comparing her with Hildreth's Cassy. Like Linda, Cassy successfully fights off the unwanted sexual advances of her enslaver before taking a lover of her choice. Not knowing otherwise, Cassy views her union with Archy as uncoerced. If the novel were told from her point of view, as *Incidents* is told from Linda's, Cassy would assert that she makes a free romantic choice. Readers, however, can readily see that Cassy's consent to marriage with Archy is problematic, to say the least. Lacking knowledge of their consanguinity, Cassy is in no position to grant consent; or, rather, the consent she believes she grants is fatally compromised by the differential between her limited knowledge of the implications of their relationship and Archy's fuller understanding.

The Linda-Sands relationship similarly proceeds in the face of significant differentials of knowledge. At the time of their initial union, to revert momentarily to the historical figures rather than their pseudonymous identities, Jacobs was fifteen and Samuel Tredwell Sawyer was twenty-eight. Jacobs had never been outside of Edenton, North Carolina, and had no formal education, whereas Sawyer was university-educated and a member of the North Carolina bar and would, within a year, become a member of the state house of representatives. Jacobs's agency in this pairing was limited from the outset by constraints attendant upon her age, race, social position, gender, and relative inexperience, sexual and otherwise. While Sawyer did not presume upon Jacobs while withholding from her something as sensational as half-siblinghood, the significant knowledge and power differentials in their relationship must be factored into any assessment of her agency.

Standards of acceptable sexual behavior change over time. Even readers of the 1980s, when *Incidents* entered the canon, may have been readier to impute sexual agency to fifteen-year-old Jacobs than readers today, newly sensitized by the Me Too movement to how power differentials have traditionally worked to promote male sexual opportunism. From a twenty-first-century perspective, the "kindness and attachment" by which twenty-eight-year-old Sands gains "control" over fifteen-year-old Linda (50), in her words, may resemble a predator grooming a target. Broadening out the conversation, students exposed to both *The Slave* and *Incidents* might be led to discuss the implications of abolitionist texts persistently discussing slavery in terms of sexual misbehavior. Besides Archy's marriage to his half-sister, *The Slave* features Col. Moore's attempt to seduce his daughter, while *Incidents*, alongside Flint's sustained harassment of Linda, includes a scene where a debilitated Southern planter indulges "the strangest freaks of despotism" involving the enslaved Luke, including acts that Jacobs describes as "too filthy to be repeated," presumably of a homosexual nature (159). Joining an existing scholarly conversation on "the erotic South" (Walters), incest as a figure for interracial sex (Sollors), and queer sexuality in *Incidents* (Abdur-Rahman), students might discuss the degree to which abolitionists do or do not deserve credit for recognizing sexual abuse as one of the defining hardships of slavery as well as whether authors such as Hildreth and Jacobs are successful at deflecting the undercurrent of sensationalism potentially implicit within these exposés.

One chapter of *Incidents* may reflect direct influence from Hildreth's novel. Chapter 12, "Fear of Insurrection," details the town's response to Nat Turner's 1831 insurrection in Southampton County, Virginia. In Jacobs's telling, a band of "country bullies and the poor whites" (57) descends on Black people's homes, looking for signs of insurrection. Jacobs pointedly emphasizes the vigilantes' comparative ignorance and illiteracy. When the "poor whites" discover letters in Linda's grandmother's home, they bring the papers to their captain, the only one among them able to read. He finds that the papers include "some verses written to [Linda] by a friend" (59), and the outraged searchers tear the letter to pieces before moving on. A similar scene transpires in chapter 39 of the expanded version of *The Slave*, published as *The White Slave*, in 1852. Having returned to America to search for his wife and son in the mid-1830s, Archy travels through Richmond, Virginia, during a period of insurrection panic. A vigilance committee charged with the suppression of incendiary publications inspects Archy's possessions, finding a letter from a banker named Tappan, a name the vigilantes erroneously conflate with well-known abolitionist Arthur Tappan. Also found in Archy's possession is Laurence Sterne's novel *A Sentimental Journey through France and Italy*, whose frontispiece includes this motto: "Disguise thyself as thou wilt, still Slavery, still thou art a bitter draught, and though thousands have been made to drink thee, none the less bitter on that account!" (254). Only the presence on the committee of some well-read, middle-class individuals who recognize the innocent nature of these texts preserves Archy from condemnation, and he notes ruefully that "before a less well-read committee of vigilance, as might easily happen in the rural districts, the having in a man's trunk a stray volume with an unfortunate frontispiece, might subject him to summary punishment as a plotter of rebellion and murder" (254).

What leads me to wonder if Jacobs may have had the scene from Hildreth's novel in mind while composing her chapter is that it was not a part of her original manuscript. Child explicitly requested that Jacobs add this chapter: "My object in writing at this time is to ask you to write what you can recollect of the outrages committed on the colored people, in Nat Turner's time. . . . Please write down some of the most striking particulars, and let me have them to insert" ("Letter" 202). Presented with the opportunity to inform readers about the depredations of roving bands of poor white vigilantes, Jacobs may have recalled Hildreth's treatment of a similar theme. In both scenes, an atmosphere of paranoia regarding insurrection leads to the empowerment of self-appointed vigilance committees, eager to seize upon written or published materials as evidence of conspiracies. In both scenes, moreover, illiterate (or barely literate) poor white people encounter literary material that confounds their limited comprehension. Finally, in both scenes, the innocent bystanders victimized by these committees narrowly avert condemnation thanks only to the intervention of better-read, more respectable middle-class white people. Whether the similarities are conscious or merely coincidental, both works show how panic over insurrections warped the administration of justice in the South, and they also suggest that the institution of slavery, far from contributing to the region's economic health, kept a class of non-enslaving white people in poverty and ignorance.

With some coaching, students could be led to explore how these books and their reception histories speak to quandaries regarding authenticity and generic status with respect to slave narratives. Undergraduates in particular might discuss whether Hildreth's writing a fictional version of a slave narrative qualifies as appropriation or whether Jacobs's reliance on fictional models compromises the status of her nonfictional narrative. Upon initial publication of *The Slave*, Hildreth posed as the volume's editor, as if bringing an authentic slave narrative before the public; reviewers quickly realized that *The Slave* was a novel, however, and treated it as such. Generic classification of *Incidents* moved in the opposite direction. After a long period during which its truth claims were disputed and it was treated as a fiction, Yellin established Jacobs's identity, and the book was recognized as a nonfictional slave narrative. Lara Langer Cohen observes that generic attribution of slavery-related works has historically depended upon perceptions of an author's racial identity (112). When *The Slave* was revealed not to be an authentic slave narrative, readers readily transitioned to seeing it as a novel by a white author, a status they were not willing to accord to slave narratives written by Black authors, narratives whose factual status was in question. The history of *Incidents* supports Cohen's point, insofar as early readers tended to resolve doubts about its authenticity by imputing authorship to its white editor, Child, a well-known literary figure, rather than the unknown woman of color, Jacobs.

Scholarship on early African American writing suggests that strict generic boundaries applied to first-person writing have only tended to obscure our critical vision. If, in the nineteenth century, factual accuracy was a slave narrative's most valuable quality, readers are comfortable now dispensing with such a rudimentary classificatory test. Students unfamiliar with this critical literature should be brought to awareness of how Jacobs imports into the slave narrative the generic conventions of the sentimental novel (Doherty) and the gothic (Wardrop) in the service of reaching her audience. Identifying shared motifs, direct influences, or crafty borrowings linking slave narratives with the wider literary culture in which they were produced enables the fullest possible appreciation of the works. If Hildreth's early experimentation with a novel ostensibly posing as a slave narrative contributed in any way to Jacobs's later exploration of unrealized novelistic possibilities within the slave narrative, the correspondences redound to the credit of both authors.

Investigating Childhood Injustice: *Incidents in the Life of a Slave Girl* and *The Tragedy of Pudd'nhead Wilson*

Jericho Williams

As one of its many strengths, Harriet Jacobs's *Incidents in the Life of a Slave Girl* illuminates the harsh realities of the enslavement of children. Jacobs personalizes the inexplicable nature of being born into slavery and experiencing childhood within deceitful circumstances so harsh and dehumanizing that an adult could easily forgive their guardians for the deliberate obstruction of the truth. Throughout *Incidents*, Jacobs appeals directly to her primary readership at the time: literate Northern white women with children of their own. For strategic and creative effect, the author incorporates elements from popular literary genres such as sentimental and gothic fiction to impart slavery's horrors to readers who are far removed from the scenes of innumerable crimes. All the while, childhood injustice remains a key component of her story.

Two decades later, the celebrated author Mark Twain would publish *The Adventures of Huckleberry Finn* (1885), perhaps the subsequent century's most lauded American novel about childhood and slavery. In the past few decades, however, the novel has prompted many discussions and debates for its casual use of the racist language of its time. While I would argue that the novel still provides valuable insight about nineteenth-century American culture, numerous slave narratives, such as Frederick Douglass's *Narrative of the Life of Frederick Douglass, An American Slave, Written by Himself* (1845) or William Wells Brown's *Narrative of William W. Brown, a Fugitive Slave* (1847), and particularly Jacobs's *Incidents*, offer far more direct examples of how children experienced slavery. The controversy surrounding *Huckleberry Finn*—because it was so popular and, for many students, has been their first introduction to Twain—has also cast a shadow on Twain's other works, especially his late-career novel *Pudd'nhead Wilson* (1894), which along with *Huckleberry Finn*, its prequel *The Adventures of Tom Sawyer* (1876), and an autobiographical travel narrative *Life on the Mississippi* (1883), form a quartet of full-length, Mississippi works.

In the context of Twain's four Mississippi books, *Pudd'nhead Wilson*, a Dr. Frankenstein–like fusion, is certainly the oddball, and it remains comparatively neglected given the great success of *Tom Sawyer* and *Huck Finn* and the more straightforward memoir *Life on the Mississippi*. However, with an emphasis on an African American mother's story and with its multilayered use of components stitched together from various literary genres to construct a very sharp condemnation of slavery, *Pudd'nhead Wilson* merits more attention and may be a more apt Twain text for our time. It also works nicely as a companion to *Incidents in the Life of a Slave Girl*. This essay details how I pair *Incidents* and *Pudd'nhead Wilson* as part of an American literature survey class at a small liberal arts institution with a majority-minority student body. By foregrounding nineteenth-century childhood in one unit, I encourage students to scrutinize the society and subcultures in which they—like Jacobs's and Twain's protagonists—were born into and have inevitably inherited. A larger purpose is examining childhood as it relates to social justice, a concept of interest to many of my students just as it was for Jacobs and Twain, albeit in their own terms. Since the greater goal is depth, what I propose by devoting a significant amount of time to *Incidents* and *Pudd'nhead* is a full-scale excavation of childhood, through five activities that accompany traditional literary discussions of each work.

Our class first considers childhood when we begin reading *Incidents*. Two of the work's more powerful sentences are the opening ones for the preface and first chapter, where Jacobs (as Linda Brent) relays, "Reader, be assured this narrative is no fiction" (5) and "I was born a slave; but I never knew it until six years of happy childhood had passed away" (9). For the current generation of students, with the advent of smartphones and the development of the personalized, carefully curated, social media self as extension of the physical self, personal testimony or a claim of truth is of great value. By describing her early childhood as an enslaved child who did not fully recognize her situation until the age of six, Jacobs opens *Incidents* in a striking way. This delayed realization invites students to contemplate child psychology and to reconsider their own childhoods. We begin our discussion of the book by defining *childhood* in a modern sense, discussing when it begins and ends and what it necessitates: the need for care and direction from adults or guardian figures.

It is not enough, though, for students to define their childhood as simply very different from Jacobs's situation. What *Incidents* accomplishes so brilliantly is the slow revelation of one's childhood limitations as set by adults and their values. An important part of comprehending what this means comes from interrogating one's perceptions of the adult world and its contradictions. For the second activity, entitled "Questioning the Adult World," I ask for a personal writing response. While this can easily be conducted on an online discussion board, I have not done so in the past because I want students to feel comfortable answering the following question without the pressure of knowing that their peers will read their response: "When did you first realize that your parent or guardian was human and could be wrong about something?" Here I suggest taking the time to explain to students that they need not write about situations that may be too disconcerting or that they might not feel OK sharing with the class. Admittedly, this is tricky because as in Jacobs's case, the answers are not always comfortable. Jacobs writes that while the woman who enslaved her taught her biblical passages such as Mark 12.31 ("Thou shalt love thy neighbor as thyself") and Matthew 7.12 ("Whatsoever ye would that men should do unto you, do ye even so unto them"), she eventually realized that her enslaver could not treat her as a neighbor because of slavery's social norms (11). The more damning implications, that antebellum white society could not uphold key biblical principles because the labor of enslaved people created and sustained its foundation, and the contradiction between what enslaving families professed to believe versus the horrific consequences of their direct actions collectively undermine the legitimacy of an entire social order. Though the lives of enslaved children and undergraduates are dissimilar, students can approximate the experience of Jacobs's initial understanding of this situation by thinking about the fracturing of their unquestioned faith in adults. As in the case of Jacobs, how they reacted at the time of their first awareness and what they think now do not often align, because as children, they, too, might have had an inkling that something was wrong, without the maturity to analyze its ramifications. For many students, the realization might be as simple as that a parent or grandparent mistakenly accused them of committing a wrong, while for others it may be as complex as the loss of a guardian to prison or a prolonged absence from their lives. In both instances and others, however, it marks a key transition of comprehending a wrong rooted in a problematic belief or situation and the destabilization of an assumption of a secure world.

From these reflections, students move on to "Irresolvable Differences," a third assignment related to identifying divides between generations that seem impossible to overcome. This one stems from a powerful passage that appears after the death of Jacobs's enslaver. In a situation that students almost always notice, the twelve-year-old Jacobs becomes the property of the deceased woman's five-year-old niece, under the supervision of the child's parents, Dr. Flint and Mrs. Flint. Jacobs befriends her new enslaver, who dotes upon and looks up to her. Students point out that their relationship, even if separated by race and social expectations, seems closer to that of sisters. The aberrant situation of a five-year-old child unknowingly retaining ownership of a twelve-year-old develops into something more complicated when the Flints later argue about their daughter's close attachment to her companion. In response to Dr. Flint's inquiry about the nature of their relationship, his wife attributes it to her daughter's fear of Jacobs. Revisiting this situation as an adult causes Jacobs to question whether her companion's actions were genuine or Mrs. Flint was simply jealous of her bond with her daughter. Realizing that this involves questioning the motives of a five-year-old, she writes, "Surely, little children are true" (21). This line captures the imposition of an adult interpretation of a situation, based upon values that manifest into coercion, when children's actions do not fall in line with expectations of a settled social order. More specifically, it calls attention to values that the children directly challenge through their actions of care and interest.

Here, the transition for students is from a time in which they realized an adult was wrong to an instance of ongoing disagreement or perceived incompatibility between themselves and a member of an older generation. It invites discussion about ways some elders might react in an effort to uphold their values. As in the case of Jacobs, my intention is to begin with an irresolvable conflict and to encourage students to discuss why certain beliefs they hold clash with those of preceding generations. Prior to class, it is important to consider class dynamics and atmosphere when thinking about discussion. Typically, I allow students to share their responses with one person they know in class and do not require them to share their topics with the entire class unless they choose to do so. I also suggest walking around the room and checking in with each student prior to returning to full-class discussion. This will minimize the potential for a major conflict in large-group discussion. It is also worth noting that how to approach this part might differ by class and instructor comfort level. During full-class discussion, students often bring up common topics from earlier argumentative writing classes related to issues such as abortion, capital punishment, the legalization of drugs, technology, and social media. In an in-class writing reflection to be shared with everyone, students choose a contentious issue, describe their beliefs about it, and then identify an elder and imagine their differing perspective about the same topic. This leads into the next assignment, which also marks the course's transition from *Incidents* to *Pudd'nhead Wilson*.

Entitled "Switching Places," the fourth activity extends from the prior assignment and also marks the transition from *Incidents* to *Pudd'nhead Wilson*. Here, students examine a perspective of someone from an older generation. Although Twain's novel features a character named David "Pudd'nhead" Wilson who becomes a key figure near the novel's conclusion, it is principally an African American woman's story projected via Twain's highly satiric point of view. The novel may be partly a mystery, a comedy, a courtroom drama, and an absurdist critique of slavery, but all of its components collectively convey the plight of an enslaved person named Roxy, who secretly swaps her infant son, Chambers, for her enslaver's infant son named Tom and then slowly observes with awe and horror how antebellum social norms foster Chambers's decline as he matures. This unique vantage point is my primary reason for teaching this novel, because Twain's multigenre concoction creatively reimagines the formation and validation of unquestioned corruption. By extension, it also allows students an avenue toward approaching those vantage points of an older generation that they may find most offensive.

With "Switching Places," they interview someone older about an issue or topic in which both parties have differing opinions. The goal for them is to temporarily trade places with this person in an imaginative sense in order to better understand how society and their experiences have shaped their beliefs. Admittedly, this activity contains two differences from Twain's story. First, their switch involves someone not their own age, and, second, the stakes are dissimilar to those that Roxy imagines when she decides to switch her child, an important point to make clear to the class. However, what students can gain from asking questions and listening is a deeper understanding about how culture and a prior time period may have nurtured what they consider to be a problematic belief. This activity has the potential to foster in-depth discussions about how one's present-day point of view may be perceived as flawed in the future. The greater goal is to encourage students to consider how perspectives of right and wrong are formed and supported and, in some cases, difficult to alter or change and to encourage them to interrogate a common assumption of linear progress or improvement.

The final phase culminates with "Blind Spot," an activity that asks students to imitate Jacobs's and Twain's cultural critiques. Rather than frame the conflict as right versus wrong, I encourage them to think deeply about the entire process from issue to interview and then respond to it analytically or creatively. Equipped with a better understanding of the conflict from the prior activity, they, like Jacobs or Roxy, are now poised to account for the generational divide and to confront injustice. To create this assignment, I draw from both Jacobs, who wrote against slavery's treatment of children from direct experience, and Twain, who wrote from observation. Students can showcase generational divides through analyses or an approved artistic rendering of the conflict, and the gist of the assignment is to identify and reflect what they perceive to be an oversight on the part of their elders. In the manner of Jacobs or Twain, they look for inconsistencies between belief or practice and its consequences; in the process, they emerge with a better understanding that they, too, are to some extent influenced by their own eras.

What makes *Incidents* and *Pudd'nhead* work well together is the horrific realization that sometimes adults are wrong and that sometimes their misguided intentions are inextricable from social, historical, and cultural norms that seemingly lock them in place. It is imperative that this not serve as an excuse for the horrors of slavery in America, a point worth emphasizing and reemphasizing while teaching these two books and engaging in the activities. The greater goal is to encourage students to consider how anyone might fall prey to problematic beliefs that influence their actions and to encourage critical thinking and engagement. Looking closely at these differences as they relate to children, partly because of what adults ostensibly owe their children and also partly due to the sometimes problematic American ideal of generational improvement, can help students in the midst of the transition between young adulthood and adulthood understand their frustration with and rejection of another generation's values. With the goal of empowering students and encouraging a depth of thinking beyond good (young) versus evil (old), this sequential approach paired with these texts provides them space to consider their differences and an anti-hierarchical means of developing and asserting their voices, while at the same time fostering thought about how they, too, will inevitably be scrutinized for how their own values shape their beliefs and actions.

A Pivotal Text: *Incidents in the Life of a Slave Girl* in a Narratives of Slavery Course

Amina Gautier

Harriet Jacobs's narrative *Incidents in the Life of a Slave Girl* is a pivotal text in my literature course on nineteenth-, twentieth-, and twenty-first-century narratives of slavery. Because the contemporary authors of neo–slave narratives "wrote from a perspective informed and enriched by the study of slave narratives" (V. Smith, "Neo–Slave Narratives" 169), reading slave narratives and neo–slave narratives side by side drives home the essential connections between these two subgenres of African American literature. Assigned chronologically, Jacobs's narrative is often the last slave narrative read before the neo–slave narratives, and its emphasis on romantic and sexual agency, the haunting presence of shame, and the importance of family render it an ideal text for such a transition. Jacobs's narrative critiques the masculine privilege of Frederick Douglass's first slave narrative (frequently read as the urtext of slave narratives) and of other male-authored slave narratives. Her focus on sexual vulnerability and the ways in which slavery perverts and warps motherhood reveals the onus on enslaved Black women to adopt and maintain sexual purity in a culture where their very agency is proscribed. Excluded from the cult of true womanhood, the enslaved woman was posited as hypersexual and culpable for her own sexual violation. In *Scenes of Subjection*, Saidiya Hartman notes, "As the enslaved is legally unable to give consent or offer resistance, she is presumed to be always willing" (81). Preyed upon by white enslavers and overseers and shamed for her own sexual victimization, Jacobs shows the enslaved Black woman to be doubly damned. Critiquing the masculine privilege of male-authored slave narratives by revealing the ways in which gender, romantic and sexual agency, and family complicate the flight of the fugitive, *Incidents* importantly prepares the way for fruitful discussions of Toni Morrison's *Beloved*, Charles Johnson's *Middle Passage*, Edward Jones's *The Known World*, and Colson Whitehead's *The Underground Railroad*, neo–slave narratives that take a similar interest in such topics and speak back to Jacobs's narrative.[1]

The students who self-select into a course on narratives of slavery will likely be familiar with Frederick Douglass's first narrative, and their familiarity will make comparisons between Douglass's and Jacobs's narratives inevitable. Therefore, students should be encouraged to move beyond simple compare-and-contrast analyses, toward a deeper exploration of the different landscapes the two texts inhabit. Unlike Douglass, who is separated at an early age from his family and has minuscule knowledge of his parents and parentage, Jacobs is reared in a multigenerational family whose members all have distinct experiences of slavery—from her grandmother, who is freed as a child and then captured and resold into slavery before gaining freedom in her old age, to Jacobs's father, who is allowed to hire himself out as a carpenter—and Jacobs deliberately begins her narrative by recounting their experiences. By embedding her personal journey within a frame of collective family experiences, Jacobs presents familial bonds that have not been destroyed by slavery and complicates the male slave narrative in which the bondsman is bound by few or no familial ties and has no extended family to speak of. *Incidents in the Life of a Slave Girl* importantly expands a field dominated by men whose quintessential narrative casts the quest for freedom as a singular, heroic, and often male endeavor predicated upon literacy. Jacobs presents a path to freedom in which literacy is neither the source "of the white man's power to enslave the black man" nor "the pathway from slavery to freedom" (Douglass, *Narrative* 364) but a practical tool to throw her enslaver[2] off her track and remove suspicion from her grandmother's home, which "would have been burned to the ground" (*Incidents* 100) if Jacobs's location had been suspected. Jacobs's narrative shows that the quest for freedom is not always straightforward but full of starts, stops, and stillness, as Jacobs flees the Flint household only to spend nearly seven years hiding nearby in her grandmother's garret. Unlike Douglass's narrative, which omits not only his courtship of his future wife, Anna Murray, but also her help in facilitating his escape, Jacobs's narrative highlights the importance of romantic choice and underscores the would-be fugitive's dependency on the aid of friends and family. Finally, rather than glossing over the sexual victimization of enslaved women or merely pointing to it to mention the hypocrisy of Christian enslavers who force enslaved women into sexual immorality, Jacobs makes the feelings and responses of victimized women a primary concern. She replaces the concept of a singular and independent journey out of slavery with that of a collective and interdependent one. Her focus on the importance of relationships, the role family plays in the enslaved person's quest for freedom, the sexual vulnerability of the enslaved woman, the radical desire for romantic agency, and the ways in which motherhood is compromised for the enslaved woman all challenge the notion of a straightforward heroic journey for the enslaved person who pursues a path to freedom.

Exploring these differences helps students to map out Jacobs's specific narrative concerns and to understand her significant assertion that "[s]lavery is terrible for men; but it is far more terrible for women. Superadded to the burden common to all, they have wrongs, and sufferings, and mortifications peculiarly their own" (68). In order to emphasize that her own story of being subjected to an enslaver's relentless pursuit is neither singular nor particular, Jacobs prefaces her experiences of victimization with anecdotes of the injustices suffered by enslaved mothers in her family and local community, and asserts that such injustices are "of daily, yea, of hourly occurrence" (18). Working as a group, students should compile a list of Jacobs's examples and keep it handy for frequent referral. From the Flints' cook, who gets frequently "locked up, away from her nursing baby, for a whole day and night" (15); to the enslaved couple Dr. Flint sells off because the husband "accused his master of being the father of her child" despite that "it was a crime for a slave to tell who was the father of her child" (16); to "a young slave girl dying soon after the birth of a child nearly white" whose enslaver taunts her on her deathbed (16); to the enslaved mother of seven whose children are all sold away from her on New Year's Day (17); to Jacobs's own grandmother, who is forced to wean Jacobs's mother early to better suckle the enslaver's child and who is separated from her five children when they are given as inheritances upon her enslaver's death (10); to Jacobs's aunt, who is prevented from carrying her pregnancies to term because she is so overworked by her enslaver (121), Jacobs lacks no shortage of examples to demonstrate the ways slavery warps motherhood for enslaved women. Furthermore, by describing the ways in which slavery thwarts motherhood *before* detailing the ways in which slavery perverts girlhood, Jacobs inverts the inextricable relationship between sex and pregnancy, thereby showing that for enslaved women childbirth is a foregone conclusion, because, with or without the benefit of marriage, sex is inescapable:

> The slave girl is reared in an atmosphere of licentiousness and fear. The lash and the foul talk of her master and his sons are her teachers. When she is fourteen or fifteen, her owner, or his sons, or the overseer, or perhaps all of them, begin to bribe her with presents. If these fail to accomplish their purpose, she is whipped or starved into submission to their will. (47)

Jacobs depicts an environment that is singularly unsympathetic to young enslaved women. The enslaved girl who reaches childbearing age automatically becomes an object of prey for the white men in an enslaver's household. Whether she is beaten or bribed, her sexual acquiescence is a presumed eventuality, and this stark claim is one with which students must come to terms.

Understanding this scarcity of sexual and romantic options is crucial for students to unpack the nuances of Jacobs's affair with Mr. Sands. Failing to see Mr. Sands as a feasible alternative, they may initially view Jacobs's affair as an ill-advised action conceived solely out of desperation and end up overlooking the "deliberate calculation" (49) that motivates her. Forbidden to marry the free Black man whom she loves "with all the ardor of a young girl's first love" (35), Jacobs is presented with two alternatives: marry an enslaved person of her enslaver's choosing or submit to her enslaver. Students who refer to their list of examples and recall that Dr. Flint sells away an enslaved couple because the wife revealed him to be the father of her child (16) will see that marriage to a fellow enslaved person does not relieve the enslaved woman from her enslaver's sexual advances. Therefore, the two choices Jacobs is given are no choices at all. Nevertheless, in an environment where sex and pregnancy are inevitabilities and in which "resistance is hopeless" (47), Jacobs strategically manages to carve out a third romantic or sexual option for herself in her relationship with Mr. Sands.

As students work to unpack her nuanced decision, they should be guided to a key passage in chapter 10 in which Jacobs explains her deliberations and another key passage in chapter 7 where Dr. Flint rejects her request to marry a free Black man. These passages will enable students to see the shrewd and strategic calculation that informs her actions and the significant assertion of agency Jacobs's act entails.

First, it is imperative to point out that Jacobs does not behave rashly. She weighs her options and surmises that if motherhood is an inevitability for the enslaved woman, then she shall choose a father for her children who has the power to buy and free them. In Mr. Sands she selects a single, unmarried man, thereby avoiding the label of adultery; and in opting for a white lover rather than an enslaved person, she selects a man over whom her enslaver has no authority. Furthermore, she picks a lover who has no legal authority over her, which she finds freeing: "There is something akin to freedom in having a lover who has no control over you, except that which he gains by kindness and attachment" (50). Significantly, she picks a man of financial means whose temperament she understands and can manipulate: "Of a man who was not my master I could ask to have my children well supported; and in this case, I felt confident I should obtain this boon. I felt sure they would be made free" (50). Before she ever bears any children, Jacobs envisions a scenario in which her future children can be bought and freed by their father, and her confidence in this projection prompts her "headlong plunge" into the affair (50). Importantly, once again, Jacobs inverts the relationship between sex and pregnancy, presuming conception prior to embarking upon a sexual relationship. Jacobs enters into an affair with the expectation that her actions will provoke her enslaver into selling her and any children she bears, and in Mr. Sands she prepares a potential buyer who she believes will free her.

Second, despite being denied the opportunity for love, marriage, and respectability with the man of her choice, Jacobs staunchly claims the right to choose her lover. When she rejects Dr. Flint's offer of a husband from among those whom he enslaves, she asks a radical question: "Don't you suppose, sir, that a slave can have some preference about marrying? Do you suppose that all men are alike to her?" (36). The enslaved person's legal inability to give consent or offer resistance, which results in the presumption of an enslaved woman's perpetual sexual willingness, undermines the concept of agency and choice on her part, but Jacobs's narrative pushes back at such presumption. By recounting her resistance to Dr. Flint's sexual overtures, her desire to make her own romantic choices, and the lengths to which she will go when such a choice is denied, Jacobs underscores the significance of romantic choice, challenges Dr. Flint's unspoken implication that any man will do for an enslaved woman, and espouses the idea that even enslaved persons should have the right to choose their partner. Jacobs's desire to marry the man of her choosing and her refusal to have a husband chosen for her forcefully bring home both the idea that marriage, courtship, love, romance, and affection are just as desirable to the enslaved and the formerly enslaved as they are to their white counterparts and the understanding that love cannot be assigned.

Jacobs's remorse over her thwarted romance with a free Black man highlights the importance of romantic agency and opens wide the door for writers of neo–slave narratives to include both the enslaved or formerly enslaved person's all-too-human desires for romantic love and affection and the ways in which slavery disrupts and warps those romantic opportunities and relationships. Romantic agency—that is, the ability to choose one's romantic partner—is a recurring theme in the four assigned neo–slave narratives. Students who read *Beloved*, *Middle Passage*, *The Known World*, and *The Underground Railroad* encounter enslaved or formerly enslaved persons who choose their partners or protest when that right is threatened. In Morrison's *Beloved*, Sethe is the only enslaved woman among a group of five enslaved men. Although all five desire her for themselves and are "sick with the absence of women," Sethe is allowed the time and freedom "so she could choose in spite of the fact that each would have beaten the other to mush to have her" (Morrison, *Beloved* 12). In Johnson's *Middle Passage*, the formerly enslaved Rutherford Calhoun balks at being forced to marry Isadora Bailey in order to relieve his debt. He warns Isadora, "You're twisting my cullions but you haven't won my consent!" (Johnson 16) and steals aboard a slave ship to escape marriage.[3] In Jones's *The Known World*, the enslaved man Elias ceases plotting his escape from the Townsend plantation after he develops feelings for Celeste, who is also enslaved, feelings that his enslaver understands are "better than chains" (102) for rooting him to the plantation. In Whitehead's *The Underground Railroad*, Cora escapes slavery with a fellow enslaved person, Caesar, yet rebuffs him and chooses Royal, an Underground Railroad station agent. The implication that enslaved people, fugitives, and the formerly enslaved should be satisfied with what they are given, should not want and desire the same things that are taken for granted by those who have been born free, whether white or Black, such as the right to choose one's romantic partner, is reputed by Jacobs and also becomes a central concern in the novels of Morrison, Johnson, Jones, and Whitehead.

These four neo–slave narratives give dramatic rendering not only to Jacobs's remorse but also to her guilt for bearing children while unmarried and her fear that separating from her children will impair her relationships with them. Jacobs suffers from the perpetual guilt of having disappointed her grandmother and other relatives, who "had pride in my good character" (51), showing that shame is a feeling the enslaved woman must deal with even when victimized. Students who transition from Jacobs's narrative to Morrison's *Beloved* or Whitehead's *The Underground Railroad* will have a foundation of contextual knowledge upon which to draw when they encounter Sethe and Cora's sexual assaults. In *Beloved*, Sethe is beaten and raped by Schoolteacher's nephews, who tore open her back and "took her milk." When she learns, years later, that her husband, Halle, inadvertently witnessed the sexual assault, she resigns herself to never seeing him again: "If he is alive, and saw that, he won't step foot in my door" (82). Her presumption of his shame triggers her own. In *The Underground Railroad*, a young Cora is raped at the onset of puberty: "Not long after it became known that Cora's womanhood had come into flower, Edward, Pot, and two hands from the southern half dragged her behind the smokehouse. . . .

The Hob women sewed her up" (21). Though Cora is an innocent victim, her shame makes her shun sexual intimacy until she meets Royal, to whom she discloses her assault: "When she told Royal about the night they took her behind the smokehouse and she apologized to him for letting it happen, he told her to hush" (285). Shame compels her to disclose her rape and apologize for her lack of virginity prior to consummating their relationship.

In *Beloved*, *Middle Passage*, *The Known World*, and *The Underground Railroad*, students will see Jacobs's grandmother's prediction that parents who abandon their children in slavery "will never have a happy moment" (80) and instead invite misery to come true, as many enslaved children may blame their parents for abandonment. In *Beloved*, Sethe's dead daughter returns as a spirit to haunt Sethe before manifesting as a young woman who punishes Sethe for "abandoning"—that is, killing her. *Middle Passage*'s Rutherford Calhoun and *The Underground Railroad*'s Cora both grow up in the wake of abandonment, believing their parents ran off for freedom while leaving them in slavery. As a consequence, Rutherford grows up hating his father "because he had cut and run" (Johnson 169). Being the child of an enslaved person who has escaped sets Cora apart on the plantation, causing the other enslaved people to fear and respect her, but leaves her wondering, "Where was she now? Why had she left her?" (Whitehead 54). In *The Known World*, the enslaved Henry Townsend is left behind after his parents purchase their freedom. As they save to buy his, he grows close to his enslaver, which precipitates his becoming an enslaver himself. His father blames Henry's enslaving others on their absence: "He wondered if all would have been different if he had bought the boy's freedom first, before Mildred's" (E. Jones 49). These four neo–slave narratives take the warning Jacobs receives from her grandmother about abandoning children in slavery and give life to it, showing how such children remain haunted by the abandonment of their parents, even into adulthood. Reading these texts together, students can readily see the influences of Jacobs's narrative on these four neo–slave narratives that expose the connective threads between Jacobs's narrative and theirs.

NOTES

1. These four novels were chosen for their critical acclaim, as each has been awarded either a National Book Award or a Pulitzer Prize or both.

2. Technically, Jacobs is the property of Dr. Flint's daughter, but because the daughter is a minor, Dr. Flint acts as Jacobs's de facto owner and enslaver.

3. Although Rutherford does ultimately marry Isadora upon return from his voyage, the decision to wed has become his choice.

Reclaiming the Role of the Enslaved Mother in Jacobs's *Incidents in the Life of a Slave Girl* and Whitehead's *The Underground Railroad*

Jennifer L. Hayes

The system of slavery in the United States was a matrilineal system. Frederick Douglass remarks in *Narrative of the Life of Frederick Douglass* that "slaveholders have ordained, and by law established, that the children of slave women shall in all cases follow the condition of their mothers" (256). When one examines the socially constructed space of mothers and mothering, women would seem to hold an elevated position within their communities. However, this elevation of status did not extend to those enslaved during the antebellum era, nor does it extend to Black mothers in the contemporary era. Angela Davis in *Women, Race, and Class* emphasizes that "a premium was placed on the slave woman's reproductive capacity. . . . In fact, in the eyes of the slaveholders, slave women were not mothers at all; they were simply instruments guaranteeing the growth of the slave labor force. They were 'breeders'—animals, whose monetary value could be precisely calculated in terms of their ability to multiply their numbers" (7). Viewing enslaved mothers in this way allowed enslavers to disregard the humanity of Black women through the creation of an ideology that encouraged the devaluation of Black women and the Black family. This ideology promoted the rape of Black women and the separation of Black mothers from their children. These abhorrent acts were justified through economic and legal systems working together to destroy Black families in the name of white supremacy and economic gain.

Teaching Harriet Jacobs's *Incidents in the Life of a Slave Girl* with Colson Whitehead's *The Underground Railroad* affords students the opportunity to evaluate a key trope within slave narratives and neo–slave narratives: the enslaved mother. In both texts, motherhood and mothers shape the lives of the protagonists. Since the system of slavery is defined through enslaved Black women's fertility, an investigation of the roles that enslaved mothers play within these works represents a fruitful place for inquiry. Additionally, slave narratives help teach students about the cultural significance of writing as a historical record. The enslaved used these texts to testify about their experiences and to promote civic engagement from their Northern readers to help topple the institution of slavery. Neo–slave narratives promote a continued understanding of the historical significance of slavery through reinterpretation and extension. While neo–slave narratives are not created from the lived experiences of enslaved people, the texts extend the historical record by interpreting historical issues that connect to slavery. The assignment that follows incorporates a close reading of Jacobs's and Whitehead's work. While other texts include similar themes, this assignment is meant to connect these works specifically. The assignment can be modified to pair a different neo–slave narrative with Jacobs's work in order to achieve the same objectives.

Striving toward Freedom through Sexual Agency in Incidents

Jacobs's life is shaped by the death of her mother: "When I was six years old, my mother died; and then, for the first time, I learned, by the talk around me, that I was a slave" (*Incidents* 10). The loss of her mother is significant because her foundation is shattered. Although her father is still alive, it is the connection to her mother that signals a transformation in her life. Eventually, she is placed with a "kind mistress" who promised Jacobs's mother on her deathbed that "her children should never suffer for anything; and during her lifetime she kept her word" (11). However, the woman's death results in a precarious situation, where Jacobs does not know what will become of her. Rather than freeing Jacobs, the woman instead bequeaths her to her five-year-old niece. As a result, Jacobs is controlled by Dr. Flint, the girl's father. Thus, the early years of Jacobs's life are marred by death and insecurity. As she develops into a young woman, Jacobs does not resign herself to the life of an enslaved person to be passed from one owner to another. She takes control over her life when she becomes sexually mature and seeks to direct her own path.

Jacobs's experience of slavery is a gendered one. As she blossoms into womanhood, she understands the problems of sexualization that she faces. Jacobs laments the troubled experience of young enslaved women when she says, "If God has bestowed beauty upon her, it will prove her greatest curse. That which commands admiration in the white woman, only hastens the degradation of the female slave" (28). Her enslaver's attraction to her creates great misery in her life, but despite Dr. Flint's ability to possess Jacobs, she demonstrates agency over her body by beginning a sexual relationship with a man of her own choosing, Mr. Sands:

> I knew nothing would enrage Dr. Flint so much as to know that I favored another; and it was something to triumph over my tyrant even in this small way. . . . I shuddered to think of being the mother that should be owned by my old tyrant. I knew that as soon as a new fancy took him, his victims were sold off to get rid of them; especially if they had children. (50)

The choice Jacobs makes is a calculated one. She chooses to start a relationship with someone whom she favors and who she hopes will secure her freedom. It is this thinking that represents the beginning of Jacobs's quest for freedom. She utilizes the one thing within the system of slavery that grants her power: her sexuality. By demonstrating sexual agency, Jacobs makes an empowering choice.

Jacobs eventually gives birth to two children: Benjamin and Ellen. These children become the focus of her energy. They symbolize her power as she attempts to ensure their freedom. Her route to freedom is not a straight one, because she feels bound to these children and as such cannot leave them. For seven years, Jacobs resides in "a small shed" attached to the upper floor of her grandmother's home (97). The small attic that she occupies allows her the opportunity to be near her children. This "loophole of retreat" emphasizes the limitations impacting enslaved mothers' lives. Jacobs is diminished by the slavery system but tries to work within the confines of her role as an enslaved person to direct her own course.

Jacobs's choice is complicated, because she lives in an environment where she maintains no legal right to her children; yet she chooses to have children with Mr. Sands. While there is an unbalanced power dynamic within her relationship with Mr. Sands, the relationship affirms her right to choose. The children born from this relationship symbolize her rebellious confrontation of the sexual exploitation of enslaved Black women. Stephanie Li argues that "for Jacobs, motherhood is not simply a politically astute literary trope and a means of describing the abuse of slavery specific to women; it is also a crucial form of female empowerment" (15). Motherhood is an extension of her sexual agency. Throughout the text, Jacobs resists the sexual advances of Dr. Flint in an effort to protect herself and future offspring from his vengeful whims. In having her children with Mr. Sands, Jacobs claims a small victory by determining the paternity of her children.

The births of Benny and Ellen create new issues as she tries to secure their freedom through her relationship with Mr. Sands. After he purchases them from Dr. Flint, Jacobs asks him "about emancipating my children" (106). Though Mr. Sands disappoints Jacobs through his inability to free the children immediately, she does not give up hope. Throughout her life, she persists in mothering them from afar. Her goal remains resolute; even though the political system she lives within diminishes her rights, she continually advocates for her children. Her drive to ensure a better future for Benny and Ellen demonstrates her humanity, because her relationship with them illustrates that Benny and Ellen are children, not chattel. The bond she shares with her children affirms the humanity of the Black family despite the barriers that often separate her from them.

Movement versus Stasis in The Underground Railroad

Two questions guide my approach to teaching *The Underground Railroad*: Why does Cora consistently stop on her journey? Why doesn't she run until she reaches freedom? Whitehead answers these questions through Cora's relationship with her memories of her mother and grandmother. When the audience first meets Cora, she has refused to join another enslaved person, Caesar, in his attempt to run away: "The first time Caesar approached Cora about running north, she said no. This was her grandmother talking" (Whitehead 3). Yet by the end of the same chapter, she has decided to embark on a journey toward freedom: "Three weeks later she said yes. This time it was her mother talking" (8). The hesitation that

Cora exhibits references her struggles with lessons she learned from her mother and grandmother.

Throughout the novel, Cora struggles with her matrilineal heritage. Cora's journey is framed by the journeys of her grandmother, Ajarry, and her mother, Mabel. Whitehead begins the novel with Cora's decision not to leave Georgia. This decision is informed by her grandmother. Whitehead then provides a historical overview of Cora's matrilineal line that hearkens back to familial histories shared in the narratives of fugitives from slavery. In short, Cora's journey is not her own. It is a continuation of Ajarry's. Ajarry's journey starts in Africa when she is separated from her family and changes hands between many owners. The slave trade teaches Ajarry about the value of her body on the market. Her position within the slavery system is connected to her productivity as a woman used to breed more enslaved people. Though she is able to bear five children, only one survives: a young girl named Mabel. As a mother, Ajarry attempts to equip her children for the challenges they will face in a society that allows slavery. She instills the values she learns through her experience being kidnapped and traded: "Ajarry bore five children by those men, each delivered on the same spot on the planks of the cabin, which she pointed to when they misstepped. That's where you came from and where I'll put you back if you don't listen. Teach them to obey her and maybe they'll obey the masters to come and they will survive" (8). Her teaching strategy develops into a focused attempt to ensure their survival. Ajarry's experience has taught her that Black women and children are not treated with human dignity. Therefore, the way to survive a brutal reality is to observe the expectations of the enslaver and conform to the environment. This strategy did not prove successful for many of her children. Her hope to ensure that they lived on was undercut by the brutality of slavery.

Ajarry never enjoys freedom after she is kidnapped from Africa, but Mabel experiences a short respite in the swamp the night after she decides to flee Georgia: "On the bed of damp earth, her breathing slowed and that which separated herself from the swamp disappeared. She was free" (300). As Mabel lies on the ground breathing deeply, she for the first time experiences a sense of independence. At one with nature, she relishes this moment as a unique defining experience. When she runs away, she experiences a feeling of empowerment that reassures her of her commitment to her daughter. Mabel's decision to run without Cora is an important one. Freedom for Mabel is about demonstrating agency over one's own life despite the expectations of her environment. Mabel claims her humanity and transforms her daughter's life in this one action.

Even though she feels free for the first time, there is an absence for Mabel. She misses her daughter and decides to return to the plantation, holding on to the brief memory of freedom she earned the night in the swamp: "She had to go back. The girl was waiting on her. This would have to do for now" (300). Nevertheless, Mabel does not make it back to her daughter and dies in the swamp after being bitten by a snake. Her death that night leaves a void within

Cora's life and changes her status on the plantation. Though Cora never learns about her mother's desire to return to her, Whitehead shares this information with the audience. Through Mabel's death on her return to the plantation, she shows the commitment and resilience of the enslaved Black mother. Mabel captured a moment for herself and wanted to share it with her daughter to empower her and promote her own survival in the years to come.

Unlike *Incidents in the Life of a Slave Girl*, *The Underground Railroad* does not focus on the life of a mother; instead, the protagonist is a daughter who seeks to reconcile the lessons left from her mother, Mabel, and her grandmother, Ajarry. Throughout the novel, Cora struggles to deal with her mother's disappearance and how her absence changed her status at the plantation: "When Mabel vanished Cora became a stray. Eleven years old, ten years, thereabouts—there was no one now to tell for sure. In Cora's shock, the world drained to gray impressions" (14). Once Mabel vanishes, Cora must learn to rely on herself: as a young child, she is dependent on her mother for protection, and without Mabel, Cora occupies a less secure position on the plantation and becomes an outcast. This devaluation in status requires her to demonstrate self-reliance in order to survive.

Synthesis: Mothering as Resistance in Slave Narratives and Neo–Slave Narratives

To emphasize the focus on mothering, I include a research paper toward the end of the unit. After students read both narratives, they examine the role of the enslaved mother in the literary genre of neo–slave narratives. This research paper requires students to investigate enslaved mother characters in both works and consider their resistance strategies. The assignment does not focus on genre but rather on character and agenda. In this way, students explore a key feature of both fugitive slave narratives and neo–slave narratives: the enslaved mother. Their investigations encourage them to reevaluate the idea of the enslaved mother. This is not merely a historical character that is acted upon. More accurately, the enslaved mother represents a human being fighting for her family's survival. Following is the prompt for the assignment:

> Throughout the semester, we have explored the role of enslaved mothers in slave narratives. The legal policy known as *partus sequitur ventrem* ensured that the child would follow the condition of the mother. As such, children born to enslaved mothers were considered property no matter their father's legal condition. As a result, enslaved mothers retained no legal rights to their children. Nevertheless, the lack of legal rights did not prevent enslaved mothers from rebelling against these principles.
>
> Write a comparison and contrast essay where you analyze enslaved mothers' resistance strategies. Identify one enslaved mother from *Incidents in the Life of a Slave Girl* and one enslaved mother from *The Underground*

> *Railroad.* Describe the limitations each mother faces within the system of slavery and argue how each mother individually fights to protect her children despite these limitations. Ultimately, your goal is to consider how these two specific enslaved mothers fought to protect their lives and the lives of their children.

This assignment creates an opportunity for synthesis. Students are encouraged to reflect on both works and consider the policies that governed the lives of enslaved people. These policies relegated Black mothers to the position of animals for breeding, yet many women fought against these dehumanizing laws. While their struggles were not always successful, studying these women and completing the assignment teaches students the ways in which the enslaved sought to protect themselves and their families from the horrors of slavery. This assignment focuses on individual protest as a strategy to convey the overarching political purposes of slave narratives. In addition to representing accounts of the impact of slavery on an individual, fugitive slave narratives also demonstrate the power of the Black family by showing the lengths to which Black mothers would go to maintain their connection to their children.

From Celia to Cyntoia: Between Love and the Law in Jacobs's *Incidents in the Life of a Slave Girl* and Perkins-Valdez's *Wench*

Colleen O'Brien

The impossibility of finding love, particularly something as powerful as "all the ardor of a young girl's first love," sets the stage for Harriet Jacobs's narrative of slavery's dehumanizing effects (58). Teaching at a regional state university in the South that serves a significant number of African American students, I often include Jacobs's *Incidents in the Life of a Slave Girl* on the reading list in my classes. Most of my students, a majority of whom are African American, appreciate Jacobs's initial love story—her desire to marry a "colored carpenter" (58). At the same time, they find Jacobs's disdain for her enslaver powerful and empathize with her struggles.

Jacobs's precarious situation was not uncommon. In 1850, a fourteen-year-old girl named Celia—with no last name—became enslaved by a septuagenarian farmer named Robert Newsom. According to the record provided by A. Leon Higginbotham, Newsom raped Celia on the way home from the slave auction and continued to do so for five years, until Celia sent warnings that she would hurt him. According to the digital records of the infamous case that are now available online, Celia had developed a relationship with a fellow enslaved person and become pregnant for the third time, unsure which man had fathered her unborn baby. But she had had enough. When Newsom disregarded her message to stay away, Celia followed through on her threat, hitting Newsom over the head with a stick. She claimed that she hadn't meant to kill him, but when she realized he was dead, she cleaned up the mess, burning his body and spreading his ashes on the pathway (Higginbotham 100).

In 2004, fourteen-year-old Cyntoia Brown (now Brown-Long) murdered Johnny Allen, a middle-aged white man who had paid $150 to have sex with her. Both Celia and Cyntoia claimed self-defense; both women faced murder convictions. Celia was hanged, and Cyntoia faced life in prison with the possibility of parole after fifty-one years. Modern-day sex trafficking captures the attention of many college students, perhaps because it involves individuals close to their average age and because Cyntoia's case in particular drew attention and support from numerous celebrities, resulting in the publication of her memoir and the production of two documentaries, *Me Facing Life: Cyntoia's Story* and the more recent *Murder to Mercy: The Cyntoia Brown Story*. Celia had no such support or recognition, of course, much like the teenage Jacobs, who suffered in silence until the publication of her own narrative decades later.

The power of narrative to reclaim one's life, for Jacobs and Brown, provides a way to resist oppression. Long before Celia invoked her common-law and natural right to self-preservation, Jacobs faced an enslaver who also constantly threatened her with rape. Jacobs's claims of self-defense hinged on the idea of sacred self-sovereignty (Stauffer 8). When Jacobs's enslaver chastises her for having an affair and conceiving a child out of wedlock, she replies, "I have sinned against God and myself . . . but not against you" (91). She thereby articulates her own right, sanctioned in the eyes of God, to control and protect her own body and to enter into sexual relations as a teenager.

Unlike Celia and Cyntoia, however, Jacobs claims to have avoided sexual abuse, and she chooses to defend herself from her enslaver's verbal abuse because of the sense of self she has gained through an intimate sexual relationship with a "lover who had always treated [her] honorably" (91). Thus, claims to the legal right of self-defense, in this case, connect integrally to the human experience of love. Jacobs's first love, "a colored carpenter, a free born man" (58), provides the model of citizenship and honor that informs her understanding of her legal right to selfhood.

While many undergraduates might recognize the hashtag #FreeCyntoia, they are less likely to grapple with the intricacies of Jacobs's language. Dolen Perkins-Valdez's 2010 novel *Wench*, however, also explores the dynamics of love, law, and self-defense within the context of slavery. Narrated through the eyes of four Black women who remain on free soil at a resort in Ohio in the 1850s to serve the sexual and domestic needs of their respective enslavers, *Wench* brings up issues similar to the stories of Cyntoia, Celia, and Harriet. The novel pairs effectively with *Incidents*, offering students the opportunity to question love and the law as they explore the parameters of selfhood outlined by Black women writers, then and now.

This essay describes how, in my undergraduate classes, I use strategically placed chapters from *Incidents* in dialogue with *Wench* to foster conversations and analyses of the dynamics of love, law, and self-defense in Black women's writing. Since many literature students set their sights on legal careers, the idea of using case history to analyze literature appeals to them. Celia's case, furthermore, now appears in digital archives that students can employ as primary sources to analyze the dynamics of sexual self-sovereignty, or lack thereof, in the antebellum era. The prevalence of sex trafficking today, furthermore, adds contemporary context to the issues at hand.

Wench, by contrast, is a twenty-first-century neo–slave narrative. Trudier Harris describes the setting of *Wench* as "striking" because it "locates a large portion of the action in Ohio, near Dayton, at Tawawa House, a resort that white southern planters use for a respite from the plantation life" (90). The striking detail is that Ohio is a free state; therefore, modern readers might wonder why, when the main character arrives in Ohio from Tennessee, she doesn't just run. As Harris goes on to say, "These white males routinely take their favored black 'wenches' with them for the month or so each summer that they reside in

Ohio" (90).[1] Nonetheless, as Harris points out, "Lizzie has no intent to take advantage of free geographical space in the North and attempt to escape. She discovers . . . that slavery is as securely intact in northern territory as it was in Tennessee" (96). Having been brainwashed by her enslaver at the age of thirteen, Lizzie believes that she loves Drayle and submits completely to his abuse.

In an era of sex trafficking, we might ask students to consider the extent to which sexual slavery is still intact today, without geographic limits. Legal and political scholars argue, after all, that the discourse of inferiority within which the United States legal system developed still pertains in the twenty-first century. In addition, the racial and sexual contracts that amend the social contract—or government's responsibility to protect bodily integrity and property—continue to set aside the rights of all women and of all races other than "white" by creating exceptions to full citizenship.

Higginbotham argues that Celia's case, because the court found that she, as property, had no right to self-defense, initiates a legal precept of inferiority that would deny future Black women the right to protection from rape. From the time that Celia records her initial statement with the justice of the peace until her conviction for murder in the first degree and death by hanging within six months, officials doubt her ability and her motive for murdering her enslaver. The fact that Newsom purchased and began raping Celia five years earlier, when she was fourteen, and continued his assaults until the moment he died just didn't matter.

More interested in the hypothetical role of Celia's chosen lover, a man also enslaved by Newsom, in the murder than they were in Celia's reason for fighting back, the concept of a woman's defending herself was beyond comprehension to the white men in charge. The court could not imagine Celia's concept of "self" as a person, as a woman, or as a legal subject; her legally invisible concept of "self" explains the legal denial of her bodily integrity (Higginbotham 100). Carole Pateman and Charles Mills indicate that the intersection of the racial and sexual contracts in the law, from the colonial period through the twentieth century, contribute to the marking of Black bodies as sexually "degenerate" and therefore unrapable (143). In other words, the law defined Black womanhood as something less than personhood and the woman's body as unworthy of defense or protection.

As is the case with *Wench*, the nonfiction cases (those of Celia, Cyntoia, and Harriet) involve "miscegenation," or forbidden interracial sexual relations. As Pateman and Mills indicate—and undergraduates can view copies of original documents online that verify this history as well—the first laws forbidding interracial sex appeared in the thirteen colonies ("Colonial Slave Codes"). The "sexual contract" of marriage between white colonists ensured racial purity, "but under the racial contract men's choice of a wife had to be limited if racial bloodlines and racial power were to be maintained. Maryland enacted the first criminal law in 1664 and this was aimed at 'freeborn English women' who had made 'shamefull Matches with African slaves'" (Cott 44). Six of the original American colonies prohibited marriage between a white person and a Black or "mulatto" person, and three of the thirteen banned interracial sex outside marriage. Nancy Cott states that "the English colonies stand out as the first secular authorities to nullify and criminalize intermarriage on the basis of race or color designations" (41). In terms of sex, legal rights are also contingent upon a white woman's privilege through marital status; Pateman and Mills "emphasized the interconnections between marriage, employment, and citizenship in *The Sexual Contract* but under the racial contract the connections were severed for African Americans in the aftermath of slavery. Slaves were prohibited from marrying, thus underlying their exclusion from civil law" (143).

Jacobs's enslaver, of course, denied her hopes for marriage. Just as Jacobs claims to have replicated her feelings for her first love, a "colored carpenter," with the white neighbor who fathers her children, one of the main characters in *Wench* professes love for a white man who is also her enslaver. Like Jacobs, whose exposure to sexual harassment begins when she is in her early teens, the character in *Wench*, Lizzie, begins to work in her enslaver's house at age thirteen, bringing her "into closer proximity to whites than she had ever been" (Perkins-Valdez 90). She eventually gives birth to a son and a daughter, like Jacobs (Celia was expecting her third child when she murdered her enslaver), and claims that she loves her enslaver, Drayle. When she tells another enslaved woman at Tawawa, the rebellious Mawu, who eventually escapes, that she doesn't "mind spending time" with the man who treats her and her children as property, Mawu responds "You don't? . . . You think you love him?" (15–16). While Lizzie never frees herself physically, she develops an expanded consciousness of her situation, much as Cyntoia Brown would during her incarceration.

The availability of *Incidents* as an e-text, combined with the web availability of *Celia v. Missouri* documents ("Celia") as well as news articles and films about Cyntoia, makes for an excellent collection of learning objects to assemble for an online learning experience that includes primary documents, fiction, nonfiction, journalism, and video. We can ask students how the life writing genre, which can include *Incidents* as well as documentary interviews with Cyntoia, informs the creation of fictional texts like *Wench*. In an interview with Sarah Broom, Lauren LeBlanc writes "while memoir is often pigeonholed as subjective and emotional, the genre is a genuine entry point for history: Collective historical narratives are drawn from individual experiences."

I remember reading *Beloved*, by Toni Morrison, as an undergraduate and being fascinated with Morrison's ability to capture a historical moment and experience so vividly. As a historical novel, *Wench* provides us the opportunity to curate learning objects that can help students map out the process of understanding slavery two hundred years ago. The urgency of understanding such a project and of theorizing how collective historical narratives consolidate the trauma and injustice that racial and gender inequality creates, presents itself because sexual slavery, or sex trafficking, still affects women as a whole and women of color disproportionately.

Celia's story, of course, differs dramatically from Harriet's or Cyntoia's, because we learn of Celia only through the accounts of white people who supported the institution of slavery. The testimony scrawled by a justice of the peace, nonetheless, is fascinatingly dispassionate:

> Celia, a slave, duly sworn, belonging to Robert Newsom says that she killed her master on the night of the 23rd day of June 1855—about two hours after dark by striking him twice on the head with a stick, and then put his body on the fire and burnt it nearly up, then took up the ashes on the morning after daylight. After breakfast, the bones were not entirely burnt up. I took up the ashes and bones out of the fireplace in my cabin where I burnt the body and emptied them on the right hand side of the path leading from my cabin to the stable.
>
> Sworn to & attested before us on this 25th day of June 1855
>
> D. M. Whyte J.P. ("Statement")

Whyte, who composed and wrote her testimony, may very well have edited or embellished her account to make her seem like a coldhearted murderer. But the absence of affect might push readers to seek comparisons in Jacobs's nonfiction prose as well as Perkins-Valdez's fiction to better understand how this infamous event took shape. By exploring the web documents and accounts of Celia's trial and comparing them with the other texts at hand, then, students can speculate on the motivations and possible emotional or psychological reactions to the murder and subsequent burning. The document emphasizes more of the aftermath of the murder, in which Celia seems to describe her actions as quotidian cleaning duties. She incinerates the body, notices that the bones remain, and emphasizes which side of the pathway she spread them upon. It is as though she describes cleaning up from a pig roast, showing no remorse for the slaughter of the pig, who was actually a white man.

One can only wonder what pushed Celia to attack Newsom. Did she "snap" after five years of abuse? Did she despise the old man who impregnated her when she was fourteen, or did she merely submit to the demands of her chosen lover, George? Was she too sick from a pregnancy that she hoped grew from a consensual relationship to bear Newsom's attack? Cyntoia's claims about her own impetus for murdering Allen seem more logical and defensible in this collective context. A woman's response to sexual abuse might channel the force of multiple experiences, of multiple girls who are only fourteen, of multiple instances when the person in power does not expect anyone to question or challenge his demands as he smothers the personhood and desires of his victim. In *Wench*, for example, Mawu begins planning to escape from the moment she arrives on free soil. Her enslaver punishes the report of her first planned attempt, delivered by Drayle via Lizzie, with alarming public ferocity. Mawu's subsequent attempt to burn her enslaver alive, in that context, seems rather justified. Neither she nor any of the Black women can exist in a world where a man's right is to deny a woman any choice whatsoever, and she meets the violent subject who tries to erase her personhood with equal wrath and self-affirming fire.

While Jacobs exacts her revenge in words, not deeds, her narrative still challenges any man's right to overcome her sense of personhood and self-sovereignty, to deny her choice. The first time Jacobs's enslaver strikes her is when she tells him that she wants to marry her first love, the free Black man. She goes on to say, "When I had recovered a little from the effects, I exclaimed, 'You have struck me for answering you honestly. How I despise you!' There was silence for some minutes. Perhaps he was deciding what should be my punishment; or, perhaps, he wanted to give me time to reflect on what I had said, and to whom I had said it" (37). She subsequently tells him that he drove her to expressing her hate, to which he responds, "Do you know that I have a right to do as I like with you,—that I can kill you, if I please?" (37). Her retort, "You have tried to kill me, and I wish you had; but you have no right to do as you like with me," illustrates her belief in a right to self-defense regardless of the unjust laws that proscribe her choices (37).

NOTE

1. For original documents regarding Tawawa House, see "Tawawa House Broadside."

Lock and Key: Systemic Literacy and Dialectical Reading in *Incidents in the Life of a Slave Girl*

Ingrid Diran

In recent years, groundbreaking works in Black feminism have read Harriet Jacobs's *Incidents in The Life of a Slave Girl* as a prism through which to glimpse the reproductive afterlives of slavery in the context of racial capitalism.[1] While these critical reorientations are of inestimable importance for scholars of New World slavery and for an understanding of racial capitalism more broadly, their theoretical fluency, not to mention their sheer complexity, pose real pedagogical challenges in the undergraduate classroom. In this essay I suggest that *Incidents* itself contains elements that elucidate some of the most salient questions in this recent theoretical literature. Indeed, I suggest that presenting *Incidents* as an autotheorization of what Alys Weinbaum calls the "race/reproduction bind" is an effective strategy for introducing students to the intersecting problematics of slavery, political economy, and literary form.

Below I offer an account of how I approached this material in a virtual first-year honors literature seminar taught in fall 2020 at the University of Wisconsin, Madison. My students mostly hailed from Wisconsin or other midwestern states, had varying degrees of preparedness but a generally high level of motivation, and were taking this class in their first semester as college students. For almost all, Jacobs's text served as a general introduction to the history of enslavement and, certainly, to the roles of gender and capital therein.

This essay unfolds in three parts. In the first, I trace the contours of Jacobs's autotheory by reading two exemplary moments in which the enslaved girl demonstrates her "premature knowledge" regarding the slavery system's weaponization of her body, desires, and desirability. I refer to this precocious understanding as a form of *systemic literacy*. Next, I place *Incidents* in dialogue with two complementary genres of secondary reading that, in my experience, help students grasp how Jacobs reimagines the interlocking strategies of racialized bondage and economic surplus. At the conclusion of this essay, I turn to two figurations of Jacobs's resistance to this system—that of the "loophole" and of the "lock and key." I suggest that these figures can be mobilized pedagogically to enable students to grasp Jacobs's importance to freedom struggles waged against racial capitalism.

Incidents of Systemic Literacy

As I have already suggested—and as many students sense almost immediately—*Incidents* is a text that evinces self-awareness and a keen attunement to the broad political, legal, economic, and theoretical ramifications of slavery. I referred to this metacognition above as systemic literacy. Its signal contours are demonstrated in two exemplary reflections appearing in the chapter called "The Trials of Girlhood," which I read below. To be sure, these moments are hardly exhaustive of the phenomenon at stake, but they have the virtue of clarifying some of the central features of systemic literacy in Jacobs's text. They do so in three ways: first, they frame certain "incidents" befalling Jacobs in particular through the shared and collective experience of enslaved girls in general; second, they describe the deforming effects of the slavery system on victims and putative beneficiaries alike; and, third, they characterize the "education" of the enslaved girl in terms of a mandatory precocity or epistemic "prematurity":

> He [Dr. Flint] told me I was his property; that I must be subject to his will in all things. My soul revolted against the mean tyranny. But where could I turn for protection? No matter whether the slave girl be as black as ebony or as fair as her mistress. In either case, there is no shadow of law to protect her from insult, from violence, or even from death; all these are inflicted by fiends who bear the shape of men. The mistress, who ought to protect the helpless victim, has no other feelings towards her but those of jealousy and rage. The degradation, the wrongs, the vices, that grow out of slavery, are more than I can describe. They are greater than you would willingly believe. (27)

> Everywhere the years bring to all enough of sin and sorrow; but in slavery the very dawn of life is darkened by these shadows. Even the little child, who is accustomed to wait on her mistress and her children, will learn, before she is twelve years old, why it is that her mistress hates such and such a one among the slaves. Perhaps the child's own mother is among those hated ones. She listens to violent outbreaks of jealous passion, and cannot help understanding what is the cause. She will become prematurely knowing in evil things. Soon she will learn to tremble when she hears her master's footfall. She will be compelled to realize that she is no longer a child. (28)

In the first passage, Jacobs transitions seamlessly from describing the effect of the fictionalized Dr. Flint's "tyranny" on "*my* soul"—a personal and intimate experience—to addressing the impersonal and institutional lack of legal protections ("no shadow of law") available to "*the* slave girl" in general, regardless of skin color. Through this exposition of her own *exemplarity*, Jacobs evinces awareness of the legal infrastructures that align her own experience with that of a potential *collectivity*. Furthermore, she extends this logic of exemplarity to Dr. Flint himself, whose cruelty, like the suffering he inflicts, is less a matter of personal fiat than an iteration of legally ascribed rights of ownership. Having thus identified the systemic basis of Flint's tyranny as well as of her own terror, Jacobs triangulates her analysis to include the figure of "the mistress," whose "jealousy and rage" is yet another tragic by-product of, and machination within, patriarchal property rights. (She notes that such rights result in parallel, if far milder, exclusions for white women.) The passage culminates in a systemic declaration that "[t]he degradation, the wrongs, the vices, that grow out of slavery" exceed descriptive capacity. We may note that they do not, however, exceed critical acumen, for Jacobs has, in fact, identified the provenance of such atrocities in the racially coded, state-sanctioned form of capitalist patriarchy.

In the second passage, Jacobs again fuses her experience with that of a representative enslaved girl, this time correlating the violence of enslavement to the end of childhood via a coercive form of sexual education. The girl's experience, she explains, requires the youth to become "prematurely knowing in evil things" and thus to develop fluency not only in the fickle depravities of enslavers but also in the institutional logics that engender extreme vulnerability and exposure. In this way, Jacobs presents her plight as simultaneously intimate and totally impersonal. The "race/reproduction bind" is lived intimately in body and socially in the enslaved community.

If we ask, in turn, what enables Jacobs to make such an extrapolation—that is, to translate the terms of her own suffering into an indictment of the slavery system—we find that her "teacher" is nothing other than the theft of childhood itself. Indeed, with the figure of "prematurely knowing," Jacobs suggests that there is an epistemic and temporal counterpart to what Hortense Spillers calls slavery's "theft of the body, a willful and violent . . . severing of the captive body from its motive will" ("Mama's Baby" 67). The paradoxical effect of this supplemental theft, as I have detailed elsewhere, is to *learn early* (and) *to think ahead.*[2] Ironically, it is precisely in her coerced precocity that the enslaved girl comes to exceed her captors' grasp of the slavery system; it is in being robbed of "innocence" that she is unfettered of any valorization of childhood that would sever personal experience from collective life. Unintentionally but inexorably, the slavery system's theft of Black childhood allows Jacobs, along with her peers of both sexes within the larger enslaved community, to grasp, better and sooner than her captors, the infrastructures of subjection—and hence, too, its loopholes.

Reading Jacobs in Community

If *Incidents* insists upon the institutional, communal, and reproducible dimensions of the enslaved girl's suffering, the text proceeds far more discreetly in limning the exemplarity of Jacobs's resistance to it. Below, I suggest how combining historical and theoretical secondary materials can help students grasp this other exemplarity of the enslaved girl: that of her economic savvy and revolutionary consciousness. To do so, I will draw on my experiences of teaching a course on the racial, political, and economic history of incarceration in which Jacobs features prominently.

To contextualize and specify the range of constraints under which enslaved women, especially those deemed "favorites," endured, I have turned to texts such as Brenda Stevenson's "What's Love Got to Do with It? Concubinage and Enslaved Women and Girls in the Antebellum South." In my course, I paired Stevenson's essay with the first half of *Incidents*, as an introduction into the erotic complications of slavery's property in persons (Locke 17) and as a text that demonstrates how commonplace were sexual predicaments such as Jacobs faced.[3]

Building upon this historical foundation, I have also turned to a range of theoretical and activist texts to elucidate the political and economic stakes of Jacobs's fugitive calculus. Key among these is Angela Davis's groundbreaking 1971 article in *The Black Scholar*, titled "Reflections on the Black Woman's Role in the Community of Slaves," which I paired with the second half of *Incidents*. Davis's article suggests the more capacious and abiding political implications of Jacobs's experience, as well as the communal matrix for its autotheorization. As I detail below, I found that this essay in particular offered students a conceptual paradigm with which to approach the political situation in *Incidents*, the economic context in which it unfolds, and its broader implications for freedom struggles more generally.

Written while Davis herself was incarcerated, and published less than a decade after the publication of the Moynihan Report, Davis's "Reflections" is of interest to students both historically and theoretically. The essay refutes the myth of Black matriarchy by attributing to the Black woman under slavery a centrality predicated not on supremacy but on radical equality. Arguing that among the "supreme ironies" of slavery is that "in order to approach its strategic goal—to extract the greatest possible surplus from the labor of the slaves—the black woman had to be released from the chains of the myth of femininity" (7), Davis shows how the Black woman wrested from "the deformed equality of equal oppression" an "immense potential" that allowed her "to ascend to the same levels of resistance which were available to her men" (8). Davis traces yet another, parallel irony in the enslaved woman's domestic duties, which, for all their drudgery and anguish, constituted "the *only* labor of the slave community which could not be directly and immediately claimed by the oppressor" (7). In this dual guise—as comrade to her man and as steward of a largely autonomous domestic sphere—the enslaved woman constitutes what Davis calls a "custodian of a house of resistance" (8). And, having thus established the revolutionary capacity of Black women, Davis concludes her essay by reframing the act of rape by enslavers as not simply gendered violence but a mode of political repression, "an unconcealed dimension of outright counterinsurgency" (8). In this light, the cunning by which Jacobs thwarts her "tyrant," by manipulating the economic calculus of another white man's desire, becomes legible not only as a brilliant stratagem but also as an act of radical political insurgency.

As students integrated the historical insight of Stevenson with Davis's insurgent critique, their reading of *Incidents* took on a new creativity and power. As I detail below, this constellation of texts enabled them to approach Jacobs's autotheorization, as well as her communally won emancipation, in a rich and dialectical manner, one that required their boldest interpretive claims to be made through, rather than at the expense of, specificity.

Making Freedom Space

After discussing as a group how Davis's dialectical presentation of the slavery system could be brought to bear on the concrete historical situation outlined by Stevenson, we discussed how one might view the particularities of the enslaved girl's experience as permutations of what Davis calls "dialectical moments in the slave woman's oppression" (12). This required grasping, as Jacobs herself does, that power relations within the slavery system are ambiguous and contestable. When students combined attention to Jacobs's systematic literacy with this focus on contestation, they began to discern that the source of Jacobs's emancipatory resolve was also what compelled the slavery system to evolve ever crueler oppressions: an abiding, collective resistance to their enslavement among the enslaved.

Readers of *Incidents* will be familiar with two motifs that recur throughout the narrative and that index, directly and indirectly, this tireless striving for freedom: the lock and key and the loophole. Each of these images exemplifies a potential for freedom that exists within and against the carceral structures of the slavery system. Their concreteness, I found, is pedagogically indispensable: students recognize that a loophole is not just a legal metaphor but an arrow slit in a wall, such as the inch-wide perforation Jacobs makes in the walls of her grandmother's garret; likewise, a key is not an abstraction of access but the material means for opening doors and floorboard hatches that imprison or conceal the fugitive. The key also contains a combination of grooves that match pins within the lock to turn it—a feature that, as I describe below, became an essential part of a culminating exercise.

After the discussion described above, I asked students to select a number of keywords from the text that were essential to Jacobs's ultimate escape. I then asked them to visualize the relation among these terms in a way that demonstrated their fundamental interdependence. To my surprise, the image several groups used was that of a key in a lock. In their visualizations, the pins on the key, whose combination alone could turn the lock, perfectly encapsulated the interdependent tactics that set Jacobs free.

Drawing on this image from my students, I created two more diagrams of the key that showed, first, how the combined pins enable Jacobs to emancipate herself and, second, how a literal revolution is implied in every turn of a lock (figs. 1 and 2).[4] Recalling Davis's argument that the enslaved woman constitutes a "custodian of a house of resistance," these two diagrams make visual and concrete the dialectical turn from oppression to resistance. Figure 1 renders the "dialectical moments" as "pins" that correspond to the grooves of Jacobs's plight—from the reality of equal exploitability of male and female enslaved people (pin 1) to the domestic setting in which the "favorite slave" (*Incidents* 30) is entrapped (pin 2) to the coerced dimensions of precocious sexual knowledge foisted upon enslaved girls in general (pins 3 and 4).

Figure 2 diagrams the revolutionary turn by which each of the previously oppressive moments, in necessary combination with each other, unlock possibilities for freedom. Perhaps most important among these pinpoints is the last: that of "deliberate calculation" (*Incidents* 49), or thinking a step ahead (pin 4). For it not only constitutes a form of resistance that Jacobs uses to outmaneuver the element of "outright counterinsurgency" signified by sexual violence; it is also what teaches Jacobs to read the institutional *complex* of slavery as a weaponized form of racial capitalism.

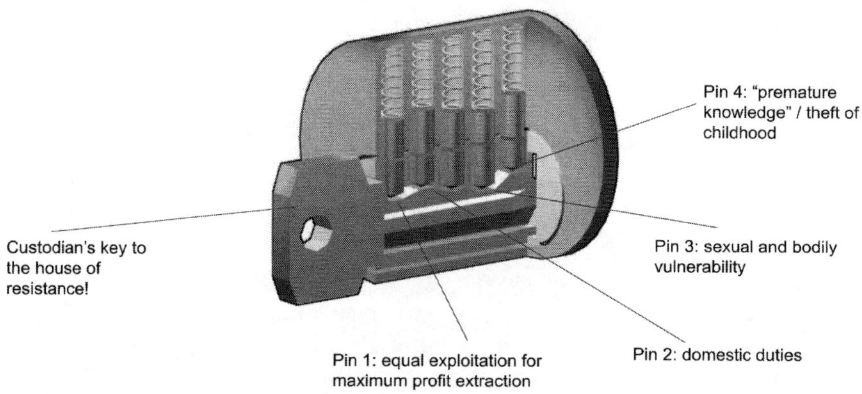

Figure 1. Dialectical moments of the enslaved girl's oppression.

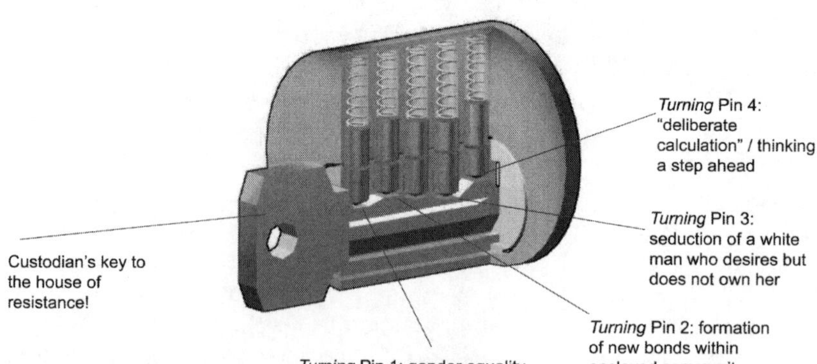

Figure 2. Dialectical moments of the enslaved girl's resistance.

Through diagrams such as these, instructors can draw upon the concept of "dialectical moments" to teach the abiding contestability of systemic oppression in New World slavery and in more contemporary iterations of expropriative violence. Such visuals not only unlock a new dimension of Jacobs's story but also link the intimate subterfuge and apparent "sophistry" of Jacobs's *Incidents* to the unfinished work of collective freedom.

NOTES

1. See, for instance, Hartman; Morgan; Spillers, "Mama's Baby"; and Weinbaum. Notably, they have reframed *Incidents* as a case study for exploring the relations among Black maternity, heritable kinlessness, and commodity production. For more on racial capitalism, see Robinson.

2. For an elaboration of this argument, see Diran.

3. Another excellent text to pair with *Incidents*, especially in the context of pregnancy and her descriptions of maternity in the context of slavery, is Morgan's *Laboring Women: Reproduction and Gender in New World Slavery*, which establishes the transatlantic provenance, character, and economy of reproduction in the context of slavery.

4. The technology of the key has, of course, become more complex since the nineteenth century. However, we may take the fact that my students visualized the nineteenth-century text via the twenty-first-century lock and key as a way of gesturing toward the contemporary salience of such questions, in a moment when both captivity and freedom take on ever more complex combinations.

From Harriet Jacobs to Assata Shakur: Connections between Past and Present

Kimberly Southwick-Thompson

Texts from the nineteenth century can be tedious reads for students in undergraduate literature courses, especially survey courses, for a number of reasons. They may find barriers in the language choices a writer has made or have difficulty understanding contexts that are crucial to the text—often a combination of these factors is what frustrates. Pairing a more contemporary text with one from a previous era, however, can allow students to think more concretely about an earlier text. Specifically, reading from Harriet Jacobs's *Incidents in the Life of a Slave Girl* and Assata Shakur's *Assata: An Autobiography* together introduces students to two writers—one a crucial and canonical writer from the nineteenth century and the other a writer and poet with a link to the Black Panther movement of the 1970s. The most obvious way Shakur's text can be read in relation to Jacobs's would be through the lens of both writers as Black women who give a female perspective on a broader theme of racism, especially in terms of the institutions they find themselves ensnared within. Drawing a line from the practices of slavery to the persecution of the Black Panthers and beyond helps students understand the twenty-first century, when systemic racism, through police brutality and the prison industrial complex, for example, still plagues America. Finding timeliness in a text like Jacobs's by reading it along with Shakur's can help them recognize how long injustices like those that twenty-first-century social justice movements fight against have existed, despite these injustices' many different masks.

Pairing a contemporary text with one from the past can be done throughout the semester in an American literature survey class, only on occasion, or even just once. Both women's texts are autobiographical prose, telling the story of their lives up until the point of the writing, which makes them a good pair not only for their subject matter but also for their genre. What autobiography is, how it has changed over time, and how a slave narrative is a certain type of autobiography are all subjects that can be addressed by looking at these women's texts together. To engage with the texts by considering their genre, students can ask, "How does each writer play to her intended audience?" An autobiography must, in order to be a reasonable length, choose representative moments from the writer's life to highlight, so asking students to answer questions about who their audiences are and how Jacobs and Shakur may have had their audience in mind lets them consider aspects of the texts such as why they have chosen these particular life moments to write about, why in this particular order, and what the intentions may be behind the supplemental commentary they provide regarding the events.

Jacobs's and Shakur's texts work so well together in the classroom in part because of similarities in subject and theme despite their temporal distance. It is not simply that both writers are Black women that unites these works but that both are treated unfairly because of their gender and race by individuals and institutions and over a century apart—one before the reconstruction period and one well after. That sexism and racism, both of which play crucial roles in these texts' conflicts, have existed for so long makes it easier for students to see why Jacobs's text, despite its publication date, is still relevant and important to read. When I taught these two texts concurrently in an upper-level women's literature course, I focused on specific chapters that highlighted their most important thematic similarities—mainly, the struggles the women detail that arise specifically from the fact that they are women imprisoned by racist institutions.

Jacobs's and Shakur's texts are both easily excerpted, and while assigning them in their entireties would make for many important conversations, focusing on relevant sections would be best for a survey class intended to cover a long period of time. Many standard anthologies of American literature already excerpt the Jacobs text, while Shakur's autobiography can be found in part on *Google Books*. Jacobs's chapter 7, "The Lover"; chapter 10, "A Perilous Passage in the Slave Girl's Life"; chapter 14, "Another Link to Life"; and chapter 41, "Freedom at Last" were the chapters I had students read. I assigned both forewords in the Shakur autobiography in addition to chapters 1 and 9, and I referred to other excerpts from the text as well. The forewords give background information students are likely unfamiliar with, specifically the political landscape of the 1970s and "the FBI's systemic surveillance of and attacks on Black groups and individuals . . . orchestrated by its counterintelligence program (COINTELPRO), which was directed specifically against what the FBI termed 'Black nationalist hate groups'" (Hinds xii). Chapter 1 details the now infamous incident where Shakur and two passengers are pulled over by cops in New Jersey and the shoot-out that leads to her arrest occurs. Chapter 9 addresses her pregnancy and childbirth while in prison.

The distance between slavery and wrongful imprisonment is condensed when students are able to draw parallels in the two women's lives. To condense that time for students, I opened class with the idea that linear progress is a myth. I had them reread the passage in the final Jacobs chapter where she sarcastically discusses her bill of sale, which culminates with this: "It may hereafter prove a useful document to antiquaries, who are seeking to measure the progress of civilization in the United States. I well know the value of that bit of paper; but much as I love freedom, I do not like to look upon it" (165). Her sardonic use of the word *progress* here and the idea that it might be measured allowed me to introduce the concept that not all cultures view time or progress as linear. I pointed out that many ancient and non-Western histories see progress as cyclical, rhythmic, or directionless rather than linear. With this in mind, students examined Jacobs's statement about measuring the progress of civilization, and I asked them to consider how her words read now, so many years after her experiences. From there, I showed the class an image from the myth of Sisyphus and briefly explained it to reinforce the idea of progress as not necessarily linear and to help highlight Jacobs's sarcastic tone.

In order to be sure that students were considering the potential nonlinearity of progress with the unfortunate truth of recent and contemporary racism and sexism in mind, we turned to a specific passage from Shakur's text, where she describes a conversation with a fellow inmate. While imprisoned in a West Virginian federal maximum security prison "designed to hold 'the most dangerous women in the country'" (Shakur 253), she notes that she and a friend agree that "sexism, like racism, was generated by capitalist, imperialist governments, and that women would never be liberated as long as the institutions that controlled our lives existed" (254). With these two quotations, one from each author's text, now fresh in students' minds, I ask them to reevaluate their notion of progress: Is it something they had previously viewed as linear, marching through time? Are women and specifically Black women "better off" today than in the past? Why or why not? After some spirited conversation that addressed the nuance a question like that demands to draw out, students were able to see how certain gains may have been made for women's rights and anti-racism and civil rights since Jacobs's and Shakur's times but ultimately that the idea of progress as an ideal is trickier to defend when some are still imprisoned, exiled, or separated wrongfully from their children. Despite gains, intersectionality teaches feminists that no woman can be considered liberated until all are.

In terms of specific subject matter, during our time with these texts we focused on how both of the enslaved women centered in these narratives have children. Both mothers are also separated from their children under different circumstances and against their will. Their experiences as pregnant women and mothers when read side by side can help students see the texts' parallel injustices. Pregnancy and childbirth are universal subjects that are often treated in literature and other media as joyful experiences; Jacobs's and Shakur's texts subvert that expectation.

When Jacobs becomes pregnant in order to escape her enslaver's advances, she is shunned by her grandmother for her sin and pitied by a friend of her mother's. She also suffers her enslaver's rage. In her narrative, she uses the word "humiliated" to describe her shame and says, "I shed bitter tears that I was no longer worthy of being respected by the good and pure" (68). Students better understand her shame when they think about her situation in blunt terms: in order to prevent being raped by her enslaver, Jacobs becomes impregnated out of wedlock by a free man who is not her first choice. Jacobs details her feelings of shame, and an important revelation for students is her desperation. That her choices in life at this point as an enslaved woman are few, and none are good, reveals a horror of slavery that some students might not have previously considered.

Shakur's pregnancy while imprisoned comes at first as a surprise to her, and though she is in jail awaiting trial for a murder she did not commit, she is happy to find herself with child, despite her complicated situation. These complications include that she is kept in solitary confinement, fed a diet that includes food it is against her religion to eat, which she refuses, and granted only a limited number of visits from the doctor of her choice. Despite her commitment to her daughter, pregnancy is a difficult time for her, compounded by the circumstances of her life during incarceration. After she gives birth, she is separated from her baby for hours, and once she is discharged from the hospital, she is again separated from her—and this time if and when she will be reunited with her is uncertain. However, the most powerful passages in the chapter about pregnancy, childbearing, and its aftermath are those containing the details of her abuse at the hands of the prison and hospital staff. There is only one doctor she trusts, and she is constantly kept from him; it is only after protests and deft navigation of legal red tape by her insistent lawyers that he is even the one who delivers her child. Shakur's distrust of most of those around her is valid, considering the abuse, and these vivid details are what sticks with students the most.

When read side by side, the women's abuse at the hands of those in an unearned position of power over them is distinct—yet despite their differences, the similarities when viewed through a broader scope are obvious. They bring attention to the choices that these women are forced to make—and how little choice they really have, considering their situations. Students, from there, should be able to point to what limits the women's choices and why they each choose as they do. Students are horrified when they read the specifics of these women's lives—pregnancy and childbirth are often heralded as important milestones in a woman's life, and the circumstances under which these women give birth impacts many students. The injustices each suffers are clear.

Through reading these texts together, students became passionate about the issues that each woman faced. During our discussion, they also came to an understanding of how racist practices today are perpetuated by lingering issues of the past—something that the connections between Jacobs, Shakur, and current news stories forged for them. Supporting resources that could be utilized are Alice Walker's essay "In Search of Our Mother's Gardens," the documentary *Thirteenth*, and excerpts from Michelle Alexander's *The New Jim Crow: Mass Incarceration in the Age of Colorblindness*. Another great complementary text would be the hip-hop song by the artist Common, titled "A Song for Assata," which covers much of the Shakur autobiography and the emcee's reactions and feelings to reading it. However, these are supplementary, considering the ground that Jacobs's and Shakur's texts alone, even when excerpted, can cover.

The direct line that can be drawn between enslavement, the Jim Crow South, mass incarceration, and police brutality should not go understated. Teaching Jacobs in the college literature classroom and including a more contemporary text beside it gives an opportunity for an instructor to stress the relationship between these afflictions. Students are drawn to Jacobs's story for its subversion and the text's ambivalent ending—a woman writing to help end the system that nearly destroyed her until she conceded to a path she found less terrible than others. The conditions of Jacobs's enslavement as a woman and the racism that made it possible—racism that continued through different but undeniable ways from the nineteenth through the twentieth century—are underlined when read next to Shakur's autobiography. This line could be traced more directly into the twenty-first century if read next to a text that directly addresses something like the police brutality that came to national attention in the 2010s and the social justice movements that came of them; Claudia Rankine's *Citizen: An American Lyric* comes to mind as a possible inclusion in that vein.

Shakur's story takes place over forty years ago, but its ties to twenty-first-century police brutality are undeniable. By connecting Shakur's experiences to the present day, it is easier for students to put Jacobs's experiences of slavery in context. Slavery can often seem like something difficult to comprehend or talk about with students. When instructors position a text that addresses the nuances of slavery beside a text that addresses issues people of color still face in the prison industrial complex, slavery as a reality of American history and literature becomes less blurred for students. They can then see the direct connections between historically wrongful practices and those that still exist in contemporary institutions. These two women's experiences are each key to understanding the unique experiences of enslaved and incarcerated women, and the parallels students are able to discover when their autobiographies are read side by side strengthen their understanding of the texts individually.

Repetition and History in *Incidents in the Life of a Slave Girl*

Molly Ball

Encountered in a survey of American literature, *Incidents in the Life of a Slave Girl* can seem to occupy a straightforward place in literary history. After all, its historical, political, and generic traits are readily apparent: *Incidents* is decidedly antebellum, decidedly abolitionist, and decidedly a slave narrative. While *Incidents* fits neatly into these categories, I take care to show my students that it is also a text that disrupts tidy literary-historical classifications. Specifically, it disrupts the dominant historical narrative in which racialized slavery existed in the antebellum South for centuries and then ended decisively with the conclusion of the Civil War. I want students to recognize that *Incidents* disturbs this historical account by troubling the bright lines often drawn between antebellum and postbellum, North and South, enslaved and free. By tracking how *Incidents* highlights continuities between these seeming oppositions, students see that while *Incidents* is certainly an abolitionist text, its political relevance does not end with the abolition of slavery. Jacobs's exhaustive description of exactly what the "advance" from slavery to freedom entails—the compromises involved, the traumatic repetitions engendered, the people left behind—leads students to question the presumption that history automatically progresses. This, in turn, forces us to consider how much our society has in fact progressed since Jacobs's era. The questions this text raises appear not only in the specific events Jacobs describes but also in the structure of the narrative itself, which is marked by repetition and ironic inversion. By calling students' attention to this structure and to the way it reflects Jacobs's unwillingness to affirm that a traumatic past can simply be left behind, I help students encounter the text's uncomfortable proximity to our own cultural moment.

Usually, in the class session just before we begin *Incidents*, I give students a brief outline of its plot and ask two questions: Why do you think we are reading this text? Why do you think we continue to read slave narratives today? They complete a free-write on these questions, and we discuss. Often, a majority of the class cites the importance of knowing history, and some students (if I've effectively cultivated an open atmosphere) state that they're not necessarily sure why we read such texts. Having briefly introduced students to the text and primed them to wonder about the utility of such texts, they begin reading, and we begin discussing at our next meeting.

I begin our first day with some theoretical framing. Many students have been taught to understand slavery and its harms in largely physical terms, as a system defined primarily by forced labor, bodily deprivation, and visible violence. In order to complicate this understanding, I introduce Orlando Patterson's concept of natal alienation, which refers to the effects of systematically severing familial ties. By denying enslaved people any enforceable, legal claim on family members, the slavery system worked to stymie the transmission of resources, culture, and knowledge from one generation to the next. Thus, the slavery system enforces "the loss of ties of birth in both ascending and descending generational time," isolating individuals within their own generation (Patterson 5). Introducing the concept of natal alienation not only helps students think with more nuance and complexity about the slavery system but also prepares them to grasp the political significance of Jacobs's concern with kinship and family. Seen in light of natal alienation, Jacobs's text does not simply argue that slavery should be abolished; rather, it contends with a system that works to sever Jacobs from both her past and her future. Thus, while her attachment to family complicates her individual bid for freedom, her refusal to simply leave constitutes a potent form of resistance against a system that denies family ties across time. In these ways, time and history—particularly insofar as they are mediated by kinship—become central concerns in the text.

Having established that Jacobs's text contends with the slavery system not just as a problem of physical violence but also as one of time and family, we can carefully examine how Jacobs frames her individual story as an interrogation of history itself. To begin this process, I typically start with the text's opening passage, which offers a deceptively simple account of Jacobs's family history going back to the Revolutionary War. Jacobs notes that her "maternal grandmother [Martha] . . . was the daughter of a planter in South Carolina, who, at his death, left her mother and his three children free, with money to go to St. Augustine, where they had relatives. It was during the Revolutionary War; and they were captured on their passage, carried back, and sold to different purchasers" (9). On our first day with the text, I ask students to contemplate the significance of starting our exploration of *Incidents* with a focus on family history—what does this suggest about the text's concerns and goals? I then ask them to consider Martha's history—how does it problematize standard narratives of US history? Students readily grasp the irony of a situation in which revolutionary Americans, while fighting for their own freedom from England, capture and reenslave an emancipated mother and her children. They also note that this moment inscribes Jacobs's family—and, by extension, all enslaved African Americans—

as part of US history from its earliest days. As we discuss these points, students see how, from the text's very inception, Jacobs quietly undermines accounts of national history that make liberty a foundational principle, suggesting that slavery's presence belies these pretensions.

As students read further in the text, we circle back to this opening passage and consider how it presages later events in the text. For instance, young Martha's capture and reenslavement threatens to repeat itself in the lives of her descendants, as Jacobs is stalked by the Flints even after establishing a life in the North. Similarly, we refer back to this passage when we discuss Jacobs's decision to begin a sexual relationship with Mr. Sands, a white man. The fact that Martha herself is the daughter of a presumably white planter reveals Jacobs's pregnancy by Mr. Sands as a repetition of the past. Jacobs occupies a similar position to that of her great-grandmother, who seems to have achieved "something akin to freedom"—albeit briefly—for herself and her children when the enslaver and father emancipates them on his deathbed (50). And, in another unfortunate repetition, Sands proves as ineffective as Jacobs's white great-grandfather at ensuring his enslaved children's freedom. While Jacobs explains her initial hope, upon beginning a sexual relationship with Sands, that he might emancipate her and any potential children, he continually fails to do this (50).

Discussing such repetitions allows us to consider several key questions that guide our reading of the text as a whole: Do these repetitions suggest that Jacobs's mission is not to free herself just from slavery but also from a cycle of exploitation that threatens to repeat in each generation? If so, *does* Jacobs break free? When in the text is she truly free, if ever? How does she achieve this state? And, finally, is it possible for her to maintain ties with her family without having those ties link her to a traumatic, ever-repeating past?

In seeking to answer these questions, I direct students to other moments of repetition in which Jacobs seems to have advanced, only to find herself facing the same threats again. For instance, we closely examine chapters 31–36, which describe Jacobs's life when she reaches the North. I point out that while Jacobs organizes her text around the movement from slavery to freedom, almost immediately upon arriving to New York she notes how it "aped the customs of slavery" (137). After presenting students with this quotation, I ask them to find examples from the text. They mention the segregated train cars and dining rooms that Jacobs encounters, the totally free hand the Flints and their agents seem to have in hunting Jacobs to reenslave her, the power white Southerners (such as Mrs. Hobbs and Mr. Thorne) have over Jacobs and her daughter even in New York, and the fact that, each summer, New York is "swarming with Southerners" (145). Clearly, the divide between South and North (and the opposition between slavery and freedom it typically signifies) breaks down in the text. Students generally recognize that while Jacobs is no longer confined to a crawlspace, her new, Northern life is more similar to her old, Southern one than might be expected.

I then ask the class to consider the repetitions that threaten Jacobs's daughter, Ellen. I put the students in small groups and assign each group two passages:

one involving Ellen, the other involving a linked moment from earlier in the text. After groups have had a chance to reread and discuss their assigned passages, we analyze them as a class. First, we examine the moment in which Jacobs, still confined in the crawlspace, learns that Mr. Sands's sister-in-law wants to adopt Ellen. Jacobs writes that while "the prospect *seemed* fair . . . [she] knew too well how lightly slaveholders held such 'parental relations'" (116). We discuss how Jacobs may be worried here about a repetition of her own experience with her first enslaver, as described in chapter 1. That woman "had been almost like a mother" and promised Jacobs's "dying mother that her children should never suffer for any thing" (11), yet she failed to emancipate Jacobs, instead bequeathing her to her five-year-old niece. Fearing a repetition of her own white mother figure's betrayal, Jacobs protests Ellen's adoption. We discuss Mr. Sands's response: he sends Ellen to the Hobbs, his relatives in Brooklyn, saying they will shelter and educate her (116). Jacobs remains suspicious, and we move to the passage in which her suspicions are confirmed. Upon meeting Ellen in New York, she finds that Ellen has received no education. Ellen's "guardian," Mrs. Hobbs, informs Jacobs that "Mr. Sands, has *given* her to my eldest daughter. She will make a nice waiting-maid for her when she grows up" (139). As the class mulls over this moment together, students usually note that, despite living in Brooklyn with her own father's relatives, Ellen seems poised to repeat her mother's trajectory. She will be forced into service to a family whose history is bound up with her own; the fact that these people are her biological *relatives* does not deter them, just as it did not deter Mrs. Flint, who, Jacobs points out, was nursed by Martha and thus is a kind of "foster-sister" to Martha's children (10). Moreover, Ellen is subjected to the same sexual threats as her mother. Mr. Thorne, a dissolute Southerner who lives with the Hobbs, "poured vile language into [Ellen's] ears" (148). This language echoes descriptions of earlier moments, in which Dr. Flint "began to whisper foul words in [Jacobs's] ear" (27). It also recalls Mrs. Flint's own whisperings as she leans over Jacobs in the night, pretending to be Dr. Flint (32). The fact that Ellen's sexual harassment begins in the North powerfully underscores the profound threat that the past poses. These repetitions are not bound by geography, nor are they laid to rest by the simple passage of time. While Ellen embodies the potential promise of a generation living beyond the yoke of slavery, she also demonstrates the very real ways in which this promise may go unrealized.

After discussing Thorne's "foul words" (148) and the way they signal the past's tendency to repeat itself in each generation, I ask students to reflect on the narrative as a whole. If the class were to plot the text's events visually, what shape would emerge? For instance, would Jacobs's life be an ascending line, in which things progressively improve with time? Would it be a jagged line, moving up and down at unpredictable intervals but never reliably progressing? Would it be a circle, moving sometimes up, sometimes down, but never deviating from the same cyclical patterns? Or would it take some other shape? I ask students to come to the board to draw their plots, and then we discuss, working toward some consensus about what shape this narrative takes and, further, what that shape suggests about its broader message. In this exercise, students engage with the text's stance on history: Does the text support or indict a model of history characterized by steady, inevitable social progress?

Having considered how narrative structure addresses history's potential to progress, we reach the pivotal—and highly ambivalent—moment in which Jacobs attains her freedom. First, we examine Jacobs's reaction to the news of her sale, in which she exclaims:

> So I was *sold* at last! A human being *sold* in the free city of New York! The bill of sale is on record, and future generations will learn from it that women were articles of traffic in New York, late in the nineteenth century of the Christian religion. It may hereafter prove a useful document to antiquaries, who are seeking to measure the progress of civilization in the United States. I well know the value of that piece of paper; but much as I love freedom, I do not like to look upon it. (165)

I ask students, Why does she not like to look upon this paper? Why all the talk of "future generations" and "antiquaries . . . seeking to measure the progress of civilization" (165)? I ask them why attaining freedom—ostensibly the goal of a slave narrative—is cast in such ambivalent terms. As we discuss, students develop an understanding that this legal transaction does not straightforwardly end her enslavement—it also inscribes the fact that she was enslaved, a fact that cannot simply be laid to rest, either for victims of enslavement or the broader community that condoned it. Thus, just two paragraphs later, when Mrs. Bruce, the employer who bought Jacobs's freedom, exclaims, "O Linda, I'm *so* glad it's all over!" (166), I ask students to free-write on the following questions: Is Mrs. Bruce right? *Is* it over? And what is "it" in this context, anyway? What is "it" for Mrs. Bruce, and what is "it" for Jacobs?

By asking these sorts of questions, I encourage students to consider the harms that Jacobs confronts in this text—not just slavery as a monolithic institution but the specific, discrete experiences it unleashes, again and again, on her and her family. These include sexual harassment, sexual exploitation, wage theft, family separation, shame, confinement, and much more. Once students have begun to articulate exactly what "it" is beyond simply "slavery," we can then discuss what is and is not ended by technical emancipation. To do this, we typically turn to the famous line from the text's penultimate paragraph, in which Jacobs notes, "Reader, my story ends with freedom; not in the usual way, with marriage," and then observes that while her situation has dramatically improved, she is not independent (167). In her words: "God so orders circumstances as to keep me with my friend Mrs. Bruce. Love, duty, gratitude, also bind me to her side" (167). I ask students, What does it mean that Jacobs describes herself as still "bound" at the end of this text? What does it mean that she still labors in a white woman's home, albeit for wages?

In posing such questions, I am not asking students to see this text as relentlessly pessimistic or despairing. I do, however, want them to contend with the ways that *Incidents* asks us to be uncomfortable, not merely on behalf of the historical Jacobs and her trials but also about the fact that we still live in a world in which the repetition of sexual, race-based, and gender-based violence persists from generation to generation. Seen in this light, *Incidents* is simultaneously an antebellum slave narrative and an alarmingly contemporary critique, one that compels us to consider how slavery, patriarchy, and sexual exploitation inscribe themselves on present-day relations.

Incidents in the Life of a Slave Girl in an American Literature Survey Course

Susanna Hoeness-Krupsaw

Undergraduate survey courses often pose special challenges deriving from the need to balance the teaching of a large amount of material with the desire to encourage depth of thought and understanding. My interactive group activity enables students to reflect on their weekly readings by bringing several authors and their texts into a conversation with one another, specifically Harriet Jacobs's *Incidents in the Life of a Slave Girl* with the transcendentalist authors Ralph Waldo Emerson and Henry David Thoreau. Students engage in close reading activities and create performances that foster empathy through "embodied" experiences with literary texts.

Background

At my public, four-year, comprehensive university, the entire sophomore-level American literature survey course is taught in a single sixteen-week semester. It is a required course for all English majors regardless of emphasis. For many of my students, this course may constitute their only extensive exposure to American literature; thus, it is crucial that I acquaint them with as many different authors as possible to prepare them for the battery of tests, such as the major field test or teacher licensure examinations, that awaits them at the end of their senior year.

The university is located in a rural to suburban area. About half of our students commute to school; the others live in campus apartments or in off-campus housing. Many of my students are first-generation college attendees, and most of my students work outside of school for at least twenty hours a week to help pay for their education, so that finding time to complete reading assignments is often difficult. Hence, I must select items that are both relevant and stimulating; owing to time constraints, I can assign only a few chapters that complement prior and subsequent assignments. Despite these constraints, I try to spend as much time as possible on establishing connections between representative texts and their historical contexts and among the literary texts themselves.

To do justice to all the facets of this survey course, I group materials into units that permit written reflection at the end of each week. These reflections usually occur in the form of weekly reader response submissions or online blog posts. Another easy and engaging means of achieving the same learning objectives is a group role-playing activity that emulates a staple of TV programming, the talk show. Our discussion of transcendentalist texts and slave narratives written before the Civil War leads to a four-participant mock talk show, which I like to call "The AmLit Show." My goals for this exercise are simple: I want students to master course content, understand the importance and relevance of the texts we are studying, and use their imagination to envision a meeting of Emerson, Thoreau, and Jacobs. If these three authors were invited to a talk show, such as *Oprah*, *Ellen DeGeneres*, *The Late Show*, or *The Daily Show*, how would they interact? What would Jacobs say to the two transcendentalist philosophers?

Methodology

Keeping in mind our course format and my objectives for the course, I embrace two pedagogical tenets to prepare the teaching activity described in this article: I have students approach the texts from a reacting-to-the-past perspective, and I embrace embodied care ethics, through which I want my students to develop a physical experience with the material they are reading so that they can experience emotions that lead them toward greater empathy and a desire to work for social justice.

My methodology is an adaptation of the popular Reacting to the Past series (from Norton Publishing, originally developed at Barnard College [reacting.barnard.edu]) and other historical game-playing or debate game approaches that are now used at over 350 colleges and universities (Flaherty).[1] Norton texts, for instance, collect historical documents and provide students with scenarios that lead them to perform cultural thought experiments. What my lesson plan accomplishes is very similar; however, I simply use our course texts as historical documents and the playful talk show format as scenario. I must also shorten the time span needed for completion of the exercise. The book series is extensive, expensive, and time-consuming. Consequently, I have adapted the concept of reacting to the past for my talk show purposes, an activity that can easily be completed in three fifty-minute class periods, with a short preparation before and a short reflection at the end of each. The adversarial and competitive element in the debate style of the book series does not align with my aims as an educator; we conduct a conversation, not a debate.

I come to the material with the idea that the study of literature and art enhances desirable empathetic behaviors that psychologists fear are in decline (Hall and Leary). Suzanne Keen, who works on narrative empathy, describes how cognitive science shows that art and literature can improve empathetic outcomes (213). The "identification with characters" can invite empathy (214). If that is indeed the case, then physically engaging in the performance of a piece of literature and stepping into a character's life further increase our empathetic experience. Scholars in performance studies, such as Beverly Whitaker Long and Mary Frances Hopkins, have long held the belief that literature can be studied through performance and that deep and meaningful engagement with texts and characters creates an experience that broadens our horizons and expands our moral compass.

This connection between literature and ethics finds further support in theories of embodiment and ethics of care. Philosopher Maurice Hamington explains that we use our imagination to figure out how another person experiences the world. Referencing eighteenth-century philosophers David Hume and Adam Smith, Hamington suggests that "the imagination fosters sympathy or empathy" (12). It enhances an individual's moral imagination, what Hamington refers to as the "caring imagination," composed of three characteristics: "empathy, critical reflection, and psychosocial context" (12). Hamington writes that "[t]he embodied dimension of care will lead to the demanding moral mandate that we experience one another, particularly those who are unfamiliar to us, which is itself a radical imperative" (7). These inspiring ideas help me justify spending a good amount of class time on a role-play activity.

The historical context for the activity is Emersonian transcendentalism. Students read Emerson's "Self-Reliance" and brief excerpts from Thoreau's *Walden* and "Resistance to Civil Government," from unit 5 of Michael O'Conner's *Digital American Literature Anthology*, to study how these philosophers promoted abolition, women's suffrage, and the Lyceum movement. Students question Emerson's seeming lack of awareness of the absence of freedom and opportunities for self-realization among the many people still in bondage in 1841, when his essay was published. Drawing on Michael Magee's research, I point out that Emerson later corrected his oversight in works such as "Address on Emancipation in the British West Indies" (1844) and "The Fortune of the Republic" (1864; Magee 110). Students expecting contemporary forms of activism remain disappointed by the often abstract nature of nineteenth-century abolitionist dissent. Even though my students often struggle with the dense texts and even denser philosophical concepts, terms such as *individualism*, *independence*, and *personal freedom* usually do capture their interest, and they are not averse to pondering the implications of Emerson's ideas.

The work of Thoreau generally generates more interest, particularly in his complaints about strong government. They see him as an early hippie, someone who dropped out of mainstream social life for a while; in fact, the tiny-house movement has opened up a whole new branch of discussion possibilities. Students also realize that what Emerson and Thoreau so beautifully outline has serious limitations: they understand that individuality to the exclusion of communal relationships comes at a cost to our understanding of society's function. Many of my students work twenty to thirty hours a week to finance their university education and shake their heads at the transcendentalists' insistence on working less and spending more time in quiet contemplation.

Thus, we contextualize the discussion and interrogate the availability of transcendentalist ideals to large portions of the population. When questions arise about reactions to transcendentalism from the African American community, I point out that scholars acknowledge Frederick Douglass's ties to the transcendentalist movement. His struggle for freedom and abolition, his emphasis on education, and his complex journey toward self-awareness are cited in this context. Rarely, however, do we find discussions of Jacobs in these analyses, even though it can easily be argued that her narrative reveals elements similar to

Douglass's. We know that after her arrival in Rochester, she made the acquaintance of other reformers while working with her brother in an abolitionist reading room (Yellin, "Written" [H. Jacobs] 214). Therefore, I like to position Jacobs's *Incidents in the Life of a Slave Girl* at the center of our class activity so that we can discuss her narrative in the light of transcendentalism.

The AmLit Show

Before we begin the activity, I remind students that it is essential that they read the assigned materials and gain a good command of Emerson's and Thoreau's ideas so that they can engage in a dialogue with Jacobs's narrative. The activity itself is easy to set up.

In terms of preparations, I start the discussion and role-playing activity by introducing Jacobs's narrative as well as her particular predicaments and publishing difficulties. I prepare a PowerPoint presentation with selected passages from Jean Fagan Yellin's article to illustrate the effort it took to rehabilitate Jacobs's work and the central role it now plays in American literature. I show slides with the prefaces by the author and by the editor. Students have seen similar introductions in our discussions of Anne Bradstreet's and Phillis Wheatley's poetry. I quickly summarize the main points of the first half of Jacobs's narrative to contextualize the assigned chapter selections. Because of time constraints, I assign only chapters 17, 18, 21, 29, 30, 31, and 41.

On day 1 of the actual activity, we go over the assigned chapters from *Incidents* and answer any questions. We try to understand Linda Brent's particular difficulties caused by Dr. Flint's harassment, her choice to take a lover, her years in the garret room, her attempt at escape and near death from a snake bite, and her final escape to the North. Students are impressed by the vivid description of Linda's years in her "loophole" and by her courage and endurance. To flesh out these ideas, I draw on the scholarship of Carolyn Sorisio, who discusses how Jacobs works toward the attainment of selfhood. Sorisio is convinced that much like Emerson, Jacobs's decisions emphasize her individuality (5). Like Sorisio, my students observe Jacobs's fortitude and determination and the tremendous self-discipline her ordeal must have required, but they also recognize that Jacobs's narrative takes into account the author's relationships with many of the individuals she meets along her arduous journey.

A short, written homework assignment asks students to make two lists, one containing questions they would like to ask of Emerson, Thoreau, and Jacobs, emphasizing elements of the authors' philosophies and experiences, and the other with questions the three historical figures would ask of each other. I remind students to review their notes for Emerson and Thoreau and to take careful notes of key points while reading Jacobs's narrative.

On day 2, we return to our task, answer any questions that have arisen since our last meeting, clarify ideas in the chapter readings, and then break into groups to begin our "reaction to the past." Group composition will vary according to class size and abilities. In highly motivated classes, I randomly assign groups with four group members. Group members draw character cards (Emerson, Thoreau, Jacobs, and their favorite talk show host) to determine their respective roles. From the questions they prepared, group members select the most interesting ones and then compose possible answers for their respective characters. In larger classes, several students work together to develop the parameters of their character after they have collectively decided what kinds of questions a talk show host would ask of them. As a group, they determine key ideas they want to hash out "onstage." Individually, they write up their portion of the dialogue for later presentation to the class. By the end of the class, I require them to compare notes so that we can watch their performances when we return on day 3.

With less motivated students, I find that we achieve more meaningful results if I assemble the groups so that each group of three includes at least one individual who I feel confident will have read and understood the texts. In this case, I serve as talk show host and prepare questions beforehand. Each group is assigned just one character, and the group will collectively write the dialogue and determine who is going to present it to the class. In either group model, I walk around the room and assist groups, answer questions, and help guide discussion.

I find that even synchronous *Zoom* classes can easily complete this kind of group work in *Zoom* breakout rooms. By joining individual rooms, I continue to provide writing assistance. *Blackboard* groups offer another effective tool for assigning group membership and asking students, outside of class, to complete some of the writing tasks. The final talk show skit is simply read to classmates instead of performed in front of the classroom. In asynchronous online classes, groups can record a video of their skit or record separate slides for a *VoiceThread* performance.

Day 3 serves as performance day, during which we watch the skits. After initial hesitations or embarrassments when asked to perform their talk show, the role play offers many benefits to the students: the experience of stepping into their roles—a physically embodied experience—makes the nineteenth-century texts come alive. Speaking the words previously read on the page changes students' outlook as they gain greater empathy for the characters they are portraying.

During the AmLit Show performances, all students are asked to take careful notes so that they can discuss later on whether groups stayed within character, which ideas they would like to investigate further, and what they learned from this exercise. After performing the skits, students reflect in written review assignments on their experiences as members of the audience and participants in the writing and performance of the skits.

If time is short and I cannot accommodate the entire role-playing activity, I assign only a written assignment in which the students write out parts of the conversation that takes place among the talk show guests. If the assignment is posted to *Blackboard* blogs, for instance, the reflection element of the activity can take place in responses to classmates' posts.

Results are mixed, of course, but we usually achieve a good review of key elements of transcendentalism in counterpoint with Jacobs's experiences. The skits emphasize close reading of selected passages that place the authors in conversation with each other. For instance, Emerson will encourage Jacobs to become more self-reliant, to which she replies that she can hardly do that as a person enslaved in Dr. Flint's household, when the only option she sees is the creation of her "loophole." Thoreau, expounding on the spiritual quality of living in nature, will innocently ask whether Jacobs enjoyed the outdoor experience in the swamp during her first attempted escape. She ignores his question and asks him whether he worried about snake bites at Walden Pond. He may praise her for her choice of a simple life, to which she replies sardonically that he should try living in a garret for seven years.

Students eventually conclude that Jacobs would have responded favorably to several ideas in Emerson's essay, including self-reliance. While students think that she probably could relate to being isolated at Walden Pond, they point out the difference between choosing such a brief exile and having to seek refuge. Especially in the latter chapters of Jacobs's narrative, students like to point out that Jacobs, like Thoreau, is critical of United States laws and policies. Overall, students observe the differences in the authors' descriptions of nature and their assessments of individualism and solitude. They are well aware of Jacobs's much greater reliance on friends and interpersonal relationships to finally gain her freedom.

Through the talk show format of this activity, students practice essential communication skills such as listening, speaking, reading, and writing. The performances themselves add a creative, kinesthetic experience to our class that provides a cognitive alternative to our routine of lecture and discussion. In addition to reading and writing, by creating their dialogues for the show students must step into the persona of their assigned character and reflect what he or she would have said in that situation, enhancing their ability to empathize with that historical literary figure. In envisioning this fictitious encounter, they test the key elements of nineteenth-century transcendentalist philosophy against the daily realities of an enslaved African American woman. The close reading and performative elements of this activity have positive implications for other classes and can easily be applied to other class activities.

NOTE

1. Role-playing activities can create problematic situations when students perform the roles of captors or enslavers. In my exercise, this is, however, not the case. The four roles are so narrowly prescribed that many students choose to read quotations from the assigned pages for their dialogues. In fact, the exercise sensitizes students to the respectful and careful use of language when they asses each other's skits.

"Home, Sweet Home": The Melodrama of *Incidents in the Life of a Slave Girl*

Alex W. Black

Teachers commonly contextualize Harriet Jacobs's *Incidents in the Life of a Slave Girl* within mid-nineteenth-century American culture by categorizing it in the genre of the sentimental novel.[1] This essay proposes a complementary way of thinking about *Incidents*: in terms of theater and performance, specifically melodrama.[2] Imported from Europe in the late eighteenth century, melodrama was popular in the United States through the early twentieth century. Onstage, melodrama was known for its use of music (*melos* is Greek for "song"), its sensational plots, and its exaggerated characterization. But melodrama was not limited to the stage. As Peter Brooks has shown, the melodramatic mode worked across medium and genre.[3] Works in the melodramatic mode featured virtuous women and innocent children who triumphed over villainous men. Within an American context, as Linda Williams demonstrates, "racial melodrama" was used in *Uncle Tom's Cabin* (the novel and the plays) to dramatize slavery's—and male enslavers'—threat to families and their homes.[4] Act 5, scene 3 of George Aiken's *Uncle Tom's Cabin* opens with Tom on the plantation of Simon Legree, who has just purchased Tom and a young woman named Emmeline. As Tom laments being brought to "the dark places," the theater's orchestra plays Stephen Foster's "Swanee River," a blackface minstrel song about an enslaved man "longing for the old plantation / And for the old folks at home." Tom starts to sing the song, when Legree enters and orders him to "[s]hut up!" Legree tells Emmeline, "We're home," at which, a stage direction indicates, she "shrinks from him." In some versions of the play, Legree is responsible for Tom's being sold away from his family in Kentucky. Here, Legree stops Tom from expressing a desire to return home.[5]

To think of *Incidents* as written in the melodramatic mode can help us interpret its themes and plot as well as its characters. Students will understand the importance of the home to Linda Brent. A "space of innocence," home is where melodrama "begins, and wants to end" (Brooks 29; Williams 28). *Incidents* begins in the "comfortable home" of the Brents (9). After the deaths of her parents, Linda finds comfort in the "snug little home" of her grandmother, Martha (18). Later in life, Linda finds refuge in Martha's garret, her "home for a long, long time" (97). That refuge is preferable to "the lonely cottage" (112) that Flint had offered her in a scheme to keep secret his mistreatment of her (50). The book ends with Linda free and wishing for "a home of my own" for herself and her children (167).

To have students think about characterization, I ask them to note the words Linda uses to describe Flint. There are, of course, her regular references to his being a doctor and his old age. Students notice that Linda describes Flint as a "tyrant," which exposes the oppression and brutality that the more common "master" conceals (50). He is her "enemy," a word that emphasizes their opposition (142). Flint is also a "villain," one of melodrama's stock characters, a word choice that implies who Linda is (109). Melodramas are peopled with villains and heroes, the latter of whom are usually heroines. The opening of "The Trials of Girlhood" chapter details in melodramatic terms what Uncle Phillip and Uncle Benjamin hinted at near the end of the previous chapter: Flint's harassment and abuse of Linda (26). Flint, she says, was "a crafty man" who "tried his utmost to corrupt the pure principles my grandmother had instilled." He was "a vile monster," one of the "fiends who bear the shape of men" (27). Linda describes herself as a "helpless victim," but like other women and girls of melodrama, she prevails (27). Just as in melodrama, Linda's weakness does not make her passive. The heroine in melodrama, Michael Booth finds, was often the most effective "in resisting and defying the villain" (26). When Flint tries to assert his authority over Linda, she declares that "never before had my puny arm felt half so strong" (*Incidents* 19).

Jacobs also uses the language of theater and performance to describe setting and action. "Scenes at the Plantation" covers the two months that Linda spends at Flint's son's plantation, her punishment for rejecting Flint's cottage scheme. The chapter's pivotal moment takes place at the cemetery where her parents are buried. Linda is "overawed by the solemnity of the scene" and imagines hearing their voices (79). As a result, she determines to free herself or die in the attempt. The chapter ends with Linda's learning of Flint's intention to bring her children "to the plantation to be 'broke in'" (82). To save the children, Linda and her family create a plan to have Sands, their father, purchase them without Flint's knowing it. As part of the plan narrated in "The Children Sold," Linda's grandmother is "requested to act as if they were really to be sent away" (91). Martha plays along, but when she sees the preparations being made to take Benny and Ellen from her home, "[t]he scene seemed too much like reality" and she "faint[s]" (92). Later, as part of the same plan, Linda herself "perform[s]" in a way that recalls the cross-dressing, and racial masquerade, of the nineteenth-century theater (96). Dressed in "sailor's clothes," her face "blackened . . . with charcoal," Linda makes her way through town to her hiding place (97).

In addition to using theatrical language, Jacobs alludes to performance culture. Students can learn more about Jacobs's and her readers' context by researching such allusions. While she waits to learn if the plan to purchase the children was successful, Linda has a startling vision that her children have been sold south rather than to Sands. Just before she has this vision, Linda hears a "band of serenaders" singing the wildly popular song "Home, Sweet Home"—itself from a play—only to hear their song transform into "the moaning of children" (93). When I teach this chapter, I play the song for students and ask them to think about Jacobs's reference.[6] Its sentiments were universally appealing, but Jacobs here wrenchingly illustrates that Linda's "exile from home" (Bishop), as one of the lyrics has it, is of an entirely different kind than what the song describes. As

Jennifer Lynn Stoever writes of this scene, "the song's conventional sentimentality remains inaccessible [to Linda], and its sound brings pain and foreboding" (60). Made aware of the power of this song, my students sense a new resonance to Linda's closing lament that "I do not sit with my children in a home of my own. I still long for a hearthstone of my own, however humble" (167). The most famous lyric of "Home, Sweet Home" is, of course, "Be it ever so humble, there's no place like home" (Bishop). Attention to this moment also brings up other, later associations for my students: a decorative pillow stitched with that adage in a family member's home, perhaps, or Dorothy Gale's wishful repetition of "There's no place like home" in *The Wizard of Oz*. For some students the song recalls "Sweet Home," the name of the plantation in Toni Morrison's *Beloved*.

"Home, Sweet Home" also connects to another reference to performance culture in *Incidents*. In a chapter titled "The Fugitive Slave Law," Linda discusses the response to the 1850 law's passage in New York City. She contrasts white New Yorkers' indifference with Black New Yorkers' panic by describing the music they consumed or produced: "[W]hile fashionables were listening to the thrilling voice of Jenny Lind in Metropolitan Hall, the thrilling voices of poor hunted colored people went up, in an agony of supplication, to the Lord, from Zion's church" (157). Lind was a celebrated singer, her manager was the showman P. T. Barnum, and "Home, Sweet Home" was in her repertoire, as it was in many other performers' repertoires.[7] Metropolitan Hall was a mile away from the African Methodist Episcopal Zion Church. Both places were on or near Broadway, the north-south thoroughfare that runs through the center of Manhattan. I ask students to think about the closeness of the two places, the differences between their music, and Jacobs's repetition of the word "thrilling." They often agree with Stoever, who writes that "Jacobs's selection of 'thrill' to describe the voices of both Lind and the black supplicants . . . indicts whites for sensationalizing what they heard as emotive entertainments while real people they knew (and often depended upon) needed advocacy and protection" (108).

Melodrama, finally, provides a way to have students consider twentieth-century historical criticism of *Incidents*. In her landmark *American Literature* essay that affirmed Jacobs's authorship, Jean Fagan Yellin responds to a historian who denied the book's authenticity: "Examining *Incidents* in a discussion of 'fictional accounts . . . in which the major character may have been a real fugitive, but the narrative of his life is probably false,' John Blassingame recently judged that 'the work is not credible'" ("Written" [*American Literature*] 480).[8] In *The Slave Community*, Blassingame judged that "the story" of "virtuous Harriet" is "too melodramatic: miscegenation and cruelty, outraged virtue, unrequited love, and planter licentiousness appear on practically every page" (233–34). Blassingame uses the term "melodramatic" in the common, depreciative sense that the *Oxford English Dictionary* defines as "characterized by sensationalism, exaggeration, or an excess of emotion" ("Melodramatic"), but a student familiar with the performance mode will recognize the features of melodrama in Blassingame's remarks about its characterization and plot.[9] Though he mentions Lydia Maria

Child's role as editor, Blassingame emphasizes internal evidence as the basis for his judgment. Yellin's case is mainly based on external evidence: Jacobs's correspondence with Amy and Isaac Post. Yellin does not address the specifics of Blassingame's charge. Indeed, in the introduction to her own edition of *Incidents*, Yellin describes Linda's statements about her relationship with Sands as "melodramatic confessions" (Introduction [*Incidents*] xiv).[10] In Yellin's edition, the table comparing the fictional names of characters with their real-life counterparts is headed "Cast of Characters," just as a printed version of a play would have it (xxxvi).[11]

NOTES

1. See, for example, V. Smith, *Self-Discovery*.

2. I have taught *Incidents* this way at large universities and at a small college in the northeastern United States. Most of the classes in which I teach *Incidents* are on the lower level of the curriculum. The classes tend to be either mostly English majors and minors or mostly general education students. In my experience, what I describe in this chapter has been productive in any of the classes in which I have taught Jacobs, including at the upper level, but the historiographical issues with which I close may be better suited for upper-level classes.

3. "The connotations of the word" *melodrama*, Brooks writes, include "the indulgence of strong emotionalism; moral polarization and schematization; extreme states of being, situations, actions; overt villainy, persecution of the good, and final reward of virtue; inflated and extravagant expression; dark plottings, suspense, breathtaking peripety" (11–12).

4. Another play that can be assigned with *Incidents* is Dion Boucicault's 1859 *The Octoroon*, which is an example of the "tragic mulatta" plot. Lisa Merrill and Theresa Saxon have a digital exhibit on Boucicault's play—which, famously, was produced with different endings—that would be useful for teachers interested in having students do archival research. More recently, Lydia R. Diamond adapted *Incidents* for the stage: *Harriet Jacobs* premiered in 2008.

5. Lyrics and a modern recording of "Old Folks at Home" are available on Stephen Railton's Uncle Tom's Cabin *and American Culture: A Multi-media Archive*, as are Aiken's scripts (Lyrics; "Aiken's *Uncle Tom*").

6. A contemporary recording and the lyrics of "Home, Sweet Home" are available on Uncle Tom's Cabin *and American Culture* (Bishop).

7. The Library of Congress's digital collections include "Jenny Lind's Home Sweet Home," an 1854 printing of sheet music that was published in New York as well as New Orleans, Detroit, and Charleston. The cover's illustration features a white mother, father, and child sitting outside a house. The song, arranged for piano, would have been played and displayed in a family's parlor.

8. Some students might be interested in learning more about the scholarly debate on Jacobs and *Incidents*; Yellin writes about it elsewhere ("Texts" 278n2).

9. For another response to Blassingame that takes gender and genre into account, see Carby.

10. For an example, see the passage in chapter 10 of *Incidents*, "A Perilous Passage in the Slave Girl's Life," that begins, "And now, reader, I come to a period in my unhappy life, which, I would gladly forget if I could" (49). In "Introduction by the Editor," Child refers to Jacobs's "lively and dramatic way of telling her own story" (6).

11. The Norton Critical Edition, in contrast, titles its table "Who's Who in *Incidents*" (xxv).

Beloved in the Attic: Harriet Jacobs's Confinement

Barbara Eckstein

Preparing a lesson and teaching a lesson are two different things. In 2017, eighteen students engaged with the curriculum I describe here in a required literature course in a predominantly white, large, public university. Four of those students were people of color from different cultural homes. I am white. Though these were not ideal demographics, the interplay of texts and student experiences proved generative and generous. This is true, in large part, because Harriet Jacobs's personal narrative of enslavement, sexual harassment and abuse, and also intergenerational love anchored the course theme of resilience and the course practice of intertextual and embodied engagement. What follows is not a description of all assignments but a focus on intertextuality with Jacobs's narrative as the touchstone.

The longer texts accompanying Jacobs's were Margaret Atwood's novel *The Handmaid's Tale*, Arthur Miller's play *The Crucible*, Ta-Nehisi Coates's personal narrative *Between the World and Me*, Dave Eggers's nonfiction narrative *Zeitoun*, and Alison Bechdel's personal graphic narrative *Fun Home.* This particular semester, instructors of the many sections of this required course chose Atwood's novel, in addition to Kiese Laymon's essay "Da Art of Storytellin" and Nathaniel Hawthorne's "The Minister's Black Veil" as the literature in common across all sections of the course. The university's general education literature program also requires that all sections of its foundations course engage a range of genres from diverse cultures and at least one major text written before 1900. In my version of the course, some lyric poems, and a greater number of short stories, helped illuminate relevant concepts in the major texts, such as gothicism, dystopia, and utopia. Hawthorne's and other authors' short stories displayed, as well, the interplay of fear and resilience. One story perhaps less well known and worthy of note is Will Mackin's "Crossing the River No Name." The university theater department's student productions of Miller's play and the musical created from Bechdel's narrative enhanced my students' enjoyment and understanding of those texts immeasurably.

The words *love* and *resilience*, especially in relation to Jacobs's narrative, might suggest optimism, but this would be a misunderstanding of the concepts and the story. To make that point about all the texts at play in the course, I required students to wade into the multiple reflections on resilience offered in the premiere issue of the environmental humanities journal *Resilience.* Reflecting again on those definitions and Jacobs's narrative, I find the resonance all the more pronounced. Twenty scholars, thinkers, writers, and activists together complicate any easy etymological understanding of *resilience* as bouncing back to where one began. Jacobs's story displays both the warnings and the wisdom offered in these twenty reflections on resilience. For example, since where we begin—enslavement, environmental degradation—is trouble, bouncing back to this starting point is not to be desired. Instead, as Cecilia Åsberg argues following Donna Haraway, our process must be to stay with the trouble, engage the instability of resilience, learning what it can be. Recognize, as Stacy Alaimo and others have said, that we do not need a resilience for the cheery, the chipper, and the ignorant, for whom denial of the trouble is, temporarily, possible. Nor should we burden one another with the imperative to be cheery, chipper, and possibly ignorant as well. Jacobs, and many others before and since, cannot, of course, so easily turn away from trouble, in any case. So she learns how to stay with that trouble, participating in the creative destruction of slavery, both in her embodied personal actions within her community and in her published narrative. But perpetual turbulence, if this be a key feature of resilience, cannot become the sole norm, writes Susie O'Brien. She argues for resilience in "a constellation of other values, including historical consciousness, justice, care, and resistance." Certainly, Jacobs longs for peace, safety, and stability for herself, her children, her grandmother, and the rest of her extended family and friends. In her comments on resilience, Ann-Elise Lewallen most particularly describes a key feature of Jacobs's ability to stay with the trouble: intergenerational thinking and commitment. She further presents herself as cultivating love and compassion wherever she finds herself, that is, not only in the debilitating attic or the snake-infested swamp but also the chaotic socioeconomic and psychic space requiring profound distrust of her insidious enslaver, of the insouciant white father of her children, and of all those who participate in or enable slavery.

The first literary text that students encountered in the course was Bruno Nadeau and Jason Lewis's "Still Standing," from the second volume of the *Electronic Literature Collection*. A short video from the website shares this art installation, which premiered in Copenhagen in 2005 (Nadeau and Lewis). In it a viewer paces in front of a full-length screen on which letters silently burble at the base. As the viewer moves, the letters react as though kicked aside. Only when the viewer stands motionless do the letters collect into recognizable words and phrases forming in lines reflecting the shape of the body of the viewer (and a poem). This evocative interaction of human body and written words invites multiple interpretations of "Still Standing." It initiates immersion in questions of confinement, resilience, attention, reading, and writing.

Kiese Laymon's essay describes how the albums of the artists OutKast reinvigorated his understanding and admiration for his grandmama. We read his essay in the first week of the course and recalled it when we began Jacobs's narrative, but, if I had the opportunity to do it over, I would invite an explicit rereading of the essay alongside Jacobs. Laymon writes of his grandmama, who was a buttonhole slicer at a chicken-processing plant, that she was the "most stylized, most efficient worker in Mississippi." She brought the same discipline and imagination to her dress for work as for church: "She understood that the audience for her work was not just her coworkers or her white male shift managers, but all the Southern black women workers who preceded her and, most importantly, all the Southern black women workers coming next." In narrating how he comes to understand the inspiration available through what he calls "Grandmama's stank or freshness," Laymon is explaining the art of his storytelling, "from whence [he] came." He concludes with a plan to visit his grandmama: "I'm going to tell Grandmama that because of her, I know what it's like to be loved responsibly."

Laymon learned from OutKast the art of storytelling "from whence he came" but also to "expect a lot more from my male heroes" than the "misogynoir" evident in their first two albums. The stark patriarchy and misogyny at the core of Margaret Atwood's dystopian world in *The Handmaid's Tale*, which we read after Laymon, emblazoned those forms of oppression on the class consciousness. When Jacobs prefaces her narrative with the words "I care to arouse the women of the North to a realizing sense of the condition of two millions of women at the South, still in bondage," even when Lydia Maria Child introduces, with restraint, this "intelligent and much-injured woman" and what "some call delicate subjects and others indelicate," the class is prepared to understand Jacobs's experience of slavery, her resilience in the face of it, and her resistance to it as particularly gendered. Offred's two-part interactions with the Commander—one as sexual cog in a patriarchal machine and the other as personal diversion for a confused man (oppressor nonetheless)—provide a fictional frame in Atwood's novel for considering the complex historical dilemma confronting "Linda" as she resists sexual violence from the conniving enslaver, Dr. "Flint," and negotiates entanglements with the untrustworthy white father of her children, Mr. "Sands."

Answers to the online journal prompt asking for comparative thinking about Atwood's novel and Jacobs's narrative directed much of subsequent class discussion toward the forms of confinement in the two stories and how Jacobs endured. The prompt asked students to reflect on how each character's capacities and vulnerabilities affect the character's ability to survive different forms of confinement. Many students, in writing and conversation, wanted to address the intergenerational love that gave Jacobs strength. This love was manifest not only among the women in Jacobs's community but also among her male relatives and male friends in the town. Beginning her narrative with the tragic death of her mother initiates her vulnerability to the violence of slavery, but it also signals the significance of the intergenerational love that will sustain her. Students were most struck by the sustenance derived from seeing and hearing her children from her attic. Atwood imagines Offred with far less access to intergenerational love and less experience, even prior to the patriarchal coup, cultivating such a safety net of love. Three hundred plus years of slavery has forced the enslaved community of Jacobs to cultivate more wisdom about, resistance to, and resilience in the face of confinement than Offred's historically recent confinement. Slowly Offred tries to create the sort of trusted community that Jacobs knows despite the extraordinary personal and systemic violence all around her.

But I did not take what now seems to me the important opportunity to consider generally, as a class, the operation of confinement, and therefore resilience and resistance, in small spaces in our current society. The students could have discussed the use of isolation rooms in educational institutions. Though not in 2017, students could now listen to a March 2019 National Public Radio interview with Albert Woodfox about his book *Solitary*, describing his forty years in solitary confinement at Angola penitentiary in Louisiana. So much important material (filmic and otherwise) exists about the effects of solitary confinement on incarcerated individuals. We might also have considered how disease can result in confinement and isolation. We might even have considered such voluntary confinement as that experienced by astronauts. We certainly could have reaffirmed our feminist concerns by considering how isolation and confinement with one's abuser intensifies the risks of domestic violence.

What we did do is follow the path of intergenerational love and the importance of bodies into the narrative by Ta-Nehisi Coates. Because Coates's extended narrative is addressed to his son, I prompted the students to write, in the online journal, a letter addressed to someone one or two generations older than they were. An earlier journal prompt had asked them to summarize one of Jacobs's letters that we had read, which answered the following questions: What kind of restrictions and freedom governed the language she chose to address her subject (*Incidents* 195–209)? What was her relationship to the recipient, and how do you understand that relationship governing what she is able to say? In subsequently assigning the intergenerational letter, I gave students the following prompt: "In your letter, address a particular topic that you both care about, but speak to the differences in the world you and your addressee occupy because of the difference in age. You may be as interior and meditative as Coates or as forthcoming and relational as Jacobs. Or something in between." I asked that the student choose someone they know or knew personally, though not necessarily someone they love.

When we turned to the narrative *Zeitoun*, there was ample opportunity to continue pursuing definitions of resilience and, especially, reflecting on the significance of intergenerational love. Dave Eggers begins his development of Abdulrahman Zeitoun with his Syrian family shaped by their proximity to the sea. Readers easily understand Zeitoun's confidence in emerging from his flooded home into the devastation of a post-Katrina New Orleans inundated by broken levees. We also understand the anxiety of his wife, Kathy, and children, who have been set adrift across the continent by their evacuation from the storm and by their inability to communicate with Zeitoun. The tragedy of his subsequent apprehension and detention, the result of racial assumptions and chaos, and even his eventual release are given a particularly horrific emphasis by the incremental starvation of neighbors' dogs trapped in a house without food and water. This trope of desperation and deprivation, memorable for the students, displays confinement laid bare by dependency and the absence of options.

Our final text, Alison Bechdel's personal graphic narrative *Fun Home*, provided an exploration of complex intergenerational love from the point of view of a maturing daughter, not the parental voice offered by Jacobs and Coates. While Jacobs struggles to create a home for her children, Bechdel suffers the confines of hers given her own lesbian identity and, more to the point, the largely unacknowledged homosexuality of her father. Witty and wise, the comic—with some careful instruction in the conventions of the form—gave the students access to the child's sense of responsibility to the parents, which we saw in glimpses with Jacobs when her son reveals he knew of her presence in the garret and when her young daughter must later keep her mother's secret. This particular 2017 class benefited from an excellent student production of Lisa Kron and Jeanine Tesori's 2015 musical adaptation of Bechdel's narrative. I want to end with a return to the mother's point of view by pointing to the song "Days and Days" sung late in the musical by Helen, Bechdel's mother, and addressed to her college-aged daughter. It begins sardonically with "Welcome to our house on Maple Avenue" and unwinds a heartbreaking expanse of days making excuses, telling and receiving lies, to accommodate a marriage to a closeted gay man. The song ends with Helen telling her daughter, "Don't you come back here. I didn't raise you to give away your days like me." The haunting song echoed in the ears of my students, awed by the art and the pain.

Beyond the end of *Incidents in the Life of a Slave Girl*, we know that Jacobs and her daughter returned, after the Civil War, to her home in North Carolina where she had been enslaved but also where intergenerational love had sustained her, even for years, in a tiny attic. Though, unlike Laymon, she does not get the opportunity to return to the South before her grandmother dies, Jacobs and her daughter go, nonetheless, to provide for the educational and material needs of the formerly enslaved community. This intergenerational commitment to the community of a particular place—home—impressed the students.

"Future Generations Will Learn from It": *Incidents in the Life of a Slave Girl* in the Archives

Carrie Johnston

In *Incidents in the Life of a Slave Girl*, Harriet Jacobs challenges her audience to recognize the hypocrisy of nineteenth-century American institutions by calling attention to the ways that United States citizens, Southern enslavers and white Northerners alike, "wrapped their crimes in the mantels of law and faith" (Fleischner 11). Jacobs's narrative exposes a legal system that sanctioned the rape of enslaved girls and women but made it a "crime for a slave to tell who was the father of her child" (*Incidents* 16). At great personal risk, Jacobs speaks of her own experiences in this system, refusing to criminalize herself or other enslaved women for breaking the silences that uphold a corrupt system. By revealing that she engaged in a relationship with Samuel Tredwell Sawyer to protect herself from sexual abuse by the man who enslaved her, Dr. James Norcom, Jacobs enlists readers' active participation in her story. If we are outraged and wish to censor or blame her, we are complicit in a violent system that insists on the silence of survivors. By contrast, to support Jacobs is to be among the "noble men and women who . . . striv[e] to help those who cannot help themselves" and to take the first step in "laboring to advance the cause of humanity" (*Incidents* 29). Jacobs demonstrates that the risks required to dismantle corrupt systems are especially incumbent upon those "whose homes are protected by law" (50), especially when the same laws violently oppress enslaved women.

I assigned *Incidents in the Life of a Slave Girl* as the first text in my Handmaids and Heroines in American Literature course, an undergraduate seminar that I taught at Wake Forest University from 2018 to 2023. Although Wake Forest's motto, *pro humanitate*, echoes Jacobs's call to "advance the cause of humanity," teaching *Incidents* at a private and predominately white institution such as Wake Forest was a humbling reminder of the indifference and complacency that often accompanies racial and socioeconomic privilege. I taught students that through such reminders Jacobs equips us with a framework for grappling with our own unconscious biases so that we do not repeat historical patterns of suppressing and silencing marginalized voices. Even though Margaret Atwood's *The Handmaid's Tale* was the namesake of this Handmaids and Heroines course, *Incidents* was the central text that taught us to actively engage with texts by women from a range of time periods and backgrounds who, like Jacobs, dared to challenge the complacency that propagates oppressive systems.

In this essay I outline an archival assignment that I designed in response to the call to action that Jacobs issues after seeing the bill of sale that secured her freedom:

> "The bill of sale!" Those words struck me like a blow. So I was *sold* at last! A human being *sold* in the free city of New York! The bill of sale is on record, and future generations will learn from it that women were articles of traffic in New York, late in the nineteenth century of the Christian religion. It may hereafter prove a useful document to antiquaries, who are seeking to measure the progress of civilization in the United States. (165)

Following Jacobs's position that "future generations will learn from it"—her bill of sale specifically and the artifacts of slavery more generally—this assignment asked students to examine bills of sale in the Wake Forest University archives after reading *Incidents in the Life of a Slave Girl.*[1] Viewing these bills of sale highlighted Jacobs's rejection of notions of "progress" and "civilization" in a nation that insists on the exchange of money for freedom. Moreover, this assignment emphasized Jacobs's reminders throughout her narrative "that women were articles of traffic" and honored her mission to bring to light that enslaved women and girls "have wrongs, and sufferings, and mortifications peculiarly their own" (68). After a series of class discussions in which we paid close attention to the ways that Jacobs dares to speak about the sexual abuse of enslaved women, students paid close attention to the names of women and girls listed on the bills of sale in the archive and were aware of the "atmosphere of licentiousness and fear" that they were most likely forced to endure (47).

The bills of sale that students consulted for this assignment are in the William Crenshaw Papers, a collection held by the Special Collections and Archives unit of Z. Smith Reynolds Library at Wake Forest University. I was introduced to Crenshaw's papers through Wake Forest's Slavery, Race and Memory Project, a university-wide initiative that acknowledges the university's "history bound up with slavery and its tragic legacies" and that "[a]ttempts to recover, understand and reckon more fully with that complex past" ("About"). William Crenshaw (1783–1861) was a founding member of the board of trustees of the Wake Forest Manual Labor Institution, and its first treasurer; his son, John M. Crenshaw, was in the first class admitted, in 1834 ("William Crenshaw Papers").[2] Crenshaw's papers include bills of sale for at least twenty enslaved African Americans, whom Crenshaw purchased and held captive on his plantation in Granville County, North Carolina. Granville County is approximately 150 miles west of Edenton, North Carolina, where Jacobs was held captive by James Norcom.

In a session held in the Special Collections and Archives classroom, students studied the handwritten bills of sale, and Megan Mulder, the Z. Smith Reynolds Library special collections librarian, provided an overview of the William Crenshaw Papers, which included pointing out the fact that these bills were originally organized with property deeds for land and livestock. During the session, each student was assigned one bill to read. They were asked to write down the names and ages of the enslaved people listed on the bill, to determine whose rights are being guaranteed in the document, to note any monetary values listed on the bill, and to pay attention to physical features of the documents, such as official seals and other markings.[3]

One challenge of the assignment is simply reading the handwritten bills. After allowing students time to look at the bills and read as much as they can on their own, I asked them to work with a partner to compare bills and detect similarities, which helped them discern the handwriting. Students found that on almost all of the bills, the seller conveys "the right and title" to the enslaved persons listed on the bill and pledges to "bind myself and my heirs to warrant and forever support unto William Crenshaw and his heirs free from the claim or claims of all persons whatsoever" ("Bill of Sale for Augustine and Jane").

It was revealing for students to read this boilerplate language, which guarantees wealth for the purchaser and his descendants while ensuring generations of poverty for the people they enslave. The class was quick to notice that these documents clear the title for a human being as one would for a piece of land. Students pointed out the hypocrisy of a legal system that grants ownership of enslaved people to Crenshaw's family in perpetuity, although, as Jacobs points out, "no promise or writing given to a slave is legally binding" (10). We discussed the long-term impact of the actions of Jacobs's "kind mistress," who died when Jacobs was a child and willed her to Norcom's young daughter (12). As a result, Jacobs's life is spent trying to untangle herself and eventually her children from this transaction. Even after Norcom ostensibly sells Jacobs's children to Sawyer, he "boasts that [the children] are still in his power. He says they were his daughter's property, and as she was not of age when they were sold, the contract is not legally binding" (116). The bills of sale we studied reiterated that this was not an isolated incident, but rather a practice codified and perpetuated by US law.

During class discussions of the legal rights conveyed by the bills, I took the opportunity to revisit the case Jacobs makes for reparations when she tells her readers of Norcom's refusal to repay a loan of $300 to her grandmother, Molly Horniblow. Norcom claims he cannot reimburse Horniblow, because the money is owed by her deceased enslaver, whose "estate was insolvent, and the law prohibited repayment" (14). Jacobs notes that Norcom keeps the silver candelabra purchased with her grandmother's money for himself, surmising that they "will be handed down in the family, generation to generation" (14). Reading this narrative detail alongside the historical document emphasized that the injustice does not end with Jacobs's grandmother but rather multiplies over generations.

After the Special Collections and Archives session, students were asked to continue to reflect on their experience handling and reading these bills of sale and to write a thesis-driven essay in which they discussed the ways these bills inform and are informed by Jacobs's narrative. I provided high-resolution digital images of the bills and a link to the Z. Smith Reynolds Library's Crenshaw Papers digital collection so students could revisit and highlight specific aspects of the documents in their essays. I found that after taking time to review the bills of sale on their own, many students chose to write about their heightened awareness of the names of the girls and women listed on the bills of sale, owing to Jacobs's discussion of the forced separation of mothers from their children and her disclosure of the widespread sexual abuse of enslaved women and girls.

Many students drew comparisons between the bills of sale and Jacobs's chapter, "The Slaves' New Year's Day," in which she tells the story of a woman whose seven children were sold away from her on New Year's Day, the designated hiring day on many Southern plantations (18). Recalling Jacobs's plea to "contrast *your* New Year's day with that of the poor bond-woman!" (17), many students also remarked that Jacobs's pleas were even more poignant when they considered the circumstances of the man described in a particular bill of sale, who is sold to Crenshaw on Christmas Eve.

There are many details from the bills of sale that align with Jacobs's experiences in slavery that students have not yet noticed, which I plan to discuss in future iterations of this class. For example, one young woman with an infant may have experienced hardships similar to those Jacobs faced when she was sent to Norcom's son's plantation to prepare for the arrival of the younger Norcom's future wife. Jacobs tells us that she was forced to leave her young daughter, Louisa, unattended at the plantation while she worked and recalls the day that Louisa wandered off and was later found asleep under the house (76). The next day Jacobs sent Louisa, "who had always been so carefully tended" (74), back to her grandmother's house where she could be properly cared for. Jacobs's reminders throughout the narrative about her good fortune to have her family nearby to take care of her children illuminated the archival silences of the young woman's life and helped us to understand the potential hardships she faced as the enslaved mother of an infant daughter.

This assignment impressed upon students the large gaps in the archival record of American chattel slavery. Engaging with the archive helped students understand that no one, not even Jacobs, can speak for those whose voices have been silenced. Instead, through reading archival documents, students could better grasp the urgency of Jacobs's mission "to kindle a flame of compassion in [readers'] hearts for my sisters who are still in bondage, suffering as I once suffered" (*Incidents* 29). Jacobs uses her voice because others cannot and reminds us that this ability to speak as a freedwoman, to read and write, and to have grown up among supportive family members and friends who championed her cause was in fact an extraordinary circumstance. As Jean Fagan Yellin notes, "Although millions of American women were held in bondage over the two hundred and fifty years that slavery was legal in the United States, Harriet Jacobs is the only woman known to leave papers testifying to her life in slavery" (Introduction [*Harriet Jacobs Family Papers*] xxix). Studying the archival record at Wake Forest and finding lists of names of enslaved women in Crenshaw's papers, with very little identifying information and no further record of their lives, highlighted the remarkable contribution that *Incidents in the Life of a Slave Girl* makes by providing context for these untold stories.

To study property deeds for enslaved people extends Jacobs's work beyond the page. Jacobs intentionally withholds her own bill of sale that she instructs us to read for evidence that "women were articles of traffic in New York, late in the nineteenth century" (165), essentially insisting that we continue her work by consulting archival records that attest to the numbers of women and girls at the mercy of a system that condoned their sexual assault. In withholding this contract that secured her freedom but was orchestrated against her wishes and without her consent, she "rejects contracts to which she cannot be a fully equal and voluntary party" (Kaplan 97). Jacobs charges her readers to continue the work of excavating and interrogating these historical documents so that "future generations can learn from it" the hypocrisy of a legal system that demands payment to the family of her abuser while "there is no shadow of law to protect her from insult, from violence, or even from death" (27).

NOTES

1. Jean Fagan Yellin has compiled historical documents that provide context for *Incidents in the Life of a Slave Girl* in *The Harriet Jacobs Family Papers.* Although volume 1 contains "Mrs. Willis's letter soliciting funds for the balance of Jacobs's purchase price," Yellin notes that "Jacobs's freedom paper has never been found" (Introduction [*Harriet Jacobs Family Papers*] xxxiv). Although we are not able to examine Jacobs's papers as she instructs future readers to do, there remains a vast archive of documentation attesting to the fact that "women were articles of traffic in New York, late in the nineteenth century" (*Incidents* 165).

2. The Wake Forest Manual Labor Institute was founded in 1834 and originally located in Wake Forest, North Carolina. It was rechartered as Wake Forest College in 1838. In 1956, the campus moved to its current location in Winston-Salem, North Carolina ("History").

3. During fall 2019 and spring 2020, I conducted this session in person, allowing students to handle the bills of sale while taking notes. In fall 2020, I conducted this assignment online because of restrictions on the size of in-person gatherings, and I shared the Crenshaw Papers Digital Collection (wakespace.lib.wfu.edu/handle/10339/94114), which is openly available. Instructors wishing to adopt this assignment can also access digitized bills of sale made available by the People Not Property project, a collaborative endeavor by the University of North Carolina, Greensboro, libraries and various North Carolina institutions (library.uncg.edu/slavery/deeds/). People Not Property is part of the *Digital Library on American Slavery*, which aggregates a number of digitized primary source documents, including race and slavery petitions and advertisements about fugitives from slavery (library.uncg.edu/slavery/).

“Something Akin to Freedom”: Recalibrating Conventions in *Incidents in the Life of a Slave Girl*

Maura D’Amore

To foreground historicized literary tropes and genres in the literature classroom is to examine the expectations and effects provoked by certain stylistic conventions and to recognize that authors shape their writing with audience and intent in mind. It is also, significantly, to grapple with the reasons for and stakes of upending norms and frustrating expectations. In this essay, I argue for the pedagogical utility of taking a comparative approach to *Incidents in the Life of a Slave Girl* to highlight how Harriet Jacobs “takes up” various conventions in an attempt to influence the response of white readers to her experience. Working with potentially limiting representations and remixing them to suit her needs, Jacobs performs a balancing act that alternately works to establish intimacies, set boundaries, create breathing room, and argue for expanded ways of thinking about victimhood and agency. Within this context, her occasional refusals to speak according to established dictates are as significant as her employment of those dictates at other times. The tensions that result from uneasy marriages of overlapping modes of address reflect the difficulty of her writerly predicament as much as her life experience. Indeed, this approach does the important work of helping students understand Jacobs herself and her narrative as something more than the sum of her biography. My ultimate goal is to provide them with the necessary tools to analyze her writing as an act of self-conscious ventriloquism and deliberate intervention.

While in this commentary I focus on two literary prototypes I have found to be especially resonant in classroom discussions of *Incidents in the Life of a Slave Girl*, namely the sentimental tale of the “tragic mulatta” and the “runaway slave” advertisement, I do so only to illustrate my method more generally. As time permits, I work to help students contextualize Jacobs’s rhetoric within a web of discourses that include the slave narrative, the seduction plot, the captivity narrative, and the domestic novel in order to attune them to her artistry. Whether contrasting *Incidents* with Frederick Douglass’s slave narrative to elucidate *Incidents*’s emphasis on differing threats posed by slavery for men in contrast to women or considering how she borrows from the genres of the seduction novel and captivity narrative to deflect criticism and make herself less of a stranger, I utilize comparisons to emphasize that Jacobs is shaping her own story. Fraught as it is for a woman of color, I want students to contemplate how the critical quotation of literary conventions might offer “something akin to freedom” (50) for Jacobs.

In her chapter on Jacobs in *Activist Sentiments: Reading Black Women in the Nineteenth Century*, P. Gabrielle Foreman warns readers that “accept[ing] the transparency between the life of Harriet Jacobs and her narrative self-construct 'Linda Brent' can limit their interpretations of the text" (19). Instead, following Sidonie Smith, she urges attention to the *graphia* in autobiography as a means to understand how Jacobs "offers her reception communities explicit directions to look for multiple modes of interpretation" (20). From the beginning of our conversations about *Incidents*, I emphasize Jacobs as a writer who quotes the culture that hems her back to itself, in order to destabilize "known" representations enough to provoke readers out of complacency. Much of my early framing, then, seeks to theorize the difficulty for Jacobs of telling her story on her own terms.[1] It takes students a while to identify the conditions (her own and those of her readers) that shape her account of her life: what parts of her experience are deemed significant (and to whom and for what reason), which details are included for purposes of authentication or revision of the historical record, and when silences or plot revisions seek to disrupt facile judgments. Jacobs's preface and Lydia Maria Child's introduction both speak to problematic tensions between the necessity of projecting "sincerity" and protecting against charges of "indecorum," and the sentimental plight of the "tragic mulatta" offered a path forward. According to Jean Fagan Yellin, "The pathos of the Tragic Mulatto rests in the contradiction between her sincere efforts to adhere to the patriarchal definition of true womanhood and the patriarchy's insistence that she violate this norm" (*Women* 72). By introducing students to this trope, I ask them to consider "Linda" as a hybrid construction. I also prime them to recognize deviations from the script as strategic.

Because I frequently teach Harriet Beecher Stowe's *Uncle Tom's Cabin* in my American literature survey courses, my students usually have an awareness of its basic outlines in the figure of Eliza (and later in the novel, Cassie). For those who do not, however, a discussion of the illustrated engravings of Eliza's escape across the Ohio, clutching her baby as she navigates ice floes in an effort to elude her pursuers and their menacing dogs, offers an illustrative introduction to the motif and larger plotline. Images by Hammat Billings for the 1853 "Splendid" edition of *Uncle Tom's Cabin* are widely available online ("Illustrations"), but it is also illuminating to share evolutions of the famous scene over time as depicted in ceramic figurines, lithographs, sheet music, and posters advertising theatrical productions. As we voice the drama of this woman's situation and the powerful ways plot drives characterization, I invite students to theorize the politics of lingering on a woman's endangered body, then and now. In what ways is the viewer similar to the enslaver, a passive observer, or a would-be savior? As they look at later representations of Eliza's escape, students can attune themselves to conventions and stylistic decisions that work to animate the imagination and encourage particular ways of viewing the woman and her situation.

To contextualize these materials, I provide a brief introduction to the term *mulatta* and some background on representations of the light-skinned, mixed-race woman in nineteenth-century print culture. I want students to have an awareness both of the particular complexities and precarities of her situation and of the range of registers in which her stereotyped character might resonate. The hue of her skin endangered her in multiple directions: as the offspring of taboo relations, her body "spoke" miscegenation in ways that could lead to mistreatment at the hands of an angry and jealous wife on a plantation, and she might be viewed suspiciously for her ability to pass. Frequently branded as "cunning" thanks to cultural anxieties surrounding racial indeterminacy, her intelligence was widely understood to be deceitful and potentially explosive. At the same time, she was valued by white men as exceptionally beautiful, which made her more vulnerable to sexual predation and violation.

For antislavery writers like Harriet Beecher Stowe and Lydia Maria Child, who wanted to mobilize white women's activism via experiences of sympathetic identification, though, the figure's proximity to whiteness was key. Ironically—notwithstanding her own lack of protection (a condition of homelessness that was thematized in narratives written about her)—under the guise of recognition and pity, the "mulatta" could serve as a safe vessel for a kind of racialized tourism. Lydia Maria Child's "The Quadroons" established a precedent for the genre in 1842, and this particular fictionalized plotline can be fascinating to examine alongside Jacobs's autobiographical account of her escape.[2] I like the class to sample Child's writing and activism prior to introducing them to her role as editor of *Incidents*, and "The Quadroons" provokes questions about the perpetuation of damaging stereotypes in works by white "allies" to the antislavery cause in addition to offering a foil for more nuanced portrayals.

Primed by these discussions, when we turn to *Incidents* the class is better able to apprehend Jacobs's rhetorical savvy. In places, she draws from the sentimental depictions endemic to this genre in order to predispose white women to judge her sympathetically, as when she states that for the Black girl hoping to live according to the "pure principles [her] grandmother had instilled" (27), "resistance is hopeless" (47), but she does so in such a way as to destabilize the categories upon which character judgment relies. When she argues, "That which commands admiration in the white woman only hastens the degradation of the female slave" (28), she exposes claims to "virtue" as dependent upon systems of legal protection that were not available to Black Americans. In this way, she troubles the "tragic mulatta" stereotype by exposing readerly sympathy as the equivalent of the "gift" of the golden chain given to her baby by a well-meaning white woman in her community ("I thanked her for her kindness, but I did not like the emblem" [70]). Nancy Bentley has suggested that writers and readers "relished the tragic perils of the Mulatta and iterated countless scenes of her shock, abuse, and betrayal" (506) in order to confirm the value of a soul that transcends "the problem of racial identity" (505). In *Incidents*, Jacobs recalibrates the performance of that suffering to reflect the realities of *her* plight. The details of her life and trauma, she makes clear, are not presented for her readers' titillation and entertainment. Refusing to offer herself up to the reader as "willing sacrificial victim" (Bentley 507), she portrays the standard plot of the "tragic mulatta" as precursor rather than main event. Trapped in a system that does not recognize the value of her humanity, Linda "deliberate[ly] calculat[es]" (*Incidents* 49) rather than submit to expectations, whether in her life or on the page. Faced with the loss of her "strongest weapon" (53) in the eyes of her readers and jurors, she "resolve[s] to match my cunning against his cunning" (107–08) to identify a loophole and widen the aperture.

Following Jacobs's lead in abandoning received tropes when they cease to suit her purposes, at the moment in the text when Linda decides to attempt an escape from slavery, I drop comparisons to the "tragic mulatta" altogether. As I detail yet another archetypal representation, that of the "runaway slave," though, I make it a point to theorize this pedagogical move. Drawing students' attention to Jacobs's thematization of the figure of the stranger in *Incidents*, I ask them to consider some of the ways alterity is packaged for readers who might be uncomfortable with, or threatened by, unfamiliar contours.[3] In lingering on the stock portrayal of the "runaway slave," a "type" made ubiquitous by the images that accompanied the text of advertisements to help them stand out amidst a page of print, I seek (as Jacobs sought, in her text, to teach her readers to suspect seemingly straightforward lines and interrogate their terms) to give them the tools to read resistantly, against the grain of inherited parameters.

The "runaway slave" advertisement was fashioned with particular audiences and goals in mind, and its form was deeply offensive and threatening to Jacobs's sensibilities.[4] It is notable, then, that she includes the text of the advertisement posted by Dr. Flint in hopes of restitution at the end of chapter 17, "Flight." As we analyze the second half of *Incidents*, I want students to consider what is gained by this more overt quotation of limited and derogatory representations of her personhood and situation.[5] Once again, I prepare them to consider the specifics of Jacobs's portrayal by familiarizing them with the broader outlines of the genre's conventions. To that end, I have found invaluable resources in two online databases: *Freedom on the Move* (freedomonthemove.org) and *N.C. Runaway Slave Advertisements* (dlas.uncg.edu/notices). Whether I gather a number of "runaway slave" advertisements to distribute in class or ask students to search and share findings in small groups, I urge them to approach these historical documents with an eye toward the ways in which motive and audience shape the description given. Together, we query the reparative potential of reimagining their personhood beyond the confines of print. This exercise foregrounds historical records as bound by biases, agendas, and silences and allows the class to see *Incidents* as an attempt to communicate a richer, more complicated version of one woman's escape from slavery.

Before sharing a "runaway slave" ad that James Norcom placed in the *American Beacon* of Norfolk, Virginia, in 1835,[6] I take them to the final chapter of the book, "Free at Last," where, in wonderment at the fact that a piece of paper—"the bill of sale"—is, in many circles, the only bond that matters, Linda reflects that it "is on record, and future generations will learn from it that women were articles of traffic in New York, late in the nineteenth century of the Christian religion. It may hereafter prove a useful document to antiquaries, who are seeking to measure the progress of civilization in the United States" (165). As if anticipating her resurrection in the archive and the classroom, a clearly frustrated Jacobs conjures a future in which "that bit of paper" (165) has the final word. In that light, we might approach the proliferation of printed documents in the text's final chapters as a ramped-up effort to help her readers do their job better. Repeatedly replying to declarations by the dominant culture with the assertion that "[*w*]*e* could have told them a different story" (123), Jacobs, through Linda, recommends tact and restraint when faced with a "text" of suffering. Differentiating between inquiry motivated by curiosity and the behavior of a "friend," she frames and guides readers' consumption of the "facts" about her life.

If Norcom's language describes Jacobs as his property, in *Incidents* Jacobs counters his claim at the same time that she frustrates readers' desires to claim or "place" her for their own (even well-meaning) purposes. Positioning her narrative in conversation with other, clearer literary precedents allows students to see Jacobs's invocation and subversion of rhetorical expectations within the text as extensions of her careful, strategic, and powerful negotiation of the conditions of her enslavement. In the words of Samantha M. Sommers, "Jacobs's treatment of print reminds us that media are medial—able to be put to a variety of uses, including liberation, although they are not inherently liberatory" ("From 'Harriet Jacobs'" 353). Throughout her text, Jacobs selectively invokes generic language and characterizations associated with certain conventions in order to guide, explain, critique, or revise interpretation. At the same time, reminding her readers "what a desolate feeling it was to be alone among strangers" (159), she implores whomever "might hear my story" (155) to attend to the particular circumstances of her situation and, more importantly, to the cadences of her speech, in any effort to understand her.

NOTES

1. Andrews's *To Tell a Free Story* is an excellent starting place for this work.

2. Hanrahan reads *Incidents* as a reply to Child's story. Her essay also includes a helpful overview of the "tragic mulatta" figure and the publication history for "The Quadroons." See also chapter 1 of Raimon's *"Tragic Mulatta" Revisited* (26–62). Raimon argues that "while [Child] did not invent the tradition that has relied upon the 'tragic mulatto,' no nineteenth-century writer was more instrumental in the trope's proliferation and circulation" (26).

3. Lloyd Pratt's articulation of "stranger humanism" in his introduction to *The Strangers Book* offers much food for thought along these lines.

4. On "runaway slave" ads as "print genre," see Waldstreicher.

5. Sommers has an excellent reading of the inclusion of this ad in *Incidents*: see "From 'Harriet Jacobs'" 356–59.

6. A facsimile is included Yale University's online collection *Harriet Jacobs: Selected Writings and Documents*: see Norcom.

"Another Link to Life": Black Feminist Geography, the Digital Humanities, and *Incidents in the Life of a Slave Girl*

Kristin Moriah

Suddenly, the world stopped. And like many others, I faced the daunting task of teaching *Incidents in the Life of a Slave Girl* during the first wave of the COVID-19 pandemic, when many postsecondary instructors were abruptly asked to stay home and teach online. Some researchers have termed that period, the mass movement to teach "all or some students remotely and adapting to rapidly changing circumstances," the "Great Pivot" (Denial et al.). For me as a Black feminist scholar, the exigencies of the Great Pivot and the necessity of sheltering in place lent new insight into the world Harriet Jacobs described. Jacobs's narrative illustrates a deep sense of what geographers might term *place*, or a very specific geographic location. I have also found that teaching students about Jacobs's investment in place alongside her search for "another link to life" (63) can illuminate contemporary discourses around the Black digital humanities. In *Incidents in the Life of a Slave Girl*, we learn that Jacobs, her enslaved family members, and their friends and relatives have sophisticated spatial awareness and an apprehension of the importance of geographic knowledge in the struggle for emancipation. In the contemporary classroom, even simple digital tools like search engines can lend insight into Jacobs's insistence on the importance of Black geography.

When Linda Brent is a young girl in Edenton, North Carolina, Black families, Black homes, and Black neighbors form the locus of her introduction to Black geographies. Jacobs begins her narrative by affirming that the "comfortable home" (9) she is raised in and the family bonds she forms there shield her from the brutal reality of chattel slavery until she is six years old (9). And yet, Jacobs's placed-based introduction lays the groundwork for her concern with truncated Black girlhood and acts as a window into her maternal motivations. Mark Rifkin posits that Jacobs's narrative "foregrounds houses as the site for tracing the state-sanctioned operation of everyday forms of racial distinction and discrimination" (75). Outlining her family lineage, Jacobs shows that her family's history is intertwined with that of her grandmother's enslavers, the owners of Edenton's Horniblow Tavern (*Incidents* 9–10). Jacobs's family and the Horniblows are deeply and dangerously connected across time and place. Jacobs informs us that "my mother's mistress was the daughter of my grandmother's mistress. In fact, my mother had been weaned at three months old, that the babe of the mistress might obtain sufficient food" (10). Under chattel slavery, the entanglement of the Horniblow and Jacobs family trees and branches means that homes and maternal care provide scant sustenance for enslaved children. In the narrative, the danger posed to Jacobs and her family intensifies as these familial ties deepen across generations and within the town of Edenton. The parasitical relationships that chattel slavery engenders are inescapable, and these elements work in tandem to intensify the horrors of chattel slavery for Jacobs. Indeed, Jacobs refers to the South as "a cage of obscene birds" (45).

Black children in Jacobs's narrative are inducted into a stifling environment where the brutality of chattel slavery is ubiquitous. And yet, Edenton's enslaved Black people also transform geographic knowledge and mobility into forms of power. Even as she is enslaved by Dr. Flint, Jacobs's knowledge of Edenton's layout, particularly her proximity to her grandmother's house, provides her with practical means of survival as well as emotional and moral support. Jacobs explains that while she suffered from neglect by her enslavers as a child, "on my various errands I passed my grandmother's house, where there was always something to spare for me" (13). Despite their fixedness in Edenton and the relentless efforts of white enslavers there, many enslaved people in *Incidents* have a keen interest in geography. And yet, this is also a cause for concern. Black geographic knowledge based on misinformation alarms Linda Brent, whose literacy allows her a more fulsome picture of the world. Linda Brent has access to newsprint, a significant form of nineteenth-century communications technology. As such, she recalls a moment in which

> [o]ne woman begged me to get a newspaper and read it over. She said her husband told her that the black people had sent word to the queen of 'Merica that they were all slaves; that she didn't believe it, and went to Washington city to see the president about it. They quarrelled; she drew her sword upon him, and swore that he should help her to make them all free. (42)

The scene can be read as a comedy or a tragedy. The woman who asks Linda Brent to read to her encapsulates the anti-Black minstrel stereotypes popularized first in print and then onstage during the mid–nineteenth century. But for Jacobs's sympathetic readers, this anecdote underscores how the program of ignorance enforced by white supremacists results in a Black vernacular knowledge of world affairs that reflects distorted truth. And yet, despite the impact of misinformation, Linda Brent's listener is not wrong, even though she is illiterate. Her main concern, global recognition of the profound injustice of chattel slavery, is accurate. Here, the desire for Black geographic knowledge provides moments of pathos in the narrative.

In the chapter "What Slaves Are Taught to Think of the North," Jacobs tells her readers how geographic knowledge is used by Southern enslavers to maintain power. Jacobs explains that among the enslaved population of Edenton, "some believe that the abolitionists have already made them free, and that it is established by law, but that their masters prevent the law from going into effect"

(42). Meanwhile, white enslavers capitalize on the geographic isolation of enslaved people in numerous ways: "when they visit the north and return home, they tell their slaves of the runaways they have seen and describe them in the most deplorable condition" (40). Their ability to travel and learn about the wider world is used to maintain the status quo: "many of the slaves believe such stories, and think it not worthwhile to exchange slavery for such a hard kind of freedom" (40). This is an example of the way, as Katherine McKittrick has argued, "that which is used geographically to displace and regulate black women during slavery, specifically patriarchal ways of seeing and white colonial desires for lands, free labor, and racial sexual domination, rests on a tight hierarchy of racial power and knowledge that is spatially organized" (40). Thus, geographic misinformation bolsters white supremacy within Edenton, North Carolina, and beyond.

"Reader, I Draw No Imaginary Pictures of Southern Homes"

Such overviews of the impact of Black geography work well alongside class discussions about some of the most dramatic episodes of the narrative, including Linda Brent's sojourn in the Snaky Swamp. Still, many questions about the relationship between teaching *Incidents in the Life of a Slave Girl* and technology remain: How do I demonstrate that Jacobs's text was not only geographically rooted in a particular time and place but also informed by technology; that her ability to evade detection and capture by her enslavers was informed by her sophisticated knowledge of space, place, and technology; that geographic and technical knowledge ties Jacobs to a larger tradition of radical maroon insurgency and resistance by enslaved people; or that Black geographic knowledge lends structure to the very text? Furthermore, how can contemporary readers use the technology at our disposal to unlock the text that Jacobs presents us with? Jacobs drives this inquiry into Black feminist geographies when she says, "Reader, I draw no imaginary pictures of southern homes" (32). But to answer this slew of concerns, I have also increasingly turned toward methodologies informed by Black feminist geography and the digital humanities, particularly maps. Catherine Knight Steele has argued that "Black American women have a technological capability built on the legacy of enslavement, rebellion, and resilience in the U.S. context. It was from this legacy that Black American women learned the skills to craft intentional discourses of resistance online" (10).

My critical awareness of the role that Black feminist geography and the digital humanities can play in helping students grasp "the shape of mystery" (104) that haunts *Incidents in the Life of a Slave Girl* is informed by my experience in the classroom at Queen's University, a medium-sized research institution located in Kingston, Ontario, and by my work as a research fellow at Pennsylvania State University's Center for Black Digital Research. Many of my students have rarely encountered Black literature on a syllabus before attending university. With them in mind, my goals for using digital technology involve enhancing their understanding of the geographic and cultural context of *Incidents in the Life of a Slave Girl*. Students in my courses have used *Google Maps* to develop a clearer sense of the main locations described in the text and their relationship to one another. So, when Jacobs describes her first experience of being punished by Mrs. Flint, we gain a richer sense of the quotidian acts of cruelty meant to grind her down, including being sent out barefoot into the town of Edenton on a "long-distance . . . errand" "in the month of February" after "several inches of snow had fallen" (20). In moments like these, a collective onscreen journey to Edenton helps students develop a critical sense of scale and distance. As Maria A. Windell posits, "it is important to recognize how Florida, California, and a series of intertextual references map a geography of possibility in her narrative. This black Transamerican Sentimentalism hemispheric imaginary marks a space known to and yet amorphous for many enslaved, formerly enslaved, and free blacks living in the eastern United States" (137–38). During the Great Pivot, the ability to use online tools and modes of communication to animate texts and to bridge the gap across time periods and distances was not just urgent but also mandatory. This shift underscored elements of Jacobs's narrative that were intertwined with geography and technology.

The attention to the spatial and geographic turns I bring to the classroom when teaching *Incidents* builds on the work of Black feminist scholars. Jacobs's sense of place is linked to her affirmation of Black humanity and is a significant intervention in Black geography. As McKittrick argues, within the narrative, the character Linda Brent's "spatial experiences and strategies illustrate how the geographic workings of slavery simultaneously produce spatial boundaries and subject-knowledges that can subvert the perimeters of bondage" (40). Maria O'Malley has shown that Jacobs "draws on the public conception of geo-political sites as opportunities to test out modes of self-sovereignty" (39). Several supplementary texts commonly taught alongside the narrative, like Michelle Burnham's "Loopholes of Resistance: Harriet Jacobs' Slave Narrative and the Critique of Agency in Foucault" and the selection from Katja Kanzler's "'To Tell the Kitchen Version': Architectural Figurations of Race and Gender in Harriet Jacobs's *Incidents in the Life of the Slave Girl*," included in the second Norton Critical Edition of the narrative, handily outline the geographic stakes of the narrative in ways that are accessible and illuminating for undergraduate students. Thinking along the lines of technology, recent scholarship by Shelleen Greene points out that Jacobs's existential split has resonances with queer forms of artificial life like BINA48. Outside of these contextual readings, each of which prompts fruitful discussions and provides clear entry points into the theoretical work of Black literary studies, the levels of spatial analysis currently offered by digital humanities, including but not limited to mapping tools, allow for a nuanced understanding of Jacobs's insurgency.

"Another Link to Life"

In the classroom, it is clear that *Incidents in the Life of a Slave Girl* is a text that can speak to readers through the generations. When my students first encounter *Incidents in the Life of a Slave Girl*, they are struck by how alive the text is, how fierce Jacobs's voice still sounds, and how striking her hard-won battles still are. For young women in particular, her struggle to resist sexual assault and exploitation, her desire for sexual autonomy, and her insistence on her right to motherhood on her terms are particularly moving and feel contemporary. It seems as if the patriarchal structures that undergirded the world that Jacobs navigated have found their way into our world, too, albeit in different forms. Young women face a world of social media that places tremendous pressure to perform circumscribed forms of femininity, from young adulthood into motherhood (Butkowski et al.). Platforms like *Instagram* have intensified scrutiny and pressure on young women to look and perform gender in narrow ways, even as they open new paths of communication. While we are often tempted to think of our contemporary moment as more permissive than the past, I wonder if the increased scrutiny and exposure my students face forces them to perform narrower forms of self-expression? What happens when young women come of age in a society not only dictated by the right to look but in which the need to be seen regulates many aspects of their lives? In what ways do these complicated relationships with technology impact students' interpretation of texts like *Incidents in the Life of a Slave Girl*? The questions raised by contemporary uses of technology are powerful reasons to link the text to the tools students use every day. I have found that a consideration of the impact of digital technology on our students' lives strengthens student analyses of *Incidents in the Life of a Slave Girl*.

Such questions about the role of technology in women's lives are not only prompted by contemporary concerns, they are suggested by the text itself. An attentive reading of the chapter "Still in Prison" reveals the impact of visual technology on Jacobs's work. In the depths of her garret, while contemplating her tribulations, Jacobs described her existential horror as "the shape of mystery," which remained inscrutable to her (104). In this chapter, the garret assumes the form of a technological apparatus, namely a camera, that affords Jacobs a critical distance from the world of chattel slavery outside her door. Using the "peephole" turned "aperture" (102), Jacobs takes on a role akin to a photographer and undermines heteropatriarchal social structures while reversing the male gaze. In vernacular terms, we might say that using the garret, Jacobs makes a way out of no way. Or, as Sydney Searchwell-Simpson, a student in my nineteenth-century African American Literature seminar, observes, "the garret is a place of both concealment and surveillance which redistributes the power from Dr. Flint to Linda. However, the garret's surveillance abilities are only formed after Linda manipulates the 'oppressive' space." Extending this observation, I would suggest that reading the garret as a camera lends new weight to the "glimpses of things out of doors" that make Jacobs "thankful for [her] wretched hiding place" (103). The refracted lens she fashions from her physical space shields her from the embodied horror of the enslaved women beneath her, each of whom offers a vision of Jacobs's potential future. The fates of any one of the women she sees beneath her, from "the bondswoman and her child" (103) sold away by her enslaver, to the wet nurse who dies by suicide to avoid being "stripped and whipped" (103), could very well be her own, save for her position behind or within the camera.

Mapping the "Shape of Mystery"

Zooming closer to Edenton in the present day, it remains helpful to retain a sense of repurposed tools and insurgent technology. Digital photography and telescopes become weapons in our present-day arsenal. Several years ago, a simple *Google* search led me to the Historic Edenton State Historic Site Visitor Center's website—a mouthful, to be sure. At that time, material from brochures that were available at the Visitor's Center was posted on the website. One of those resources was a brochure of downtown Edenton, which mapped out the main locations that Jacobs writes about in her narrative (fig. 1). The map on the brochure is rudimentary, and the material is no longer freely available on the web, but it remains an invaluable tool that has opened up new forms of inquiry in my classroom. For example, the closeness of Dr. Norcom's home to Samuel Tredwell Sawyer's home is made visible by the map and suggests, among other things, the minute degrees of difference between the two men. The short distance between Molly Horniblow's home and Dr. Norcom's home (and the very real danger posed by the location of Harriet's garret) is put into stark relief too.

With the map and its key sites in mind, I have asked students to use basic online tools like *Google Maps* to explore Edenton and the places Jacobs describes. I am mindful of the work of the Colored Conventions Project (coloredconventions.org) when I tell students that "these tools are not intended to perform analysis for us automatically. Rather, these tools provide a set of instruments for exploring different kinds of questions at varying scales" (Foreman et al., *Colored Conventions* 15). In-class group assignments in which students map the town of Edenton lend nuance to Jacobs's descriptions of her daily life during childhood, in the Flint household, and as a fugitive. This form of digital exploration gives students a thick sense of the terrain around Edenton, particularly the Snaky Swamp, where Jacobs retreats temporarily, and the town's strategic position on Edenton Bay. They come to understand Edenton as being not only a significant site of chattel slavery and maroonage but a key node in the antebellum commercial shipping routes that sustained and enabled bondage on a global scale. For practical reasons, Black abolitionists were often silent about geographic details that would have revealed how they achieved freedom. Frederick Douglass chided abolitionists who were too public about the details of their business, claiming that "the practice of publishing every new invention by which a slave is known to have escaped from slavery, has neither wisdom nor

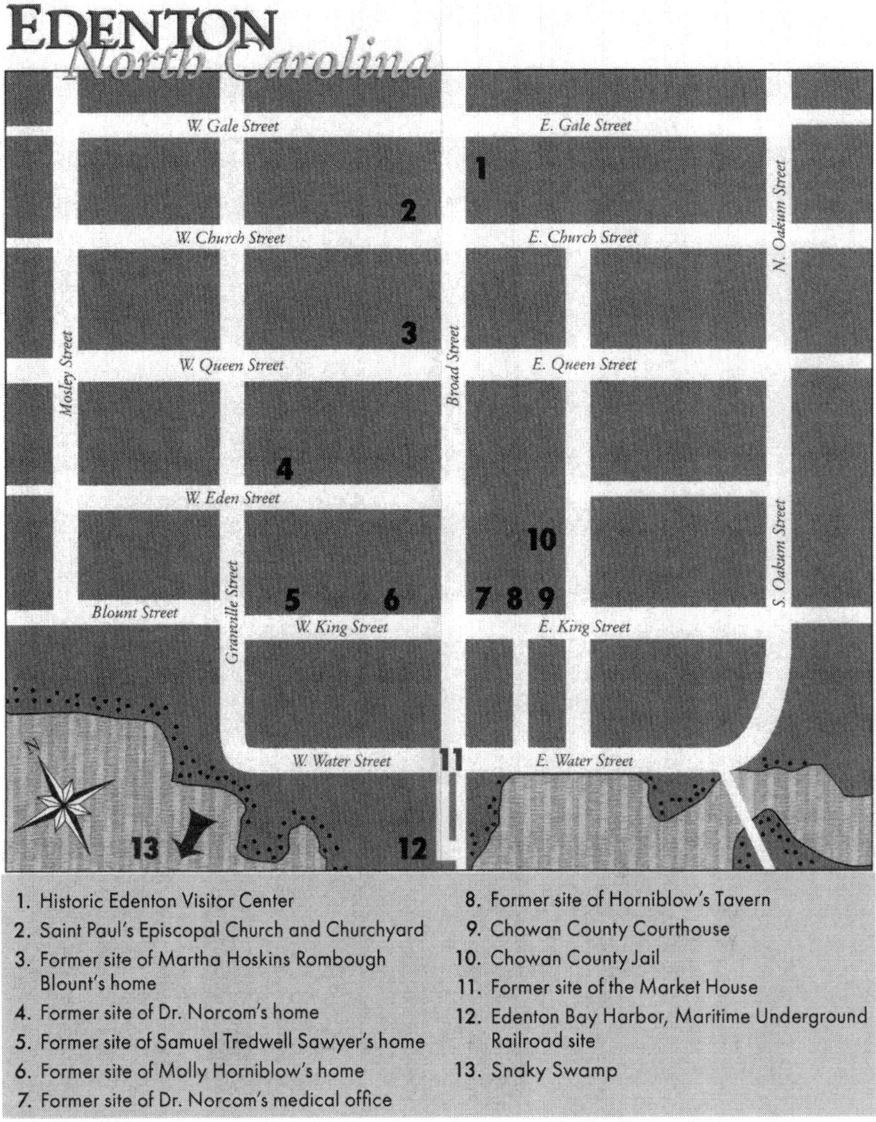

1. Historic Edenton Visitor Center
2. Saint Paul's Episcopal Church and Churchyard
3. Former site of Martha Hoskins Rombough Blount's home
4. Former site of Dr. Norcom's home
5. Former site of Samuel Tredwell Sawyer's home
6. Former site of Molly Horniblow's home
7. Former site of Dr. Norcom's medical office
8. Former site of Horniblow's Tavern
9. Chowan County Courthouse
10. Chowan County Jail
11. Former site of the Market House
12. Edenton Bay Harbor, Maritime Underground Railroad site
13. Snaky Swamp

Figure 1. Historic Edenton map. Courtesy of the North Carolina Department of Natural and Cultural Resources.

necessity to sustain it" (*My Bondage* 323). Douglass believed that in publishing such accounts, "the anti-slavery man addresses the slaveholder, not the slave; he stimulates the former to greater watchfulness, and adds to his facilities for capturing his slave" (324). Jacobs's reticence around Black geography within the narrative serves a similar function, even as it informs her daily life and her journey to freedom. Jacobs is careful to omit from *Incidents* many details about abolitionist uses of antebellum commercial shipping routes and maroon insurgency. Her opacity was a strategy of survival and solidarity. But it is incumbent upon us as contemporary readers to turn our critical lenses toward the text by any means necessary.

The result of this collective Black feminist geographic work is the knowledge that digital technology can expose the ties that bind us together across vast distances and periods. The digital environments spawned by the pandemic are often ill-suited for collective work and a sense of group cohesion among students. But by adopting insurgent Black feminist attitudes toward technology, the very kind that Jacobs displays, we can not only reconcile ourselves to the position we are in but also use that position to develop deep insight into nineteenth-century Black literature. Black feminist geographies and Black digital technologies work together to reveal yet another facet of the text and another glimpse at Jacobs's brilliance.

Incidents in the Life of a Slave Girl in a Gender and Women's Studies Course: Students as Agents of Change

Heidi M. Hanrahan

In the closing pages of *Incidents in the Life of a Slave Girl*, Harriet Jacobs points out that despite her manumission, her struggle is not over. She remains separated from her children and longs for "a home of [her] own . . . however humble" (156). Clearly, she leaves her audience with work to do. If readers have been paying attention, the text spurs them to action—to take up the cause of all those who are oppressed. Jacobs insists on engagement. As such, *Incidents* plays a key role in the interdisciplinary Introduction to Gender and Women's Studies course I teach with two colleagues, a class structured around the theme of "gender, confinement, and freedom" with a goal of helping students see themselves as agents of change. Our team (a historian, a sociologist, and a literature specialist) combines our research and teaching interests through this organizing principle, with Jacobs's text as a cornerstone.[1]

Incidents serves as a powerful component of our course, as it fully embodies the interconnected ideas of gender, race, power, confinement, freedom, and engagement. Illustrating how a marginalized woman finds (limited) power and freedom in the midst of captivity, the text perfectly complements other aspects of our course, including a visit to a women's prison and readings and discussions on topics as varied as contemporary family structures, Queen Elizabeth I, and questions of women writers and canonicity. Finally, since *Incidents* invites—in fact, demands—an engaged, activist audience, it echoes our call for students to see themselves as agents of change with responsibility beyond the classroom.[2] In this essay, I begin with the genesis of our course and the role *Incidents* plays in its structure. Next, I discuss why in later iterations we incorporated more reflective writing and a service-learning component into the class. Our assessment revealed that, especially when we thought about Jacobs's text, we could be doing more to connect the classroom to the world beyond academia.

My coinstructors and I have been teaching Introduction to Gender and Women's Studies, which is always team-taught by faculty members from history, English, and the social sciences, every other fall semester since 2012. While planning our first collaboratively written syllabus, we met to brainstorm ideas. The conversation took a promising turn when we began discussing the field trip that the original team of instructors traditionally took their students on—usually to a museum and a play. Where did we want to take our students? Amy, the sociologist, explained that when teaching about social inequalities and deviant behavior, she had taken classes to tour men's prisons, but she had never toured a women's prison. That idea interested us and caused us to suddenly recognize an overlap in our academic interests: Sally, the historian, regularly studies and teaches about the anchorites, medieval religious women who walled themselves up in tiny rooms in churches. I work mostly in nineteenth-century literature, with an interest in how marginalized writers and characters access power. In short, we shared an interest in how institutions have constrained people along the lines of gender and how people responded to those constraints, finding forms of freedom and sites of resistance within those confines. By the end of that meeting, we had settled on a visit to a women's prison and on a course theme: "Gender, Confinement, and Freedom." Finally, we selected the end-of-course text we would all read together: *Incidents*, which, with its interdisciplinary possibilities, insistence on social change and action, and nuanced depictions of intersectionality, encapsulated everything we wanted to talk about.

The course is divided into four parts: three "discipline perspective" units and a final unit on *Incidents*, which also serves as a space of synthesis and reflection. Amy begins with a sociological perspective, introducing students to concepts like how we "learn" gender through socialization and how gender impacts family and workplace dynamics. She also invites guest speakers, including a political science professor who speaks on women in politics and upcoming elections and a professor from social work who speaks about gender and incarceration. Next, Sally takes students through an introduction to how gender and history have shaped each other, with an emphasis on religious traditions and political and economic agency. My section, which features writers as wide-ranging as Nathaniel Hawthorne, Alice Dunbar Nelson, and Randall Kenan, focuses on how literature itself is often gendered, reflecting and shaping our understandings of religion, the individual, marriage, family, sex, and sexuality. About halfway through the class, we take our field trip to the women's prison—always one of the most impactful parts of the course—and spend the subsequent class period discussing it. Finally, the last several classes are devoted to Jacobs's text and reflecting on the class as a whole.

By the time we arrive at *Incidents*, students are ready to put the text into conversation with everything we've been working on all semester. We talk about the book's careful depiction of gender dynamics in enslaved people's lives. For instance, students appreciate the plight of enslaved men, particularly Linda's father, who despite telling his son to come to him when he calls him, lives in a world where he is so powerless to protect that child that the boy is better off listening to the woman who is his enslaver (12). Jacobs, though, notes that because of their sexual exploitation and the burdens of motherhood, "slavery . . . is far more terrible for women" (64). Indeed, Jacobs's focus on the specific horrors of slavery for women highlights Linda's intersectional identity: a young Black woman with no legal control over her body yet with an expectation that she conform to Christian morality, even as her enslaver pursues her with impunity. Again and again, students see how she fights back in the midst of confinement, insistent on exercising her freedom and will. Together, we read Linda's agonized justification of her choice to sleep with Sands, a choice she makes with "deliberate calculation" (46). It is, she notes, "less degrading to give one's self, than to submit to compulsion," adding, "There is something akin to freedom in having a lover who has no control over you" (47). For students, these poignant claims reflect a sad lack of choice and a fierce assertion of agency.

Of course, students are always keenly interested in Linda's ongoing battle with Dr. Flint, whose role as a conflation of the enslaver, father, and doctor roles serves as a powerful symbol for how entrenched the patriarchy is, especially in his hostility to marginalized women. Students thrill in Linda's "competition in cunning" with Flint as she sends him letters claiming she's up north when she's really often only feet away from him (102–03). Students easily connect Linda's hiding in the garret to the medieval anchorites and the prisoners we met on our field trip. These women can see glimpses of the world and interact with it in limited ways but remain separated from it. For Linda, this is sometimes a blessing (as when she sees an enslaved woman being pursued and feels "thankful" for her own "wretched" hiding place) and sometimes a curse (as when she sees her son bleeding from a dog bite but is unable to help him) (97, 93). Discussing Benny's injury, students often bring up the visitor room at the prison and the separate "mommy and baby" room, spaces that are tinged with sadness. They remember guards telling us that some women don't want their children to visit; it's just too hard.

In fact, our class spends a great deal of time talking about how motherhood gives Linda strength even as it limits and confines her. Students are reminded of pieces we've read together, like Charlotte Perkins Gilman's "The Yellow Wall-Paper," where a woman loses her mind in part because of her maternal guilt. They also make connections to earlier class discussions about why women do not enter politics or rise in the workplace at the same rates as men. Linda, like others we discuss, loves her children but pays a price for that love. At her lowest moments, she says she would gladly die if not for them (65). Yet, as students note, just a few pages later in some of the book's most powerful prose, she points to the children as a key source of her power: "I had a woman's pride, and a mother's love for my children. . . . My master had power and law on his side; I had a determined will. There is might in each" (70). Students see how in a hierarchically raced and gendered world, nothing is straightforward or easy for those without power.

On the final day of discussion, we look at extratextual documents, like Lydia Maria Child's letters and Jacobs's letters to Amy Post. I also pass around Jean Fagan Yellin's biography, and students pour over the photos she includes. When students learn that "Mr. and Mrs. Bruce" are actually N. P. Willis and his wife, and I tell them about her connections to Fanny Fern and Harriet Beecher Stowe (both of whose work we read), they are excited to see how Jacobs's life intersected with many other important protofeminist figures of her time. Importantly, we discuss how she is not just the passive recipient of their aid, charity, or advice. The letters to Post, especially, illustrate Jacobs's shaping of her own narrative, a reminder that though her writing was always "mediated" by Child and white audience expectations (Tricomi 219), even in the textual space, she found ways to exercise agency in the midst of confines. In Benjamin Fagan's words, she's a "rogue reader," someone who "understands print and its pathways as necessarily open and available to revision and manipulation" (21).

Our students' writing on *Incidents* shows them discussing our course themes with nuance, avoiding easy generalizations. Melanie[3] latches on to the types of freedom the text explores: "The freedom [Linda] desires is multilayered: she desires freedom over her mind, her body, her actions, her children." In an essay connecting *Incidents* to the history section of the class, Tara makes specific connections to the anchorites, writing that Linda, like these medieval women, "finds herself most free when she is actually being physically confined." So, too, does Rachel make a powerful comparison between Jacobs's book, the suffragist Alice Paul (whom they discussed in the history portion), and our field trip, specifically a passage in which Linda discusses the "stifling" air in her hiding space (128). In the prison, Rachel remembers, "[m]ore often than not, the air was stale and foul smelling. Alice Paul recalls when she and other suffragettes broke the windows in their jail cells in order to breathe in fresh air. Linda does not have this opportunity, but undoubtedly if she had, she would have done the same." Rachel's insight, linking three very different kinds of women from different periods of history, is precisely the kind of moment we had hoped for when planning the class. In short, Jacobs's text is perfect for facilitating these moments of interdisciplinary insight.

After three iterations of the course, my coteachers and I assessed how well we were achieving our goals and found that while we were succeeding in two of them (students understood our course themes and employed interdisciplinary perspectives), we were falling short of the third goal: helping students see themselves as agents of change, capable of making connections between our course work and their work in the world beyond the classroom. As we wrote about that assessment, "we gave them a vocabulary for action and hope, but we did not get them actively involved in working for social justice, reform, or change. We pushed them right up to the point, but stopped short" (Hanrahan et al. 110). We were reminded of Miss Fanny, the kind white woman who sometimes recognizes her agency (she buys and frees Linda's grandmother when Dr. Flint tries to sell her) but ultimately gives in to a sense of powerlessness, telling Linda, "she wished that I and all my grandmother's family were at rest in our graves" (73). In other words, Miss Fanny sees injustice and pain but feels nothing can be done, a claim Jacobs rejects, insisting she will bring peace to her family through securing their freedom. When we saw that our students would not or could not see themselves making a change in their world right here and now—that we were leaving "dream[s] . . . not yet realized" (*Incidents* 156)—we decided to take up Jacobs's call to action. We added specific reflective assignments and a service-learning component to allow students to see themselves more clearly as agents of change.

Adding service learning to a class involves planning and coordination. We read up on best practices and quickly understood that it needed to be fully incorporated, not just used as an add-on component.[4] We worked with our university's service-learning liaison, who connected us with a women's shelter, where students helped paint, clean, organize, and prepare and serve meals. We also worked with a grassroots organization fighting Amendment 1, a West Virginia ballot initiative that would restrict access to abortion. Students who chose this option worked the phone banks. We volunteered alongside them when we could. We also had them keeping a log of their experiences and regularly discussed their experiences in class. At the semester's end, their final writing assignment asked them this question: How has this course, with all of its components (the interdisciplinary units, the field trip, the service learning, and *Incidents*), helped you see yourself as an agent of change in the world, someone capable of using what you learned in this class to improve the world outside the classroom?

These final essays show that, while we still have improvements to make, students did see themselves as agents of change, people who could do the kind of work Jacobs calls us to do. For instance, even though Amendment 1 passed, students still felt empowered about the work they did. Georgiana writes, "Talking to people at the phone bank solidified to me that there really is something I can do to help women, even if it's just calling people to sign a petition or bill." She adds that she now wants to work with incarcerated women, specifically to provide low-cost health care, since they "deserve a second chance at life." Other students pointed to specific service ideas they came up with while volunteering and ways that they had begun to think about the intersections of their career plans and their budding activism. Above all, the students wrote of their realization that they could make small but meaningful differences. As Casey put it, "Before this class, I consistently told myself that I was too small to generate change. This course has shifted my viewpoint. . . . Being an agent of change means starting small and contributing to a larger cause."

Ultimately, we remain convinced that *Incidents in the Life of a Slave Girl*, a text that calls its readers to action, is a perfect choice for a change-focused, interdisciplinary approach to a gender and women's studies course. In answer to Jacobs's plaintive description of her dreams "not yet realized," we offer the words of our student Maria in her final reflection: "People are out here suffering, and I don't want to just sit and feel powerless any longer."

NOTES

1. Thanks to Sally Brasher and Amy L. DeWitt, my coteachers, for allowing me to talk about our work in this venue and for their continued collaboration.

2. For more on this idea, see Hanrahan.

3. Students' names have been changed. We obtained IRB approval to collect and study our students' written work and kept written records of our in-class discussions.

4. Seethaler's and Rojas's articles were especially helpful.

Seeing a "True and Just Account": *Incidents in the Life of a Slave Girl* and Visual Culture

Melissa J. Lingle-Martin

Teaching Harriet Jacobs's *Incidents in the Life of a Slave Girl* in its visual culture contexts helps instructors meet learning objectives common to a range of literary studies and humanities courses and invites students to perceive some of the text's key thematic concerns and cultural contributions. Appealing to the visual is also a reliable way to increase student engagement. We live in a world saturated with images. Importantly, the antebellum era, too, was a visual age, when new technologies of vision, like photography, were invented and graphics could be widely distributed through the developing efficiency of the printing press and increasing modes of transport. Scholars have shown that Jacobs was aware that she "work[ed] with words during a profoundly visual cultural moment" (Blackwood 94). Indeed, debates about slavery were particularly ocularcentric.[1] As an abolitionist, especially one who worked for a time in an antislavery reading room, Jacobs would have been very familiar with what Phillip Lapsansky describes as the "graphic discord" of the abolitionist and antiabolitionist print wars (201). Furthermore, *Incidents* elaborates connections among reading, vision, truth, and justice. For instance, Linda Brent, *Incidents*'s pseudonymous narrator, asserts, "Reader, I draw no imaginary pictures of southern homes. I am telling you the plain truth" (32). The language of this quotation indicates that Jacobs links truth and storytelling. It also suggests that Jacobs envisioned her narrative as correcting errors propagated by the dominant propaganda, both visual and textual, of the age, the "imaginary pictures." Here, as throughout the text, Jacobs reinforces Brent's authority as one able to share eyewitness testimony—truth-telling intended to destroy slavery and seek justice. However, justice, Jacobs shows, requires new ways of seeing.[2] Therefore, as Lena Hill argues, *Incidents* is intentionally visually pedagogic and "emphasiz[es] slave vision as a means of instructing readers" (51). Thus, most importantly, a visual studies approach to the text honors Jacobs's own focus on vision. In what follows, I share strategies instructors can use to engage students in meaningful analysis of *Incidents* and its visual culture contexts as one way to invite students to explore the function of genre, the complexity of Jacobs's interventions in multimedia and ideological contexts, and the continued relevance of the text.

When teaching lower-level courses, such as a high school American studies course or a general education American literature survey, I situate our reading of *Incidents* in antebellum visual culture to provide context for Jacobs's work, especially as an antislavery text, and to help students identify and analyze the functions of genre. In particular, I address confusions that stem from students' unfamiliarity with textual slave narratives and from Jacobs's use of a pseudonym.

Sometimes students read *Incidents* as either a highly polemic journalistic account, devoid of personal, intellectual, and imaginative insight, or a fictional account—a novel. I strive to help them explore how Jacobs's text, yes, has a very specific political agenda and testifies of atrocities to evoke in readers "a realizing sense of the condition of two millions of women at the South," as the preface by the author that opens *Incidents* explains (5). But I also prepare them to experience the text as an individual's personal, artful, and intellectual pursuit of truth and justice that exceeds and defies conventional generic constraints. To do this, I often share excerpts from Jacobs's 21 June 1857 letter to Amy Post, where Jacobs explains that she has "[s]triven faithfully to give a true and just account of my own life in slavry" and elaborates complex and compelling notions of truth and justice (*Incidents* 200). In this letter, she notes that she has omitted some things from the narrative because of modesty, sexism, and prejudice; she nonetheless asserts her authority, truthfulness, and good intentions. She writes "not to tell you what I have heard but what I have seen—and what I have suffered" in order to seek sympathy for others rather than for herself (200). Hers is truthful, firsthand testimony based on what she has both seen and felt, information gathered from a variety of senses, from living. Here and throughout the text, Jacobs artfully negotiates the conventions and stereotypes of the time in order to reach readers and more. She also writes for justice beyond sympathy, a justice she helps us perceive through her construction of the text. As P. Gabrielle Foreman points out, Jacobs "gauge[s] the distance between the strict truth that falls short and [undertells her story] to match what we might call delicate expectations, while simultaneously indicating to receptive readers that more is apparent for those who choose to look" ("Politics" 321). While, at the surface level, Jacobs shares what she has seen, she also encourages readers to learn to "look" and think anew. This looking anew, looking carefully and critically, offers readers a way to apprehend both truth and justice.

To help students read *Incidents* as engaging with ways of seeing, early in our encounter with the text we survey some of the many graphics, the "illustrated books and tracts, lithographed prints, and broadsheets with woodcuts; monthly periodicals . . . annual almanacs; and a wide variety of printed ephemera, including candy wrappers, envelope stickers, song sheets, and stationary" that Lapsansky vividly describes as "[r]olling off the presses" in the antebellum era (202).[3] For example, and importantly for our preparation for reading *Incidents*, I share the cover vignette from *The American Anti-Slavery Almanac, for 1843*, compiled by Lydia Maria Child, the abolitionist writer and activist who edited *Incidents* (*Oh, Hail Columbia!*).[4] This image introduces students to the rhetorics of sentiment and patriotic iconoclasm at work in the abolitionist movement and in Jacobs's text. We examine the brutal irony of the cover picture, which depicts a Black woman, presumably enslaved, huddled on the ground in front of the US Capitol Building. The woman cowers, trying to protect an infant cradled in her arms, as a massive eagle digs its claws into her back and threatens further harm. The iconoclastic juxtaposition of the cowering woman and endangered child with the eagle, Capitol Dome, and the flag waving above—three key American icons usually connected with liberty and protection—pushes readers to see how slavery betrays national ideals. Analysis of this image prepares students to recognize some of the antislavery arguments of *Incidents* and especially the patriotic iconoclasm of its opening pages. It also allows us to consider how Jacobs's text functions differently from—and sometimes critiques—mainstream abolitionist media.

When we turn to the text, students are quick to recognize how Brent highlights the incongruity of the institution of slavery in Revolutionary era America through her recounting of her grandmother's reenslavement: "It was during the Revolutionary War; and they were captured on the passage, carried back, and sold to different purchasers" (9). The simple juxtaposition of enslavement and the Revolutionary War—the purported fight for freedom—enacts the same patriotic iconoclasm as the print examined above. Yet while the print is allegorical, Brent's representation is specific. Moreover, the narrative's consistent focus on parents' desperate struggles to protect their children—her father's "strongest wish was to purchase his children," we learn on the very first page—offers eyewitness testimony about the crimes the image can represent only allegorically (9). This analysis shows that Jacobs was involved in a shared discourse: abolitionists used similar consciousness-raising strategies across mediums, in allegorical graphics and in first-person texts. We also recognize the increased truth-telling power of Jacobs's testimony: this is the very personal story of Jacobs's family. Students understand that despite Jacobs's use of a pseudonym, "this narrative is no fiction," as Jacobs asserts in the very first line of the preface (5).

These class discussions pave the way for a workshop that invites students to further analyze how *Incidents* engages with the visual culture of the era, especially abolitionist and proslavery propaganda, and provides not only what William Andrews helpfully calls "eye-witness" and "I-witness" testimony ("Introduction") but also ideological and imaginative challenges that push viewers to see beyond the simplified optics of both the antiabolitionist and abolitionist visual campaigns. This exercise works best after students have read at least half of the book or all of the selections provided in most anthologies and can certainly be done as a culminating activity if students have read the entire narrative. Before the workshop, I prepare a shareable *Google Slides* file with a variety of antebellum graphics. While I often tailor my selection to images that seem most appropriate to previous class discussions, I regularly include the following images: an unattributed illustration used in several antislavery pamphlets, including Child's *Authentic Anecdotes of American Slavery* (1838); *Slavery as It Exists in America. Slavery as It Exists in England*, a proslavery broadside by John Haven (1850); *Oh Carry Me Back to Ole Virginny*, an image romanticizing slavery and reproduced on tobacco package labels by Robertson, Seibert, and Shearman (1859); and *The Negro in His Own Country* with its companion, *The Negro in America*, both engravings from Joseph Priest's *Bible*

Defense of Slavery (1853). While in upper-level college seminars I sometimes have students explore digital collections of images on their own and then bring relevant findings to class discussion or share them on a class blog, selecting images beforehand and distributing them to small groups in class often best facilitates active engagement with the texts in high school or survey-level classes. In those cases, I usually separate students into groups of three to four, assign each group one specific image or direct them to select the one they have the most questions about, and then share the following instructions:

> Examine the image. Discuss its basic argument or message and record a two- to three-sentence response.
>
> Discuss how *Incidents* and other course materials engage with that argument. Identify at least one specific line or passage that supports your claim.
>
> Note how the narrative and other course materials implicate vision—or the lack of it—in the perpetuation of slavery, racism, and injustice.

As students work through this process, I circulate among the groups, tracking their progress and helping them find passages and attend to specific language. Because the goal of this workshop is to have students engage with the text and images, not to search for scenes they can remember but not easily find, I aim to be present enough in the small groups so that I can help locate quotations and think through connections.

When we reconvene as a class, groups who analyzed *Incidents*'s engagement with the proslavery graphics report that the images, each in their own way, suggest that enslavement in America is benevolent, edifying, and even enjoyable for the enslaved. Specifically, *The Negro in His Own Country* and *The Negro in America* (a pair we treat as one composite), suggests that life for enslaved people in America allows them to experience cultivation and even salvation in ways that life in an imagined Africa does not. *Slavery as It Exists in America. Slavery as It Exists in England* contrasts a depiction of the supposedly carefree life of enslaved people in America with the sordid struggles of laborers in England, suggesting the former is far preferable. Rendered in a more realistic tone than the previous cartoon-like broadside, *Oh Carry Me Back to Ole Virginny* nonetheless deceptively portrays enslaved life as carefree and comfortable, a life that allows young families to relax together with music and dance in apparently ample leisure time.

Incidents is full of eyewitness testimony that refutes these images' claims. To begin with, in *The Negro in America* and *Oh Carry Me Back to Ole Virginny* enslaved people appear in a comfortable family group. *Incidents*, students swiftly note, repeatedly relates stories about the separation of families, especially mothers and children. For instance, in chapter 3, "The Slave's New Year's Day," Brent documents the realities of enslaved people being transferred among enslavers. "On one of these sale days," Brent states, "I saw a mother lead seven children to the auction block. She knew that *some* of them would be taken from her; but they took *all*" (18). The mother is thus devastated, and Brent witnesses her mourning: "her wild, haggard face lives to-day in my mind" she says (18). This is clearly eyewitness testimony. As she often does throughout the text, Brent prefaces a description of one of slavery's many atrocities with "I saw." In another example, when her grandmother is separated from one her children, Brent's uncle, Brent describes the scene in particularly heart-wrenching and even more ocularcentric language: "Could you have seen that mother clinging to her child, when they fastened the irons upon his wrists; could you have heard her heart-rending groans, and seen her bloodshot eyes wander wildly from face to face, vainly pleading for mercy; could you have witnessed that scene as I saw it, you would exclaim, *Slavery is damnable!*" (24). As with the previous passage, these lines function as clear eyewitness testimony. This is also what Andrews would term "I-witness," for Brent shares her family's experience and strong personal response. Moreover, the text here emphasizes the importance of perception and empathy, of seeing and experiencing the world as someone else might live it. If readers could see and live through the scene as Brent did, they would see differently. These are just two of the many scenes of family separation documented in *Incidents*, and students remark how vividly, in language that appeals to our eyes, ears, touch, and emotions, these scenes contradict the idealized vision of slavery proffered in proslavery images.

Furthermore, students frequently note that the domestic life depicted in *Incidents* differs strikingly from that envisioned in *The Negro in America*, with its scene of seeming cultivation and civil regard. Brent's experiences in the Flint drawing room are filled with harassment and abuse. "The degradation, the wrongs, the vices, that grow out of slavery, are more than I can describe," Brent explains, with exasperation (27). Yet describe them she does, and after detailing how both Mrs. and Dr. Flint persecute her, Brent, acknowledging the sometimes unbelievable nature of the scenes, declares, "Reader, I draw no imaginary pictures of southern homes. I am telling you the plain truth" (34). Students speculate that Jacobs had exactly the proslavery images we have examined in mind when she presents her narrative as an alternative to "imaginary pictures."

Incidents's direct refutation of proslavery claims that a society built on slavery is better than a society built on free labor offers yet more evidence that the narrative counters the idea of slavery as a benevolent institution and offers, simultaneously, eyewitness testimony and pointed critiques of racist ways of seeing. Students scouring the text for testimony against the claims of *Slavery as It Exists in America. Slavery as It Exists in England* point to Brent's assertion that "I would ten thousand times rather that my children should be the half-starved paupers of Ireland than to be the most pampered among the slaves of America" (29). While her motivation for this specific statement is her desire to be virtuous, elsewhere the narrative documents the mistreatment and poverty of the enslaved. For example, Brent and her brother rely on their grandmother for sufficient food and clothing and for moral guidance (13). Moreover, Brent explains throughout the narrative that enslavers "regard" enslaved people, even their own children, to be "as marketable as the pigs" (34) and "on a par with the animals" (45). "These God-breathing machines are no more, in the sight of their masters, than the cotton they plant, or the horses they tend," Brent asserts (12). Again, Brent emphasizes "sight" and suggests that slavery relies on certain ways of seeing, including dehumanizing disregard, and this also directly contradicts the seeming civil regard depicted in images like *The Negro in America*. This disregard, I urge students to consider, is one manifestation of the injustice against which Jacobs writes. To support this claim, I point to the opening chapter, where Brent identifies injustice for the first time in her enslaver's disregard: "My mistress had taught me the precepts of God's Word: 'Thou shalt love thy neighbor as thyself.' 'Whatsoever ye would that men should do unto you, do ye even so unto them.' But I was her slave, and I suppose she did not recognize me as her neighbor" (11). This lack of recognition is the first "act of injustice" that Brent identifies as such (12), as injustice, but throughout the narrative, as we have seen, she highlights the disregard of enslavers for those they enslave—those they consider merely "merchandise" (9) or, as noted above, beasts.

Importantly, the cover vignette from *Authentic Anecdotes of American Slavery* also raises questions about recognition and justice. Here, in a simple black-and-white print, a presumably enslaved Black woman bows, pleading, holding up her chained wrists, at the feet of what appears to be a white allegorical figure, a woman holding scales and thus seeming to represent justice. This Justice bends ever so slightly and reaches out one arm toward the enslaved woman's hands. Even before they have finished the narrative, groups analyzing this image usually point out that *Incidents* highlights Brent's fierce battle for agency and manifests Jacobs's exertion of agency through writing, agency this image seems to deny. As Jean Fagan Yellin notes of this and graphics like it, "With the inclusion of an empowered white chain-breaking liberator, the enchained black supplicants are seen as powerless" (*Women* 19). Moreover, the text on the image, "Remember them that are in bonds as bound with them," could be interpreted to suggest that viewers respond with "interiorized feeling but not exteriorized action" (22). In response to such a possible reading of this image and its implication that justice is internal and personal, groups often note that Jacobs has Brent envision a very different Justice. At the end of chapter 8, Brent's longing for a "Queen Justice" to whom "the President was subordinate" imagines women as powerful and poised to take action not only by sympathizing but also by changing the system, "mak[ing] them all free," as an enslaved woman with whom Brent speaks thinks a "queen of 'Merica" might (42). When I highlight that this invocation of a "Queen" in an American context could be considered iconoclastic, ironic, or both (as Lauren Berlant puts it, "no American president could be subordinate to any queen—of America or of Justice" [*Queen* 226]), we then consider how this sort of incongruity differs from the iconoclasm of other abolitionist imagery. Here, Brent's imagined scene seems to fulfill American ideals and shows how American icons, like Lady Justice, might actually do justice. Jacobs's is a generative iconoclasm. Students, though, usually do justice to the image: they connect the image and its call for adherence to a sort of golden rule, to Brent's early hope that her enslaver would regard her as a neighbor (11). In the image, the kneeling woman and Justice lock eyes and seem to be looking intently at each other. This detail paired with the words above the image aligns with *Incidents*'s call for recognition. Such observations help us go beyond the dismissive binary of image versus word. The two can work together. Indeed, Jacobs had hoped to include images in *Incidents*![5]

On the whole, through this workshop and our discussions students develop a clearer sense of how the text exists beyond the limits of genre, and they analyze its pursuit of truth and justice in its cultural context. We also recognize that one specific way Jacobs pursues those ends is by writing to cultivate critical visual literacy. Later, when students have finished the narrative, we discuss how this critical purchase of *Incidents* is even more evident in another passage refuting the proslavery claims of *Slavery as It Exists in America. Slavery as It Exists in England*:

> I have heard much about the oppression of the poor in Europe. The people I saw around me were, many of them, among the poorest poor. But when I visited them in their little thatched cottages, I felt that the condition of even the meanest and most ignorant among them was vastly superior to the condition of the most favored slaves in America. . . . Their homes were very humble; but they were protected by law. . . . I do not deny that the poor are oppressed in Europe. I am not disposed to paint their condition so rose-colored as the Hon. Miss Murray paints the condition of the slaves in the United States. A small portion of my experience would enable her to read her own pages with anointed eyes. (152–53)

Students remark that this passage, too, suggests that Jacobs intended to confront misconceptions propagated in the media, both image and text. It also attests to the truthfulness of Brent's portrayals—no "rose-colored" paintings—and the power of her perception. As Lena Hill argues, Jacobs "stress[es] the exceptional nature of black American visual observation" and "demonstrate[s] how their truthful spectatorship portrays the need for a morally grounded national identity" (42). Indeed, while Brent asserts her freedom at the end of *Incidents*, she qualifies that it is not perfect: "We are as free from the power of slaveholders as are the white people of the north; and though that, according to my ideas, is not saying a great deal, it is a vast improvement in *my* condition" (167). Here again we see patriotic iconoclasm, celebrating freedom while also announcing its faults. "The dream of my life is not yet realized," Brent admits (167), yet she fights and writes for it, for herself and for all people.

Reading *Incidents* in American Studies in the fall of 2020, after having also read selections from *The 1619 Project*, my students and I were struck by how the patriotic iconoclasm running throughout the project and especially Nikole

Hannah-Jones's introductory essay parallels the rhetoric and determination of *Incidents*. Both works encourage critical literacy regarding texts, media, history, and lives. Both highlight the generative power of such critical vision. As Hannah-Jones compellingly puts it, "despite being violently denied the freedom and justice promised to all, black Americans believed fervently in the American creed. Through centuries of black resistance and protest, we have helped the country live up to its founding ideals" (16). When read in both its current and contemporary contexts, Jacobs's "true and just account" helps us recognize the injustice—the very functioning—of racist ways of seeing and helps us more critically imagine and perhaps then achieve our ideals.

NOTES

1. Clytus's "Keep It before the People," Cutter's *The Illustrated Slave*, and Lapsansky's "Graphic Discord" are just three of the many works that provide helpful overviews of the "ocularcentric ethos," as Clytus puts it (291), of antebellum debates about slavery and offer compelling analyses of the cultural work of images.

2. In her analysis of Frederick Douglass's and Jacobs's engagements with portraiture of fugitives from slavery and with early technologies of vision, photography in particular, Blackwood also notes that "Jacobs provide[s] a counternarrative to other antebellum descriptions of how (and what) to see" (121).

3. Instructors can find a wealth of images to analyze in conversation with *Incidents* in the following digital archives: *A House Divided* (www.digitalhistory.uh.edu/exhibits/ahd/index.html), *Images of African American Slavery and Freedom* (www.loc.gov/rr/print/list/082_slave.html), *Documenting the American South* (docsouth.unc.edu/index.html), *The New York Public Library Digital Collections* (digitalcollections.nypl.org/divisions/schomburg-center-for-research-in-black-culture-manuscripts-archives-and-rare), Uncle Tom's Cabin *and American Culture* (utc.iath.virginia.edu/abolitn/abgall.html), *Harpweek* (www.harpweek.com), and *Slavery Images* (www.slaveryimages.org/s/slaveryimages).

4. This image and many more from several issues of the *Almanac* are available to download and reproduce without restrictions from the digital collections of the Schomburg Center for Research in Black Culture at the New York Public Library.

5. In an 1854 letter to Amy Post, Jacobs asked Post to try to get a daguerreotype of Jacobs's brother to include in *Incidents*. Jacobs explained, "[I]f this said Book should ever come in existence I want to have an Illustrated Edition and the whole family in" (Yellin, *Harriet Jacobs Family Papers* 1: 210). Analyzing the work of text and image in *Incidents*, Blackwood writes, "Nowhere in *Incidents*, however, does text or image alone possess enough representational capacity to put the entirety of the slave experience before the reader or viewer. Nowhere, either, does the truth alone possess the power to encompass the entirety of the slave experience" (120).

Incidents in the Life of a Slave Girl and Literature by Women

Lorraine Dubuisson

I teach Harriet Jacobs's *Incidents in the Life of a Slave Girl* as part of a senior-level undergraduate literature survey called Literature by Women that examines women's writing within its social, historical, and theoretical contexts. Topics include Renaissance and medieval women writers, feminist theory and criticism, and contemporary poetry by women. Because we are a multicampus institution, this course has traditionally been taught as a hybrid, with face-to-face class meetings for cohorts on multiple campuses coupled with an online component in which all the cohorts participate together. The students taking this class are generally English majors who are enthusiastic about the subject matter and whose participation in online activities is robust.

I begin the course with Virginia Woolf's *A Room of One's Own* and its famous argument that women need financial independence, privacy, and leisure in order to become successful, professional writers (243); also woven throughout the text is the implication that a historical absence of these assets means that women writers lack a literary history to which their writing can respond. That argument is immediately undercut when the class discusses Alice Walker's "In Search of Our Mother's Gardens," in which Walker contends that Woolf leaves women of color entirely out of the equation (1298–99) and offers numerous examples of an alternative artistic history for women independent of Woolf's formula for success (1300–02). All the texts we read in this course are evaluated in terms of these competing arguments. This becomes a quite powerful basis for analysis of the slave narrative of a woman who not only lacks wealth and leisure but who also lacks autonomy and spends a significant portion of her life hiding in a cramped and deeply physically uncomfortable attic in order to be near her children.

The bulk of our class discussions about *Incidents* revolves around Jacobs's multilayered argument against slavery, particularly her assertions that slavery is damaging to both the enslaved and the enslaver and that slavery is an affront to Christian values. Most of my students expect to read about the horrors of slavery for the enslaved in a slave narrative. When Jacobs writes, "He told me I was his property; that I must be subject to his will in all things" (27), she is commenting on the aspect of slavery students expect to encounter in the text. The students who take this course do not fit into a single demographic mold; for example, the typical roster contains traditional and nontraditional students as well as students who come from a variety of racial and ethnic backgrounds and who occupy a variety of positions on the gender continuum. Uniting many of them, however, is their surprise when they discover how much of Jacobs's discussion of slavery focuses on its dangers to the psyche and morality of enslavers, particularly female enslavers, as a function of the white, Northern, female audience she is attempting to reach.

Jacobs argues that slavery destroys the integrity of the enslavers; it makes male enslavers rapists and torturers and makes those who are not actively participating in sexually menacing the enslaved, like the wives of enslavers, complicit in those activities. For Jacobs, one of the overwhelming perversions of slavery is that it erodes the bonds of sisterhood that she asserts should exist between white women and Black women, for "the mistress, who ought to protect the helpless victim, has no other feelings towards her but those of jealousy and rage" (27). In this and other passages like it, Jacobs claims that the camaraderie that should flourish between two women because they are women and despite racial differences cannot occur between an enslaved woman and her female enslaver because the institution of slavery destroys the female enslaver's capacity for compassion toward enslaved women. Many of the texts we read in this class are about female solidarity, about women supporting each other through difficult circumstances, and *Incidents* provides a counterpoint to that prevailing narrative of the course.

Jacobs also argues that slavery cheapens marriage, the bedrock of nineteenth-century Western society, and leaves women no choice but to behave immorally. If enslaved women cannot truly be married (because they have no legal status), then all their marriages are shams and their children illegitimate (*Incidents* 35). If enslaved women must submit to the sexual degradation demanded by their enslavers, they cannot live up to the prevailing ideal of womanhood—purity, chastity, piety—expected of all American women in this time period, making them inappropriate marriage partners if they could legally marry (27–29). Even though rape, extramarital affairs, and sex outside the sanctity of marriage are understood as wrong, slavery tempts male enslavers, especially, to commit all these immoralities; as a result, the enslavers' marriages are broken by slavery (34). A great deal of the syllabus is devoted to texts that foreground marriage, but most of these texts are about marriages between white people; while many of them focus on injustices to women in the context of marriage, *Incidents* is the only text we read that illuminates the specific challenges matrimony and extramarital sexual encounters (including rape) posed for enslaved Black women.

Additionally, Jacobs comments extensively on parenthood in *Incidents*. Slavery leads both male and female enslavers to disavow the children that are generated from relationships with enslaved people. Jacobs depicts a world in which white men own their children, beat their children, and sell their children as property, alongside white women who are only too glad for them to do so or who participate in punishing these children for even existing (33–34). Although Jacobs does mention a few exceptional white women who help the children of their husbands' relationships with enslaved people (34), most of the female enslavers Jacobs discusses in *Incidents* behave like the "incarnate fiend" (16) who welcomes the death of the enslaved person her husband has impregnated. The callous disregard for familial bonds by white enslavers is contrasted throughout with the profound devotion of Black families. For example, Jacobs loves her children so deeply that she endures terrible living conditions to secure their freedom and to be near them as they grow up. She writes, "I was not comfortless [in the attic]. I heard the voices of my children. There was joy and there was sadness in the sound" (98). Many of the fiction and nonfiction pieces I assign in this course are written from the point of view of women who are ambivalent about motherhood, while some of them feature women who feel actively oppressed by their children. *Incidents* presents a complicated portrayal of motherhood and parenthood in general that prompts meaningful discussion of these topics.

By the time students read *Incidents*, they have read other texts that make for interesting comparisons. For example, Julian of Norwich's *A Book of Showings* and Margery Kempe's autobiography both showcase the potential transformative power of suffering, an idea that resonates with Jacobs's transformation from enslaved to freed after a lifetime of suffering in a variety of ways. Aphra Behn's *Oroonoko; or, The Royal Slave* critiques slavery within a Christian context, like *Incidents*, and also features sexual violence against women. Eliza Haywood's *Fantomina; or, Love in a Maze* is about a young woman who sexually pursues a man over a protracted period of time and using a variety of disguises; this text raises issues of consent and issues of the power of female sexuality while also commenting on the double standard that governs what sexual behavior is appropriate for men and women, issues that are discussed at length in *Incidents*. After reading *Incidents*, students read three short speeches by Sojourner Truth that allow the class to discuss the complications of assigning authorship to works that have been transcribed by others or that have, as in Jacobs's case, been heavily edited by others. Finally, students read Margaret Atwood's short story "Rape Fantasies," which offers an opportunity to discuss the ways in which women have been blamed for their own sexual assaults.

All students read two articles about *Incidents*, Caleb Smith's "Harriet Jacobs among the Militants: Transformations in Abolition's Public Sphere, 1859–61" and Patricia D. Hopkins's "Seduction or Rape: Deconstructing the Black Female Body in Harriet Jacobs' *Incidents in the Life of a Slave Girl*." Smith's article focuses on Lydia Maria Child's editing of *Incidents* and argues that her decision to omit a chapter of Jacobs's manuscript elides Jacobs's sympathy with more militant factions of abolitionists than she is typically associated with. Hopkins's article explores the sexual relationship Jacobs initiates with Mr. Sands and whether that relationship is one of agency or coercion, among other issues. One student is assigned to present the Smith article to the class and another to present the Hopkins article. The presenting student makes a post on the discussion board providing questions to lead discussion; the remaining students in the class are expected to respond to those questions, and the presenting student is expected to facilitate the conversation during the duration of the discussion. Examples of discussion prompts might include the following:

What arguments do the assigned articles make about Jacobs, contemporaneous responses to her work, differences of opinion within the abolitionist movement, and sexuality and the Black female body as represented in Jacobs's writing?
What problems for reading and understanding *Incidents* are posed by Child's suppression of Jacobs's final chapter?

The online component of Literature by Women includes a variety of elements such as discussions about the week's reading, the article presentation assignment, and information about the midterm and final exams. Examples of discussion prompts based on *Incidents* might include the following:

Discuss the multilayered argument Jacobs creates against slavery.
In what ways does slavery damage both the enslaver and the enslaved?
How does slavery destroy Christian values?
What call to action is Jacobs making specifically for a Northern audience? What does she want Northerners to do (or not do, as the case may be)?
How is motherhood (and parenthood in general) presented in this text?

Students are encouraged to make at least some of their discussion posts in video format. I participate heavily in the weekly discussions. I comment on student posts throughout the week, and after I grade each discussion, I post a discussion overview in which I recap what the students have said. I mention each student by name, clarify any misconceptions revealed in the discussion, and add any additional information I think students will need to perform successfully on future assignments for the course. Sometimes I deliver this overview in text format, and sometimes I post in video format. Students consistently comment that my sustained participation in the discussions makes that aspect of the class meaningful for them. When I mention them by name and respond explicitly and publicly to comments they have made, they feel as if their voices are being heard and that I'm not merely assigning them a grade without truly engaging with their ideas.

Incidents in the Life of a Slave Girl is a vital component of Literature by Women. It provides the class an opportunity to discuss the intersection of race and gender and to explore a variety of themes that are present in other texts read throughout the semester. It also provides an opportunity for students to engage critically with ideas like those in *A Room of One's Own* that often form the nucleus of women's studies courses. Unlike Woolf's Judith Shakespeare "[scribbling] some pages up in an apple loft on the sly" (Woolf 241) and then burning them unpublished before killing herself (242), Jacobs belongs to "the far-reaching world of the creative black woman" (A. Walker, "In Search" 1300) that Walker celebrates; she is part of that literary history of women's writing that Woolf denies and a vital voice in the tradition of Black women's writing in America.

NOTES ON CONTRIBUTORS

Marilyn Judith Atlas is professor of English at Ohio University. She specializes in American literature, particularly experimental and ethnic literature and literature of place. She is the former director of the Women's Studies Program at Ohio University and studies minority and immigrant writers, how race and gender intersect in women's writings, the power of absence in literature, and how different art forms influence one another. In 2004 she received the Society for the Study of Midwestern Literature MidAmerica Award. She has written and lectured extensively on the Chicago Renaissance and Toni Morrison's fiction.

Molly Ball teaches in the Department of American Studies at the University of Minnesota, Twin Cities. She is interested in the intersections of race and gender in early American literature, and her work has appeared in journals such as *ESQ*, *Legacy*, and *Early American Literature*. She is currently revising a book-length project titled "Writing out of Time," which examines how nineteenth-century populations deemed to have no future within the nation both represent and dispute that temporal status through experiments with forward-moving narrative forms.

Alex W. Black is associate professor of English at Hobart and William Smith Colleges. He studies the print and performance cultures of nineteenth-century American and African American literature. His research, which has been supported by the Historical Society of Pennsylvania and the Library Company of Philadelphia, has been published in *American Literary History*, *American Quarterly*, and *J19*. With Brigitte Fielder and Johanna Ortner, he coedited Frances Ellen Watkins Harper's *Forest Leaves* for Just Teach One: Early African American Print.

Ashley Burge is assistant professor of African American literature at Augustana College, IL. A Toni Morrison scholar who specializes in the neo–slave narrative and Black women's subjectivity in African American literature, Burge emphasizes Black feminism and ecocriticism in her scholarship, centering both her teaching and research on race, gender, sexuality, and class. She has published essays in *The North Carolina Literary Review*, *African American Culture: An Encyclopedia of People, Traditions, and Customs*, *The Pennsylvania Communication Annual*, and the critical anthology *Through Mama's Eyes*. Her current book project uses Morrison's oeuvre to develop a theoretical paradigm that transmutes tragedy to healing and subjectivity.

Maura D'Amore is professor of English at Saint Michael's College. She is the author of *Suburban Plots: Men at Home in Nineteenth-Century American Print Culture* (2014).

Chereka Dickerson is associate professor of English at Metropolitan State University of Denver. Dickerson's research areas include African American literature and culture, contemporary US women's literature, hip-hop studies, and life writing studies.

Ingrid Diran is assistant professor of English at the University of Wisconsin, Madison.

Lynn Domina teaches English at Northern Michigan University. She is the author of several books, including most recently an annotated edition of Nella Larsen's novel

Passing. She has written on N. Scott Momaday, Leslie Marmon Silko, Denise Levertov, and many other literary figures.

Josh Doty is associate professor and chair of the Department of English Literature and Language at St. Mary's University. His essays on American literature, science, and medicine have been published in journals such as *Early American Literature*, *Nathaniel Hawthorne Review*, and *Leviathan: A Journal of Melville Studies*. His book, *The Perfecting of Nature: Reforming Bodies in Antebellum Literature*, was published in 2020.

Lorraine Dubuisson is professor of English at Middle Georgia State University. Her areas of interest include Victorian literature, early American literature, and the scholarship of teaching and learning. She is currently the president of the Georgia Philological Association.

Barbara Eckstein was professor of English and a faculty member in the Center for Global and Regional Environmental Research at the University of Iowa. Focusing on environmental humanities, she embraced teaching nonmajors in a required literature course as another opportunity to think and act across disciplines. She retired in 2019. Her most recent publications are in the journal *Urban History* and in the collection *City Scripts: Narratives of Postindustrial Urban Futures*.

Amina Gautier is associate professor of English at the University of Miami. She specializes in nineteenth-century American literature and African American literature. Gautier is the author of three short story collections, *At-Risk*, *Now We Will Be Happy*, and *The Loss of All Lost Things*. She is a recipient of the Pen/Malamud Award for Excellence in the Short Story. Her critical essays and reviews have appeared in *African American Review*, *The Cambridge Companion to the American Short Story*, *Critical Insights: Frederick Douglass*, *Daedalus*, *Journal of American History*, *Libraries and Culture*, *Nineteenth-Century Contexts*, and *Whitman Noir: Essays on Black America and the Good Grey Poet*.

Heidi M. Hanrahan is professor of English at Shepherd University, where she also serves as the assistant dean of interdisciplinary and integrative studies. She teaches literature, literary theory, composition, and gender and women's studies. Her research interests include nineteenth-century American and British literature, composition, and pedagogy. Her articles have appeared in journals including *The New England Quarterly*, *Poe Studies*, *MELUS*, *Studies in American Humor*, *Feminist Teacher*, and *Transformations* and in collections including *Narratives of Community* and *Liminality, Hybridity, and American Women's Writing*. She was named the 2018 West Virginia Professor of the Year by the Faculty Merit Foundation.

John Hay is associate professor of English at the University of Nevada, Las Vegas, and a specialist in nineteenth-century American literature. He is the author of *Postapocalyptic Fantasies in Antebellum American Literature* (2017) and the editor of *Apocalypse in American Literature and Culture* (2020). His articles have appeared in journals such as *Early American Literature*, *ESQ*, and *The New England Quarterly*. He is currently working on a book about the mid-nineteenth-century American novel.

Jennifer L. Hayes is associate professor of English at Tennessee State University. Her research interests include African American drama and Black feminist theory. Her manuscript *Teaching African American Literature through Experiential Praxis: African*

American Writers in Europe considers different approaches to teaching African American literature in study abroad courses.

Susanna Hoeness-Krupsaw is professor of English at the University of Southern Indiana and has over thirty years of experience teaching undergraduate and graduate students, including in courses on authors such as Amy Tan and Margaret Atwood. Her research interests include modern American and Canadian fiction, women's literature, and graphic narratives. She has recently published on John Lewis's *March*, Maxine Hong Kingston's *The Woman Warrior*, and the graphic novel adaptation of Octavia E. Butler's *Kindred*. She coedited *Performativity, Cultural Construction, and the Graphic Narrative*, a collection of essays that draws on performance studies.

Jolene Hubbs is professor of American studies at the University of Alabama. She is the author of *Class, Whiteness, and Southern Literature*.

Carrie Johnston is the director of research and scholarly initiatives at Southern Methodist University Libraries. She was formerly the digital humanities research designer at the Z. Smith Reynolds Library at Wake Forest University, where she also taught in the Department of English. Her teaching and research focus on women's literature and its intersections with technology and political discourse in the early twentieth century. Her work has appeared in *American Quarterly*, *Amerikastudien / American Studies*, *College Literature*, and *Studies in the Novel*.

Melissa J. Lingle-Martin has read and analyzed *Incidents* with students at the University of Baltimore, Florida Gulf Coast University, the American University in Bulgaria, and the North Carolina School of Science and Mathematics (NCSSM). Most recently, she has explored the text with high school students in American studies and women's, gender, and sexuality studies courses at NCSSM. Lingle-Martin specializes in nineteenth-century American literature and culture.

Corrie Catlett Merricks has taught composition, writing, and rhetorical theory for nineteen years at five institutions. She is currently teaching at a public high school, and her experience teaching writing at the college level informs her ability to prepare high school students to succeed academically.

Clark Moreland is lecturer of English and founding director of the Heimmermann Center for Engaged Teaching at the University of Texas of the Permian Basin, where he has taught since 2005. Among other honors, in 2014 he received the prestigious University of Texas Regents' Outstanding Teaching Award, and in 2023 he was elected as a fellow of the University of Texas Academy of Distinguished Teachers. He writes about the intersections of race, religion, disability, and literature in early American culture. He is the author of *Will: Parenting at the Crossroads of Disability and Joy*, a memoir about raising a son with Down syndrome, and is preparing a book about the rhetoric of Christian pacifism in the works of C. S. Lewis and Dr. Martin Luther King, Jr.

Kristin Moriah is assistant professor of English at Queen's University, Canada. She is the codirector of the Black Studies Summer Institute. Her academic work can be found in *American Quarterly*, *PAJ: A Journal of Performance and Art*, *Theatre Research in Canada / Recherches théâtrales au Canada*, and *Canadian Theatre Review*. Her research interests include sound studies and Black feminist performance. Her work has been supported by fellowships from the Social Sciences and Research Council of Canada, the Rare Book School at the University of Virginia, and the Harry Ransom Center.

Colleen O'Brien is professor of English, African American studies, and women and gender studies at the University of South Carolina, Upstate, and the author of *Race, Romance, and Rebellion: Literatures of the Americas in the Nineteenth Century* (2013), which includes a chapter on Harriet Jacobs.

Carl Ostrowski is professor of English at Middle Tennessee State University, where he has taught since 1999. He is the author of *Literature and Criminal Justice in Antebellum America* and *Books, Maps, and Politics: A Cultural History of the Library of Congress, 1782–1861,* which won the Eliza Atkins Gleason Book Award, presented every third year to recognize the best book written in English in the field of library history.

Amy Schmidt is assistant professor of English at Williams Baptist University. Her work has appeared in *Southern Literary Journal*, *Arkansas Review*, and *The Americanist*, and she is associate editor of *The Civil Rights Reader: American Literature from Jim Crow to Reconciliation*. Her current research examines the role rice plays in southern women's literature.

Kimberly Southwick-Thompson is assistant professor at Jacksonville State University. She is the founder and editor-in-chief of the literary arts journal *Gigantic Sequins*. She currently lives in Alabama.

Eric Sterling is distinguished teaching professor of English at Auburn University, Montgomery, where he has taught for the past thirty years. He directs the master's program in liberal arts. Sterling has published four books and ninety refereed articles, and he has won awards for teaching excellence.

Abbey Whigham is a graduate student at the University of Chicago's Crown Family School of Social Work, Policy, and Practice. She volunteers with a grassroots anti-violence organization in Chicago and is an advocate, speaker, and organizer within the transracial adoptee community.

Jericho Williams is assistant professor of English at University of Alaska, Fairbanks. His research focuses on American and African American literature. He is the editor of *Critical Insights: Ralph Waldo Emerson* (2023) and *Critical Insights: Frederick Douglass* (2020), and he has written about environmental education and injustice in American slave narratives in *Ecogothic in Nineteenth-Century American Literature*, childhood in the fiction of Nella Larsen in *South Atlantic Review*, and literary naturalism and the novels of Claude McKay in *The New Centennial Review* and *Studies in American Naturalism*. His forthcoming research projects examine the works of William Wells Brown, Zora Neale Hurston, and Alice Walker.

SURVEY RESPONDENTS

Marilyn Judith Atlas, *Ohio University*
Molly Ball, *University of Minnesota, Twin Cities*
Catherine Becker, *Northwest Nazarene University*
Alex W. Black, *Hobart and William Smith Colleges*
MaryJo Bona, *Stony Brook University*
R. J. Boutelle, *University of North Carolina, Greensboro*
Ashley Burge, *Augustana College, IL*
Maura D'Amore, *Saint Michael's College*
Alice Anita Deck, *University of North Carolina, Charlotte*
Gerry Del Guercio, *YMCA*
Chereka Dickerson, *Metropolitan State University of Denver*
Josh Doty, *St. Mary's University*
Lorraine Dubuisson, *Middle Georgia State University*
Barbara Eckstein, *University of Iowa*
James Finley, *Texas A&M University, San Antonio*
Theresa Gaul, *Texas Christian University*
Amina Gautier, *University of Miami*
Regina Hamilton, *University of Kentucky*
Heidi M. Hanrahan, *Shepherd University*
John Hay, *University of Nevada, Las Vegas*
Jennifer L. Hayes, *Tennessee State University*
Tamara D. Hill, *Edward Waters College*
Susanna Hoeness-Krupsaw, *University of Southern Indiana*
Jolene Hubbs, *University of Alabama*
Tammie Jenkins, *Independent Scholar*
Amanda Louise Johnson, *Rice University*
Carrie Johnston, *Wake Forest University*
Christina Katopodis, *Graduate Center, City University of New York*
Melissa J. Lingle-Martin, *Independent Scholar*
Corrie Catlett Merricks, *West Jessamine High School, Nicholasville, KY*
Clark Moreland, *University of Texas of the Permian Basin*
Kristin Moriah, *Queen's University, Canada*
Colleen O'Brien, *University of South Carolina, Upstate*
Carl Ostrowski, *Middle Tennessee State University*
Anita Patterson, *Boston University*
Elaine Roth, *Indiana University, South Bend*
Amy Schmidt, *Williams Baptist University*
Jelena Sesnic, *University of Zagreb*
Jane Smith, *Richland College*
Stephanie A. Smith, *University of Florida*
Kimberly Southwick-Thompson, *Jacksonville State University*
Eric Sterling, *Auburn University, Montgomery*
Ashley Tellis, *Independent Scholar*

Allison L. Tharp, *Virginia Commonwealth University*
Michael Torregrossa, *Bristol Community College*
Candace J. Waid, *University of California, Santa Barbara*
Pierre A. Walker, *Salem State University*
Lisa West, *Drake University*
Jericho Williams, *University of Alaska, Fairbanks*

WORKS CITED

Abdur-Rahman, Aliyyah. "'The Strangest Freaks of Despotism': Queer Sexuality in Antebellum African American Slave Narratives." *African American Review*, vol. 40, no. 2, 2006, pp. 223–37.

"About the Slavery, Race and Memory Project." *Slavery, Race and Memory Project*, Wake Forest University, srmp.wfu.edu/. Accessed 5 Sept. 2023.

Adichie, Chimamanda Ngozi. "The Danger of a Single Story." *TED*, 2009, www.ted.com/talks/chimamanda_ngozi_adichie_the_danger_of_a_single_story.

"Aiken's *Uncle Tom*." Uncle Tom's Cabin *and American Culture: A Multi-media Archive*, U of Virginia, 1998–2009, utc.iath.virginia.edu/onstage/scripts/aikenhp.html.

Alaimo, Stacy. "Bring Your Shovel!" *Resilience: A Journal of the Environmental Humanities*, vol. 1, no. 1, Jan. 2014, www.jstor.org/stable/10.5250/resilience.1.1.02.

Alexander, Michelle. *The New Jim Crow: Mass Incarceration in the Age of Colorblindness*. New Press, 2010.

Allen, Francine L. "Sacred and Undesirable: Examining the Theological Import of Hiding Places in Exodus and Harriet Jacobs's *Incidents in the Life of a Slave Girl*." *Priscilla Papers*, vol. 29, no. 3, summer 2015, pp. 21–27.

Andrews, William L. "An Introduction to the Slave Narrative." *Documenting the American South*, U of North Carolina, Chapel Hill, docsouth.unc.edu/neh/intro.html.

———. *To Tell a Free Story: The First Century of Afro-American Autobiography, 1760–1865*. U of Illinois P, 1988.

Applegate, Debby. "Roman à Clef." *American Literary History*, vol. 7, no. 1, 1995, pp. 151–60.

Aquinas, Thomas. "New English Translation of St. Thomas Aquinas's *Summa Theologiæ* (*Summa Theologica*)." By Alfred J. Freddoso, 11 July 2023, nd.edu/~afreddos/summa-translation/TOC.htm.

Åsberg, Cecilia. "Resilience Is Cyborg: Feminist Clues to a Post-Disciplinary Environmental Humanities of Critique and Creativity," *Resilience: A Journal of the Environmental Humanities*, vol. 1, no. 1, 2014, www.jstor.org/stable/10.5250/resilience.1.1.03.

Atwood, Margaret. *The Handmaid's Tale*. 1986. Anchor Books, 1998.

———. "Rape Fantasies." Gilbert and Gubar, vol. 2, pp. 1210–17.

Augustine. *Enchiridion: On Faith, Hope, and Love*. Translated by Albert C. Outler, Westminster Press, 1955.

Baker, Houston A. *Blues, Ideology, and Afro-American Literature: A Vernacular Theory*. U of Chicago P, 1984.

Baldwin, James. *Go Tell It on the Mountain*. 1952. Vintage Books, 2013.

Bean, John C. *Engaging Ideas: The Professor's Guide to Integrating Writing, Critical Thinking, and Active Learning in the Classroom*. 2nd ed., Josey-Bass, 2011.

Bechdel, Alison. *Fun Home.* 2006. Mariner Books, 2007.

Behn, Aphra. "Oroonoko; or, The Royal Slave." Gilbert and Gubar, vol. 1, pp. 186–231.

Bentley, Nancy. "White Slaves: The Mulatto Hero in Antebellum Fiction." *American Literature*, vol. 65, no. 3, 1993, pp. 501–22.

Berlant, Lauren. *The Queen of America Goes to Washington City: Essays on Sex and Citizenship.* Duke UP, 2002.

———. "The Queen of America Goes to Washington City: Harriet Jacobs, Frances Harper, Anita Hill." *American Literature*, vol. 65, no. 3, 1993, pp. 549–74.

Berry, Sarah L. "'[No] Doctor but My Master': Health Reform and Antislavery Rhetoric in Harriet Jacobs's *Incidents in the Life of a Slave Girl.*" *Journal of Medical Humanities*, vol. 35, no. 1, 2014, pp. 1–18.

"Bill of Sale for Augustine and Jane." William Crenshaw Papers, Wake Forest University, ZSR Library, Special Collections and Archives, wakespace.lib.wfu.edu/handle/10339/93524.

Bishop, Henry R. "Home, Sweet Home." Uncle Tom's Cabin *and American Culture: A Multi-media Archive*, U of Virginia, 1998–2009, utc.iath.virginia.edu/sentimnt/sweethomef.html.

Bitzer, Lloyd. "The Rhetorical Situation." *Philosophy and Rhetoric*, vol. 1, no. 1, 1968, pp. 1–14.

"Black Lives Matter Mural in Alabama Has Historical Significance." *Today*, 1 July 2020, www.today.com/video/black-lives-matter-mural-in-alabama-has-historical-significance-86676037732.

Blackwood, Sarah. *The Portrait's Subject: Inventing Inner Life in the Nineteenth-Century United States.* U of North Carolina P, 2019.

Blaisdell, Bob, editor. *From the Origins through the Civil War.* Dover Thrift Editions, 2014. Volume 1 of *The Dover Anthology of American Literature.*

Blassingame, John W. *The Slave Community: Plantation Life in the Antebellum South.* Oxford UP, 1972.

Bolton, Philathia, et al., editors. *Teaching with Tension: Race, Resistance, and Reality in the Classroom.* Northwestern UP, 2019.

Booth, Michael R. *English Melodrama.* Herbert Jenkins, 1965.

Boucicault, Dion. *The Octoroon.* Edited by Sarika Bose, Broadview Press, 2014.

Braiterman, Zachary. *(God) after Auschwitz: Tradition and Change in Post-Holocaust Jewish Thought.* Princeton UP, 1998.

Braxton, Joanne M. *Black Women Writing Autobiography: A Tradition within a Tradition.* Temple UP, 1989.

Brontë, Charlotte. *Jane Eyre.* 1847. Norton Critical Edition, 4th ed., W. W. Norton, 2016.

Brooks, Peter. *The Melodramatic Imagination: Balzac, Henry James, and the Mode of Excess.* Yale UP, 1976.

Brown, Claude. *Manchild in the Promised Land.* 1965. Simon and Schuster, 2012.

Brown, William Wells. "Narrative of William W. Brown, A Fugitive Slave." 1847. Clotel *and Other Writings*, by Brown, Library of America, 2014, pp. 1–54.

Brownson, Orestes A. *The Spirit-Rapper: An Autobiography*. Little, Brown, 1854.

Bryant, John. Introduction. *Typee: A Peep at Polynesian Life*, by Herman Melville, Penguin Books, 1996, pp. ix–xxx.

Burnham, Michelle. "Loopholes of Resistance: Harriet Jacobs' Slave Narrative and the Critique of Agency in Foucault." *Arizona Quarterly: A Journal of American Literature, Culture, and Theory*, vol. 49, no. 2, 1993, pp. 53–73. *Project Muse*, https://doi.org/10.1353/arq.1993.0028.

Butkowski, Chelsea P., et al. "Quantifying the Feminine Self(ie): Gender Display and Social Media Feedback in Young Women's Instagram Selfies." *New Media and Society*, vol. 22, no. 5, May 2020, pp. 817–37.

Carby, Hazel V. *Reconstructing Womanhood: The Emergence of the Afro-African Woman Novelist*. Oxford UP, 1988.

"Celia, a Slave Trial (1855)." *Famous Trials*, created by Douglas O. Linder, University of Missouri, Kansas City, School of Law, 1995–2023, famous-trials.com/celia.

Chaney, Michael A. "Keeping Pictures, Keeping House: Harriet and Louisa Jacobs, Fanny Fern, and the Unverifiable History of Seeing the Mulatta." *ESQ: A Journal of the American Renaissance*, vol. 59, no. 2, 2013, pp. 262–90.

Chappell, Bill, and Richard Gonzales. "Brandt Jean's Act of Grace toward His Brother's Killer Sparks a Debate over Forgiving." *NPR*, 3 Oct. 2019, npr.org/2019/10/03/766866875/brandt-jeans-act-of-grace-toward-his-brother-s-killer-sparks-a-debate-over-forgi.

Charles, Julia. *That Middle World: Race, Performance, and the Politics of Passing*. U of North Carolina P, 2020.

Cherniavsky, Eva. *That Pale Mother Rising: Sentimental Discourses and the Imitation of Motherhood in Nineteenth-Century America*. Indiana UP, 1995.

Child, Lydia Maria. *Authentic Anecdotes of American Slavery*. Charles Whipple, 1838. *Library of Congress*, www.loc.gov/item/92838862/. Accessed 5 Sept. 2023.

———. "Communications: Archy Moore." *The Liberator*, 18 Mar. 1837, p. 47.

———. "Introduction by the Editor." H. Jacobs, *Incidents* [Foster and Yarborough], pp. 6–7.

———. "Letter to Harriet Jacobs." H. Jacobs, *Incidents* [Foster and Yarborough], pp. 202–03.

———. "The Quadroons." *The Liberty Bell*, Anti-Slavery Fair, 1842, pp. 115–41. Uncle Tom's Cabin *and American Culture: A Multi-media Archive*, U of Virginia, 1998–2009, utc.iath.virginia.edu/abolitn/abfilmcat.html.

Clytus, Radiclani. "'Keep It before the People': The Pictorialization of American Abolitionism." *Early African American Print Culture*, edited by Lara Langer Cohen and Jordan Alexander Stein, U of Pennsylvania P, 2012, pp. 290–317.

Coates, Ta-Nehisi. *Between the World and Me*. Spiegel and Grau, 2015.

Cohen, Lara Langer. *The Fabrication of American Literature: Fraudulence and Antebellum Print Culture*. U of Pennsylvania P, 2012.

Cohen, Lara Langer, and Jordan Alexander Stein, editors. *Early African American Print Culture*. U of Pennsylvania P, 2014.

Collins, Patricia Hill. *Black Feminist Thought: Knowledge, Consciousness, and the Politics of Empowerment*. 2nd ed., Routledge, 2000.

"Colonial Slave Codes." *Maryland State Department of Education*, archives .marylandpublicschools.org/NR/rdonlyres/F68E8866-61CB-4AF5-8AE6 -F9275A9CEE9C/33050/23_ColonialSlaveCodes_July2012.pdf. Accessed 12 Oct. 2023.

Common. "A Song for Assata." *Like Water for Chocolate*, Geffen Records, 2000. *Spotify*.

Copeland, M. Shawn. "'Wading through Many Sorrows': Toward a Theology of Suffering in Womanist Perspective." *Moral Issues and Christian Responses*, edited by Patricia Beattie Jung and Loyle Shannon Jung, 8th ed., Fortress Press, 2013, pp. 37–45.

Cott, Nancy. *No Small Courage: A History of Women in the United States*. Oxford UP, 2000.

Covey, Herbert C. *African American Slave Medicine: Herbal and Non-herbal Treatments*. Lexington Books, 2007.

Crafts, Hannah. *The Bondwoman's Narrative*. Edited by Henry Louis Gates, Jr., Grand Central, 2014.

Crowe, Eyre. *With Thackery in America*. Charles Scribner's Sons, 1893.

Cutter, Martha J. "Dismantling 'The Master's House': Critical Literacy in Harriet Jacobs' *Incidents in the Life of a Slave Girl*." *Callaloo*, vol. 19, no. 1, 1996, pp. 209–25, https://doi.org/10.1353/cal.1996.0010.

———. *The Illustrated Slave: Empathy, Graphic Narrative, and the Visual Culture of the Transatlantic Abolition Movement, 1800–1852*. U of Georgia P, 2017.

Daly, Mary. *Beyond God the Father: Toward a Philosophy of Women's Liberation*. Houghton Mifflin, 1974.

Daniels-Rauterkus, Melissa. "Civil Resistance and Procreative Agency in Harriet Jacobs's *Incidents in the Life of a Slave Girl*." *Women's Studies*, vol. 48, no. 5, 2019, pp. 498–509, https://doi.org/10.1080/00497878.2019.1628758.

Darby, Flower, and James M. Lang. *Small Teaching Online: Applying Learning Science in Online Classes*. Wiley, 2019.

Davis, Angela. "Reflections on the Black Woman's Role in the Community of Slaves." *The Black Scholar*, vol. 3, no. 4, 1971, pp. 2–15.

———. *Women, Race, and Class*. Vintage Books, 1981.

Davis, Charles T., and Henry Louis Gates, Jr. *The Slave's Narrative*. Oxford UP, 1985.

Deck, Alice A. "Whose Book Is This? Authorial versus Editorial Control of Harriet Brent Jacobs' *Incidents in the Life of a Slave Girl: Written by Herself*." *Women's Studies International Forum*, vol. 10, no. 1, 1987, pp. 33–40.

Denial, Cate, et al. "After the Great Pivot Should Come the Great Pause." *The Chronicle of Higher Education*, 25 Feb. 2022, www.chronicle.com/article/after-the -great-pivot-should-come-the-great-pause.

Diamond, Lydia R. *Harriet Jacobs: A Play*. Northwestern UP, 2011.

Dickinson, Emily. "Tell all the Truth but tell it slant—." *The Complete Poems of Emily Dickinson*, edited by Thomas H. Johnson, Little, Brown, 1961, pp. 506–07.

Diller, Christopher G. "The Prefaces to *Uncle Tom's Cabin*." *New England Quarterly*, vol. 77, no. 4, 2004, pp. 619–45.

Diran, Ingrid. "Scenes of Speculation: Harriet Jacobs and the Biopolitics of Human Capital." *American Quarterly*, vol. 71, no. 3, 2019, pp. 697–718.

Doherty, Thomas. "Harriet Jacobs' Narrative Strategies: *Incidents in the Life of a Slave Girl*." *The Southern Literary Journal*, vol. 19, no. 1, 1986, pp. 79–91.

Douglass, Frederick. *My Bondage and My Freedom. Documenting the American South*, U of North Carolina, Chapel Hill, 2000, docsouth.unc.edu/neh/douglass55/douglass55.html.

———. *Narrative of the Life of Frederick Douglass, an American Slave, Written by Himself. The Classic Slave Narratives*, edited by Henry Louis Gates, Jr., Signet, 2002, pp. 323–436.

———. "We Welcome the Fifteenth Amendment." *The Speeches of Frederick Douglass: A Critical Edition*, edited by John R. McKivigan et al., Yale UP, 2018, pp. 267–77.

Downs, Doug. "Rhetoric: Making Sense of Human Interaction and Meaning-Making." *Writing about Writing*, edited by Elizabeth Wardle and Downs, 4th ed., Bedford / St. Martin's, 2020, pp. 369–95.

Driscoll, Ellen. *The Loophole of Retreat.* 16 June 2006–7 Jan. 2007, New York Historical Society, New York City.

Du Bois, W. E. B. *The Souls of Black Folk*. 1903. Penguin Classics, 2018.

duCille, Ann. *The Coupling Convention: Sex, Text, and Tradition in Black Women's Fiction*. Oxford UP, 1993.

Edwards, Mary K. Bercaw. "Questioning *Typee*." *Leviathan*, vol. 11, no. 2, 2009, pp. 24–42.

Eggers, Dave. *Zeitoun*. McSweeney's Books, 2009.

Ellison, Ralph Waldo. *Invisible Man*. 1947. Vintage Books, 1995.

Emerson, Donald E. *Richard Hildreth*. Johns Hopkins Press, 1946.

Ernest, John, editor. *The Oxford Handbook of the African American Slave Narrative*. Oxford UP, 2014.

———. "Qualified Knowledge: Douglass and Harriet Jacobs." *Approaches to Teaching* Narrative of the Life of Frederick Douglass, edited by James C. Hall, Modern Language Association of America, 2000, pp. 110–16.

Fagan, Benjamin. "Harriet Jacobs and the Lessons of Rogue Reading." *Legacy: A Journal of American Women Writers*, vol. 33, no. 1, 2016, pp. 19–21.

Faulkner, William. *As I Lay Dying*. 1930. Norton Critical Edition, W. W. Norton, 2009.

Fern, Fanny. Ruth Hall *and Other Writings*. Edited by Joyce W. Warren, Rutgers UP, 1986.

Fetterley, Judith. *The Resisting Reader: A Feminist Approach to American Fiction*. Indiana UP, 1978.

Flaherty, Colleen. "Minds on Fire." *Inside Higher Education*, 27 Aug. 2014, www.insidehighered.com/news/2014/08/27/book-advocates-reacting-past-pedagogy.

Fleischner, Jennifer. "A New Voice for Freedom." *Incidents in the Life of a Slave Girl*, by Harriet Jacobs, edited by Fleischner, Bedford / St. Martin's, 2010, pp. 1–21.

Floyd-Thomas, Stacey, and Juan Floyd-Thomas. "Patchwork Redemption: Suffering and Joy in Racial Perspective." *The Table Podcast*, hosted by Evan Rosa, Biola University Center for Christian Thought, 22 Apr. 2019, cct.biola.edu/patchwork-redemption-ethics-race.

Forbes, Erin E. "Do Black Ghosts Matter? Harriet Jacobs' Spiritualism." *ESQ: A Journal of the American Renaissance*, vol. 62, no. 3, 2016, pp. 443–79.

Foreman, P. Gabrielle. *Activist Sentiments: Reading Black Women in the Nineteenth Century*. U of Illinois P, 2009.

———. Introduction. *Our Nig; or, Sketches from the Life of a Free Black*, by Harriet E. Wilson, Penguin Books, 2009, pp. xxv–lv.

———. "Manifest in Signs: The Politics of Sex and Representation in *Incidents in the Life of a Slave Girl*." Garfield and Zafar, pp. 76–99.

———. "The Politics of Sex and Representation in Harriet Jacobs's *Incidents in the Life of a Slave Girl*." H. Jacobs, *Incidents* [Foster and Yarborough], pp. 318–41.

———. "Who's Your Mama? 'White' Mulatta Genealogies, Early Photography, and Anti-Passing Narratives of Slavery and Freedom." *American Literary History*, vol. 14, no. 3, 2002, pp. 505–39.

Foreman, P. Gabrielle, et al. *The Colored Conventions Movement: Black Organizing in the Nineteenth Century*. U of North Carolina P, 2021.

Foreman, P. Gabrielle, et al. "Writing about Slavery / Teaching about Slavery: This Might Help." *NAACP Culpeper*, 26 Mar. 2021, naacpculpeper.org/resources/writing-about-slavery-this-might-help/.

Foster, Frances Smith. "Resisting *Incidents*." H. Jacobs, *Incidents* [Foster and Yarborough], pp. 255–74.

———. *Written by Herself: Literary Production by African American Women, 1746–1892*. Indiana UP, 1993.

Franklin, John Hope. *From Slavery to Freedom*. 9th ed., McGraw Hill, 2011.

Gallagher, Catherine. "The Rise of Fictionality." *The Novel: History, Geography, and Culture*, edited by Franco Moretti, vol. 1, Princeton UP, 2006, pp. 336–63.

Gandhi, Mohandas. "The Gita and Satyagraha." *Selected Writings*, edited by Ronald Duncan, Dover Publications, 2005, pp. 45–72.

Garfield, Deborah M., and Rafia Zafar, editors. *Harriet Jacobs and* Incidents in the Life of a Slave Girl*: New Critical Essays*. Cambridge UP, 1996.

Gates, Henry Louis, Jr., editor. *The Classic Slave Narratives*. Signet, 2012.

———, editor. *Collected Black Women's Narratives*. Oxford UP, 1988. The Schomburg Library of Nineteenth-Century Black Women Writers.

———. Introduction. *The Bondwoman's Narrative*, by Hannah Crafts, edited by Gates, Grand Central, 2014, pp. xli–cxii.

———. *"Race," Writing, and Difference*. U of Chicago P, 1986.

———. *The Signifying Monkey: A Theory of African-American Literary Criticism*. Oxford UP, 2007.

Genovese, Eugene. *Roll Jordan Roll: The World the Slaves Made*. Vintage Books, 1976.

Gilbert, Sandra M., and Susan Gubar, editors. *The Norton Anthology of Literature by Women: The Traditions in English*. W. W. Norton, 2007. 2 vols.

Gilkey, Langdon. *Message and Existence*. Seabury Press, 1979.

Gilman, Sander L. "Black Bodies, White Bodies: Toward an Iconography of Female Sexuality in Late Nineteenth-Century Art, Medicine, and Literature." *"Race," Writing, and Difference*, edited by Henry Louis Gates, Jr., U of Chicago P, 1985, pp. 223–61.

Glenn, Cheryl. "Remapping Rhetorical Territory." *Rhetoric Review*, vol. 13, no. 2, 1995, pp. 287–303. *JSTOR*, www.jstor.org/stable/465834.

Glymph, Thavolia. *Out of the House of Bondage: The Transformation of the Plantation Household*. Cambridge UP, 2008.

Goldsby, Jacqueline. "'I Disguised My Hand': Writing Versions of the Truth in Harriet Jacobs's *Incidents in the Life of a Slave Girl* and John Jacobs's 'A True Tale of Slavery.'" Garfield and Zafar, pp. 11–43.

Gomaa, Sally. "Writing to 'Virtuous' and 'Gentle' Readers: The Problem of Pain in Harriet Jacobs's *Incidents* and Harriet Wilson's *Sketches*." *African American Review*, vol. 43, nos. 2–3, 2009, pp. 371–81.

Gordon-Reed, Annette. *The Hemingses of Monticello: An American Family*. W. W. Norton, 2009.

Grasso, Linda. *The Artistry of Anger: Black and White Women's Literature in America, 1820–1860*. U of North Carolina P, 2002.

Greene, Shelleen M. "Bina48: Gender, Race, and Queer Artificial Life." *Ada: A Journal of Gender, New Media, and Technology*, no. 9, 2016. *Scholars' Bank*, U of Oregon, May 2016, scholarsbank.uoregon.edu/xmlui/handle/1794/26811.

Grendler, Marcella, et al. "Guide to Religious Content in Slave Narratives." *Documenting the American South*, University Library, U of North Carolina, Chapel Hill, 2019, docsouth.unc.edu/neh/religiouscontent.html.

Guy-Sheftall, Beverly. "The Body Politic: Black Female Sexuality and the Nineteenth-Century Euro-American Imagination." *Skin Deep, Spirit Strong: The Black Female Body*, edited by Kimberly Wallace-Sanders, U of Michigan P, 2002, pp. 13–35.

Hall, James C., editor. *Approaches to Teaching* Narrative of the Life of Frederick Douglass. Modern Language Association of America, 2000.

Hall, Judith, and Mark Leary. "The U.S. Has an Empathy Deficit." *Scientific American*, 17 Sept. 2020, www.scientificamerican.com/article/the-us-has-an-empathy-deficit/.

Hamington, Maurice. *Embodied Care: Jane Addams, Maurice Merleau-Ponty, and Feminist Ethics*. U of Illinois P, 2004.

Hannah-Jones, Nikole. "The Idea of America." *The 1619 Project: New York Times Magazine*, 18 Aug. 2019, pp. 14–26.

Hanrahan, Heidi M. "Harriet Jacobs's *Incidents in the Life of a Slave Girl*: A Retelling of Lydia Maria Child's 'The Quadroons.'" *New England Quarterly*, vol. 78, no. 4, 2005, pp. 599–616.

Hanrahan, Heidi M., et al. "Gender, Confinement, and Freedom: Team Teaching Introduction to Women's Studies." *Feminist Teacher*, vol. 26, nos. 2–3, 2016, pp. 94–114.

Harper, Frances E. W. *Iola Leroy; or, Shadows Uplifted*. Penguin Books, 2010.

"Harriet Jacobs Wanted Poster." *WikiTree*, www.wikitree.com/photo/jpg/Jacobs-3831-1. Accessed 6 Sept. 2023.

Harris, Trudier. "'Does Northern Travel Relieve Slavery? 'Vacations' in Dolen Perkins-Valdez's *Wench*.'" *South Atlantic Review*, vol. 78, nos. 3–4, 2013, pp. 90–109. *JSTOR*, www.jstor.org/stable/43739217.

Hartman, Saidiya. *Scenes of Subjection: Terror, Slavery, and Self-Making in Nineteenth-Century America*. Oxford UP, 1997.

Haven, John. *Slavery as It Exists in America. Slavery as It Exists in England*. *Library of Congress*, www.loc.gov/pictures/item/2008661524/. Accessed 5 Sept. 2023.

Hawthorne, Nathaniel. "The Minister's Black Veil." *Twice-Told Tales*, by Hawthorne, edited by John B. Russell, American Stationers, 1837, pp. 53–77.

Haywood, Eliza. "Fantomina; or, Love in a Maze." Gilbert and Gubar, vol. 1, pp. 276–95.

Heilbrun, Carolyn C. *Hamlet's Mother and Other Women*. Columbia UP, 1990.

Hentz, Caroline Lee. *The Planter's Northern Bride*. T. B. Peterson and Brothers, 1854. *HathiTrust Digital Library*, hdl.handle.net/2027/osu.32435008298911.

Higginbotham, A. L. *Shades of Freedom: Racial Politics and Presumptions of the American Legal Process*. Oxford UP, 1996.

Hildreth, Richard. *The Slave; or, Memoirs of Archy Moore*. John H. Eastburn, 1836.

———. *The White Slave; or, Memoirs of a Fugitive*. Tappan and Whittemore, 1852.

Hill, Heather N. "Tutoring for Transfer: The Benefits of Teaching Writing Center Tutors about Transfer Theory." *The Writing Center Journal*, vol. 35, no. 3, 2016, pp. 77–101.

Hill, Lena. *Visualizing Blackness and the Creation of the African American Literary Tradition*. Cambridge UP, 2014.

Himes, Kenneth R. "Social Sin and the Role of the Individual." *The Annual Society of Christian Ethics*, vol. 6, 1986, pp. 183–218.

Hinds, Lennox S. Foreword. *Assata: An Autobiography*, by Assata Shakur, Lawrence Hill Books, 2001, pp. xi–xviii.

"History: How We Got Here." *Wake Forest University*, about.wfu.edu/history/. Accessed 24 Oct. 2020.

Hoeveler, Diane Long, and Tamar Heller, editors. *Approaches to Teaching Gothic Fiction: The British and American Traditions*. Modern Language Association of America, 2003.

The Holy Bible: New International Version. Zondervan, 1984.

hooks, bell. *Ain't I a Woman: Black Women and Feminism*. South End Press, 1981.

Hopkins, Patricia D. "Seduction or Rape: Deconstructing the Black Female Body in Harriet Jacobs' *Incidents in the Life of a Slave Girl*." *Making Connections: Interdisciplinary Approaches to Cultural Diversity*, vol. 13, no. 1, 2011, pp. 4–20.

Hurston, Zora Neale. *Their Eyes Were Watching God*. 1937. Harper Perennial, 2006.

"I Be So Glad . . . When the Sun Goes Down." *YouTube*, uploaded by ALilyAmongst-Thorns, 2 June 2011, www.youtube.com/watch?v=C-zlSq4mWiE&t=45s.

"Illustrations for the 'Splendid Edition.'" Uncle Tom's Cabin *and American Culture: A Multi-media Archive*, U of Virginia, 1998–2009, utc.iath.virginia.edu/uncletom/illustra/53illf.html.

Jacobs, Harriet. *Incidents in the Life of a Slave Girl*. Edited by Frances Smith Foster and Richard Yarborough, Norton Critical Edition, 2nd ed., W. W. Norton, 2019.

———. *Incidents in the Life of a Slave Girl*. Edited by Henry Louis Gates, Jr., Oxford UP, 1990. The Schomburg Library of Nineteenth-Century Black Women Writers.

———. *Incidents in the Life of a Slave Girl*. Edited by Koritha Mitchell, Broadview Press, 2023.

———. *Incidents in the Life of a Slave Girl, Written by Herself*. Edited by Jennifer Fleischner, 2nd ed., Bedford / St. Martins, 2019.

Jacobs, John S. "Antislavery Office and Reading Room." *The North Star*, 23 Mar. 1849.

Johnson, Charles. *Middle Passage*. Scribner, 1990.

Jones, Anne Goodwyn, and Susan V. Donaldson, editors. *Haunted Bodies: Gender and Southern Texts*. U of Virginia P, 1997.

Jones, Edward P. *The Known World*. Amistad, 2004.

Jones, Tayari. *An American Marriage*. Algonquin Books, 2018.

Jones-Rogers, Stephanie E. *They Were Her Property: White Women as Slave Owners in the American South*. Yale UP, 2019.

Julian of Norwich. "A Book of Showings to the Anchoress Julian of Norwich." Gilbert and Gubar, vol. 1, pp. 38–45.

Kanzler, Katja. "'To Tell the Kitchen Version': Architectural Figurations of Race and Gender in Harriet Jacobs's *Incidents in the Life of the Slave Girl*." H. Jacobs, *Incidents* [Foster and Yarborough], pp. 341–50.

Kaplan, Carla. "Narrative Contracts and Emancipatory Readers: *Incidents in the Life of a Slave Girl*." *The Yale Journal of Criticism*, vol. 6, no. 1, 1993, pp. 93–119.

"Kara Walker: The Emancipation Approximation." *Buffalo AKG Art Museum*, 2023, www.albrightknox.org/art/exhibitions/kara-walker-emancipation-approximation.

Keckley, Elizabeth. *Behind the Scenes: Forty Years a Slave and Four Years in the White House*. Oxford UP, 1988.

Keen, Suzanne. "A Theory of Narrative Empathy." *Narrative*, vol. 14, no. 3, 2006, pp. 207–36. *JSTOR*, jstor.org/stable/20107388.

Kempe, Margery. *The Book of Margery Kempe*. Gilbert and Gubar, vol. 1, pp. 46–59.

King, Martin Luther, Jr. "I Have a Dream." *The Essential Martin Luther King, Jr.*, Beacon Press, 2013.

———. *Strength to Love*. Fortress Press, 2010.

Koenigs, Thomas. *Founded in Fiction: The Uses of Fiction in the Early United States*. Princeton UP, 2021.

Krawczynski, Keith. "American Slavery Part 1." *Kaltura*, www.kaltura.com/tiny/6ihd3. Accessed 17 Oct. 2023.

———. "American Slavery Part 2." *Kaltura*, www.kaltura.com/tiny/uw7pt. Accessed 17 Oct. 2023.

———. "American Slavery Part 3." *Kaltura*, www.kaltura.com/tiny/un38g. Accessed 17 Oct. 2023.

———. "American Slavery Part 4." *Kaltura*, www.kaltura.com/tiny/q3ccv. Accessed 17 Oct. 2023.

———. "American Slavery Part 5." *Kaltura*, www.kaltura.com/tiny/18qzu. Accessed 17 Oct. 2023.

———. "American Slavery Part 6." *Kaltura*, www.kaltura.com/tiny/dumdx. Accessed 17 Oct. 2023.

———. "American Slavery Part 7." *Kaltura*, www.kaltura.com/tiny/r9nmv. Accessed 17 Oct. 2023.

Lapsansky, Phillip. "Graphic Discord: Abolitionist and Antiabolitionist Images." *The Abolitionist Sisterhood: Women's Political Culture in Antebellum America*, edited by Jean Fagan Yellin and John C. Van Horne, Cornell UP, 1994, pp. 201–30.

Lauter, Paul, editor. *The Heath Anthology of American Literature*. Vol. B, 7th ed., Cengage, 2014.

Laymon, Kiese. "Da Art of Storytellin' (A Prequel)." *Oxford American*, no. 91, winter 2015, oxfordamerican.org/magazine/issue-91-winter-2015/da-art-of-storytellin-a-prequel.

LeBlanc, Lauren. "How to Write the Book No One Wants You to Write." *The Atlantic*, 25 Sept. 2019, www.theatlantic.com/entertainment/archive/2019/09/sarah-m-brooms-yellow-house-historical-feat/596464/.

Lee, Julia Sun-Joo. *The American Slave Narrative and the Victorian Novel*. Oxford UP, 2010.

"Legacies: Contemporary Artists Reflect on Slavery No. 3 of 3." *YouTube*, uploaded by New-York Historical Society, 30 May 2008, www.youtube.com/watch?v=5z5JFsAyFDM.

Levander, Caroline. "'Following the Condition of the Mother': Subversions of Domesticity in Harriet Jacobs' *Incidents in the Life of a Slave Girl*." *Southern Mothers: Fact and Fiction in Southern Women's Writing*, edited by Nagueyalti Warren and Sally Wolf, Louisiana State UP, 1999, pp. 28–38.

Levine, Robert S. "The Early African American Novel." *The Cambridge History of the American Novel*, edited by Leonard Cassuto, Cambridge UP, 2011, pp. 267–82.

Levine, Robert S., and Sandra M. Gustafson, editors. *The Norton Anthology of American Literature*. Vol. B, 10th ed., W. W. Norton, 2022.

Levy, Andrew. "Dialect and Convention: Harriet A. Jacobs's *Incidents in the Life of a Slave Girl*." *Nineteenth-Century Literature*, vol. 45, no. 2, 1990, pp. 206–19.

Lewallen, Ann-Elise. "Resilience Embodied." *Resilience: A Journal of the Environmental Humanities*, vol. 1, no. 1, 2014. *JSTOR*, www.jstor.org/stable/10.5250/resilience.1.1.11.

Lewis, C. S. *The Problem of Pain*. HarperCollins Publishers, 1996.

Li, Stephanie. "Motherhood as Resistance in Harriet Jacobs's *Incidents in the Life of a Slave Girl*." *Legacy: A Journal of American Women Writers*, vol. 23, no. 1, 2006, pp. 14–29.

Locke, John. *Second Treatise on Government.* Barnes and Noble, 2004.

Long, Beverly Whitaker, and Mary Frances Hopkins. *Performing Literature: An Introduction to Oral Interpretation.* Prentice-Hall, 1982.

Lyons, Mary E. *Letters from a Slave Girl: The Story of Harriet Jacobs.* Atheneum, 2007.

Lyrics to "Old Folks at Home." Uncle Tom's Cabin *and American Culture: A Multimedia Archive,* U of Virginia, 1998–2009, utc.iath.virginia.edu/minstrel/oldfolksf.html.

MacKethan, Lucinda H. *Daughters of Time: Creating Woman's Voice in Southern Story.* U of Georgia P, 1990.

Mackin, Will. "Crossing the River No Name." *The New Yorker,* 29 May 2017, www.newyorker.com/magazine/2017/06/05/crossing-the-river-no-name.

Magee, Michael. "Emerson's Emancipation Proclamations." *Raritan: A Quarterly Review,* vol. 20, no. 4, 2001, pp. 96–116. *EBSCO,* research.ebsco.com/linkprocessor/plink?id=fb502714-0a90-33f0-8b59-cb8dbcf221dc.

Mansouri, Leila. "Slave Narratives, Black Disenfranchisement, and the Electoral Limits of Black Freedom," *J19,* vol. 8, no. 2, 2020, pp. 355–62.

Martin, Joan. "By Perseverance and Unwearied Industry." *Cut Loose Your Stammering Tongue: Black Theology in the Slave Narratives,* edited by Dwight N. Hopkins and George C. L. Cummings, 2nd ed., Westminster John Knox Press, 2003, pp. 107–30.

McEntee, Grace. "The Ethos of Motherhood and Harriet Jacobs' Vision of Racial Equality in *Incidents in the Life of a Slave Girl.*" *The Literary Mother: Essays on Representations of Maternity and Child Care,* edited by Susan C. Staub, McFarland, 2007, pp. 200–23.

McKittrick, Katherine. *Demonic Grounds: Black Women and the Cartographies of Struggle.* U of Minnesota P, 2006.

Medeiros, Peggi. *Harriet Jacobs in New Bedford.* History Press Library Editions, 2020.

Me Facing Life: Cyntoia's Story. Directed by Daniel H. Birman, Daniel H. Birman Productions / ITVS, 2011.

"Melodramatic, *Adj.*" *Oxford English Dictionary,* Oxford UP, 2023, https://doi.org/10.1093/OED/8226366234.

Melville, Herman. *Typee: A Peep at Polynesian Life.* Penguin Books, 1996.

Merrill, Lisa, and Theresa Saxon. *The Octoroon Archive.* Hofstra University, digitalexhibits.hofstra.edu/s/octoroon/page/home.

Miller, Arthur. *The Crucible.* 1953. Penguin Books, 2016.

"Montgomery Public Schools." *US News and World Report,* 2023, www.usnews.com/education/k12/alabama/districts/montgomery-county-102843.

Moody, Joycelyn K., editor. *A History of African American Autobiography.* Cambridge UP, 2021.

Morgan, Jennifer L. *Laboring Women: Reproduction and Gender in New World Slavery.* U of Pennsylvania P, 2004.

Morrison, Toni. *Beloved.* 1987. Vintage Books, 2004.

———. *Jazz.* 1992. Vintage Books, 2004.

———. "On *Beloved*." *The Source of Self Regard: Selected Speeches, Essays, and Meditations*, by Morrison, Random House, 2019, pp. 416–22.

———. *Sula*. 1973. Vintage Books, 2004.

———. *Tar Baby*. 1981. Vintage Books, 2004.

Mulford, Carla, editor. *Teaching the Literatures of Early America*. Modern Language Association of America, 2000.

Murder to Mercy: The Cyntoia Brown Story. Directed by Daniel Birman, Netflix, 2020.

Nadeau, Bruno, and Jason Lewis. "Still Standing." *Electronic Literature Collection*, Electronic Literature Organization, 2022, collection.eliterature.org/2/works/nadeau_stillstanding.html.

The Negro in America. *Digital History*, 2021, www.digitalhistory.uh.edu/exhibits/ahd/slavery19b.html.

The Negro in His Own Country. *Digital History*, 2021, www.digitalhistory.uh.edu/exhibits/ahd/slavery18.html.

Nichols, Mary Gove. *Mary Lyndon; or, Revelations of a Life: An Autobiography*. Stringer and Townsend, 1855.

Norcom, James. Advertisement. *American Beacon*, 4 July 1835. *Harriet Jacobs: Selected Writings and Documents*, Yale University, 2023, glc.yale.edu/sites/default/files/files/Ad%20for%20the%20capture%20of%20HJ.pdf.

O'Brien, Susie. "Creative Destruction and a Sliver of Hope." *Resilience: A Journal of the Environmental Humanities*, vol. 1, no. 1, 2014. *JSTOR*, www.jstor.org/stable/10.5250/resilience.1.1.13.

O'Conner, Michael, editor. *Digital American Literature Anthology*. Millikin University, 2019, digitalamlit.millikinenglish.org.

Oh Carry Me Back to Ole Virginny. *Library of Congress*, www.loc.gov/item/93510468/. Accessed 5 Sept. 2023.

Oh, Hail Columbia! Happy Land! The Cradle Land of Liberty! . . . . *The New York Public Library Digital Collections*, 2023, digitalcollections.nypl.org/items/510d47da-753a-a3d9-e040-e00a18064a99.

O'Malley, Maria. "Imagining Massachusetts: Political Geography and Sexual Control in Harriet Jacobs's 'Incidents in the Life of a Slave Girl.'" *Journal of Narrative Theory*, vol. 46, no. 1, 2016, pp. 39–69.

Otter, Samuel. "Philadelphia Experiments." *American Literary History*, vol. 16, no. 1, 2004, pp. 103–16.

Ozick, Cynthia. *The Shawl*. 1980. Vintage Books, 1983.

Painter, Nell Irvin. *Southern History across the Color Line*. U of North Carolina P, 2002.

Parini, Jay. Introduction. *The Norton Book of American Autobiography*, edited by Parini, W. W. Norton, 1999, pp. 11–22.

Pateman, Carole, and Charles Mills. *Contract and Domination*. Polity, 2007.

Patterson, Orlando. *Slavery and Social Death: A Comparative Study*. Harvard UP, 1982.

Perkins-Valdez, Dolen. *Wench*. Amistad, 2011.

Petersen, Emily, et al. "Vital Signs: Pregnancy-Related Deaths, United States, 2011–2015, and Strategies for Prevention, 13 States, 2013–2017." *Morbidity and Mortality Weekly Report*, vol. 68, no. 18, 2019, pp. 423–29.

Peterson, Carla. *Doers of the Word: African American Women Speakers and Writers in the North, 1830–1880*. Rutgers UP, 1998.

"*The Piano Lesson* (1995)." *YouTube*, uploaded by Dreams of 1619, 8 July 2022, youtube.com/watch?v=R2iWteE2GQc&t=4647s.

Porter, James E. "Intertextuality and the Discourse Community." *Writing about Writing*, edited by Elizabeth Wardle and Doug Downs, 4th ed., Bedford / St. Martin's, 2020, pp. 416–31.

Pratt, Annis. *Archetypal Patterns in Women's Fiction*. Indiana UP, 1981.

Pratt, Casey. "'These Things Took the Shape of Mystery': *Incidents in the Life of a Slave Girl* as American Romance." *African American Review*, vol. 47, no. 1, 2014, pp. 69–81.

Pratt, Lloyd. *The Strangers Book: The Human of African American Literature*. U of Pennsylvania P, 2015.

Radcliffe, Ann. *A Sicilian Romance*. Edited by Alison Milbank, Oxford UP, 2008.

Raimon, Eve Allegra. *The "Tragic Mulatta" Revisited: Race and Nationalism in Nineteenth-Century Antislavery Fiction*. Rutgers UP, 2004.

Rankine, Claudia. *Citizen: An American Lyric*. Graywolf Press, 2014.

Rauschenbusch, Walter. *A Theology for the Social Gospel*. Macmillan, 1917.

Reed, Austin. *The Life and Adventures of a Haunted Convict*. Edited by Caleb Smith, Modern Library, 2016.

Remnick, David. "Blood at the Root." *The New Yorker*, 28 Sept. 2015, newyorker.com/magazine/2015/09/28/blood-at-the-root.

"Review 1—No Title." *The Liberator*, 12 June 1846.

Richardson, Lisa, et al. "Patterns and Trends in Age-Specific Black-White Differences in Breast Cancer Incidence and Mortality—United States, 1999–2014." *Morbidity and Mortality Weekly Report*, vol. 65, no. 40, 2016, pp. 1093–98.

Rifkin, Mark. "'A Home Made Sacred by Protecting Laws': Black Activist Homemaking and Geographies of Citizenship in *Incidents in the Life of a Slave Girl*." *Differences*, vol. 18, no. 2, 2007, pp. 72–102.

Robbins, Hollis, and Henry Louis Gates, Jr., editors. *The Portable Nineteenth-Century African American Women Writers*. Penguin Books, 2017.

Robertson, Robert John, and Shannon Riggs. "Collaborative Assignments and Projects." *High-Impact Practices in Online Education: Research and Best Practices*, edited by Kathryn E. Linder and Chrysanthemum Mattison Hayes, Routledge, 2018, pp. 71–84.

Robinson, Cedric J. *Black Marxism: Making of the Black Radical Tradition*. U of North Carolina P, 2020.

Rohrbach, Augusta. *Truth Stranger than Fiction: Race, Realism and the U.S. Literary Marketplace*. Palgrave Macmillan, 2002.

Rojas, Maythee. "Stepping Up and Out: Strategies for Promoting Feminist Activism within Community Service-Learning." *Feminist Teacher*, vol. 24, nos. 1–2, 2015, pp. 83–98.

Rosenberg, Charles. *The Cholera Years: The United States in 1832, 1849, and 1866*. U of Chicago P, 1962.

Rossetti, Christina. "Goblin Market." *The Complete Poems*, by Rossetti, Penguin Books, 2001, pp. 5–19.

Royster, Jacqueline Jones, and Gesa E. Kirsch. *Feminist Rhetorical Practices: New Horizons for Rhetoric, Composition, and Literacy Studies*. Southern Illinois UP, 2012.

Rushdy, Ashraf. *Neo–Slave Narratives: Studies in the Social Logic of Literary Form*. Oxford UP, 1999.

Sanchez-Eppler, Karen. *Touching Liberty: Abolition, Feminism, and the Politics of the Body*. U of California P, 1993.

Santamarina, Xiomara. "Black Womanhood in Women's Slave Narratives." *The Cambridge Companion to the African American Slave Narrative*, edited by Audrey A. Fisch, Cambridge UP, 2007, pp. 232–45.

Seethaler, Ina C. "Feminist Service Learning: Teaching about Oppression to Work toward Social Change." *Feminist Teacher*, vol. 25, no. 1, 2016, pp. 39–54.

Shakur, Assata. *Assata: An Autobiography*. Lawrence Hill Books, 2001.

Shapiro, Deborah, and Joseph Cuseo. *High Engagement Practices for Teaching and Learning*. AVID Press, 2018.

"Slave House Preservation." *Saving Slave Houses*, created by Jobie Hill, 2023, www.savingslavehouses.org/saving-slave-houses-project/home-page-2019/.

Smith, Caleb. "Harriet Jacobs among the Militants: Transformations in Abolition's Public Sphere, 1859–61." *American Literature*, vol. 84, no. 4, 2012, pp. 743–68.

Smith, Sidonie. *A Poetics of Women's Autobiography: Marginality and the Fictions of Self-Representation*. Indiana UP, 1987.

Smith, Valerie. "Form and Ideology in Three Slave Narratives." H. Jacobs, *Incidents* [Foster and Yarborough], pp. 220–34. Originally published in *Self-Discovery and Authority in Afro-American Narrative*, 1987.

———. "Neo–Slave Narratives." *The Cambridge Companion to the African American Slave Narrative*, edited by Audrey Fisch, Cambridge UP, 2007, pp. 168–85.

———. *Self-Discovery and Authority in Afro-American Narrative*. Harvard UP, 1987.

Smyth, William D. "O Death, Where Is Thy Sting? Reverend Francis J. Grimke's Eulogy for Harriet A. Jacobs." *The Journal of Negro History*, vol. 70, winter-spring 1985, pp. 35–39.

Sollors, Werner. *Neither Black nor White yet Both: Thematic Explorations of Interracial Literature*. Oxford UP, 1997.

Sommers, Samantha M. "From 'Harriet Jacobs and the Recirculation of Print Culture.'" H. Jacobs, *Incidents* [Foster and Yarborough], pp. 351–64.

———. "Harriet Jacobs and the Recirculation of Print Culture." *MELUS*, vol. 40, no. 3, 2015, pp. 134–49.

Sorisio, Carolyn. "'There Is Might in Each': Conceptions of Self in Harriet Jacobs's *Incidents in the Life of a Slave Girl, Written by Herself*." *Legacy: A Journal of American Women Writers*, vol. 13, no. 1, 1996, pp. 1–18. *JSTOR*, www.jstor.org/stable/25679182.

Spillers, Hortense J. "Interstices: A Small Drama of Words." *The Routledge Language and Cultural Theory Reader*, edited by Lucy Burke et al., Routledge, 2000, pp. 197–204.

———. "Mama's Baby, Papa's Maybe: An American Grammar Book." *Diacritics*, vol. 17, no. 2, 1987, pp. 64–81.

———. "Notes on an Alternative Model—Neither/Nor." *Black, White, and in Color: Essays on American Literature and Culture*, by Spillers, U of Chicago P, 2003, pp. 301–18.

Srikanth, Siddharth. "Fictionality and Autofiction." *Style*, vol. 53, no. 3, 2019, pp. 344–63.

Starr, Paul. *The Social Transformation of American Medicine: The Rise of a Sovereign Profession and the Making of a Vast Industry*. Basic Books, 2008.

"Statement of Celia to Justice of the Peace June 25, 1855." *Famous Trials*, created by Douglas O. Linder, University of Missouri, Kansas City, School of Law, 1995–2023, famous-trials.com/celia/184-statement. html.

Stauffer, John. *The Black Hearts of Men: Radical Abolitionists and the Transformation of Race*. Harvard UP, 2004.

Steele, Catherine Knight. *Digital Black Feminism*. New York UP, 2021.

Stein, Gertrude. *Three Lives*. Penguin Books, 1990.

Stevenson, Brenda E. "What's Love Got to Do with It? Concubinage and Enslaved Women and Girls in the Antebellum South." *The Journal of African American History*, vol. 98, no. 1, 2013, pp. 99–125.

Stoever, Jennifer Lynn. *The Sonic Color Line: Race and the Cultural Politics of Listening*. New York UP, 2016.

Stover, Johnnie M. "Nineteenth-Century African American Women's Autobiography as Social Discourse: The Example of Harriet Anne Jacobs." *College English*, vol. 66, no. 2, 2003, pp. 133–54.

Stowe, Harriet Beecher. *A Key to* Uncle Tom's Cabin. John P. Jewett, 1853.

———. *Uncle Tom's Cabin*. Edited by Elizabeth Ammons, Norton Critical Edition, 3rd ed., W. W. Norton, 2018.

Tatar, Maria. *The Heroine with 1,001 Faces*. Liveright, 2021.

Tate, Claudia. *Domestic Allegories of Political Desire*. Oxford UP, 1992.

Taves, Ann. "Spiritual Purity and Sexual Shame: Religious Themes in the Writings of Harriet Jacobs." *Incidents in the Life of a Slave Girl*, by Harriet Jacobs, W. W. Norton, 2001, pp. 209–22.

"Tawawa House Broadside." *Ohio Memory*, 2013, ohiomemory.org/digital/collection/p267401coll32/id/16868/.

Thirteenth. Directed by Ava DuVernay, Netflix, 2016.

Thompson, Samuel. *New Guide to Health; or, Botanic Family Physician*. 3rd ed., J. Howe, 1832.

Thurman, Howard. *Jesus and the Disinherited*. Beacon Press, 1996.

Titus, Mary. "'This Poisonous System': Social Ills, Bodily Ills, and *Incidents in the Life of a Slave Girl*." Garfield and Zafar, pp. 199–215.

Tompkins, Jane. *Sensational Designs: The Cultural Work of American Fiction, 1790–1860*. Oxford UP, 1986.

Tricomi, Albert H. "Harriet Jacobs's Autobiography and the Voice of Lydia Maria Child." *ESQ: A Journal of the American Renaissance*, vol. 53, no. 3, 2007, pp. 216–52.

Truth, Sojourner. "Ain't I a Woman?" Gilbert and Gubar, vol. 1, pp. 510–11.

———. "Keeping the Thing Going while Things Are Stirring." Gilbert and Gubar, vol. 1, pp. 512–13.

———. "What Time of Night It Is." Gilbert and Gubar, vol. 1, pp. 511–12.

Twain, Mark. *The Adventures of Huckleberry Finn*. 1885. W. W. Norton, 1998.

———. *The Adventures of Tom Sawyer*. 1876. W. W. Norton, 2007.

———. *Life on the Mississippi*. 1883. Signet, 2009.

———. *Pudd'nhead Wilson*. 1894. W. W. Norton, 2005.

The Upanishads. Translated by F. Max Muller, part 2, Clarendon Press, 1900.

Waldstreicher, David. "Reading the Runaways: Self-Fashioning, Print Culture, and Confidence in Slavery in the Eighteenth-Century Mid-Atlantic." *The William and Mary Quarterly*, no. 562, 1999, pp. 243–72.

Walker, Alice. *The Color Purple*. 1982. Mariner Books, 2003.

———. "In Search of Our Mother's Gardens." Gilbert and Gubar, vol. 2, pp. 1296–1303.

Walker, Kara Elizabeth. *The Emancipation Approximation*. 25 Oct. 2003–8 Feb. 2004, Buffalo AKG Art Museum, Buffalo, NY.

Wallace-Sanders, Kimberly, editor. *Skin Deep, Spirit Strong: The Black Female Body in American Culture*. U of Michigan P, 2002.

Walpole, Horace. *The Castle of Otranto: A Gothic Story*. Edited by Nick Groom, Oxford UP, 2014.

Walters, Ronald G. "The Erotic South: Civilization and Sexuality in American Abolitionism." *American Quarterly*, no. 25, 1973, pp. 177–201.

Wardrop, Daneen. "'What Tangled Skeins Are the Genealogies of Slavery!': Gothic Families in Harriet Jacobs's *Incidents in the Life of a Slave Girl*." *The Literary Griot*, vol. 14., nos. 1–2, 2002, pp. 23–43.

Washington, Harriet A. *Medical Apartheid: The Dark History of Medical Experimentation on Black Americans from Colonial Times to the Present*. Doubleday, 2007.

Washington, Margaret. "'From Motives of Delicacy': Sexuality and Morality in the Narratives of Sojourner Truth and Harriet Jacobs." *The Journal of African American History*, vol. 92, no. 1, 2007, pp. 57–73, https://doi.org/10.1086/jaahv92n1p57.

Wearn, Mary McCartin. *Negotiating Motherhood in Nineteenth-Century American Literature*. Routledge, 2008.

Weinbaum, Alys Eve. *Wayward Reproductions: Genealogies of Race and Nation in Transatlantic Modern Thought*. Duke UP, 2004.

Weinstock, Jeffrey Andrew, editor. *The Cambridge Companion to American Gothic*. Cambridge UP, 2017.

Welter, Barbara. "The Cult of True Womanhood, 1820–1860." *American Quarterly*, vol. 18, no. 2, summer 1966, pp. 151–74.

Wharton, Edith. *The Age of Innocence*. 1920. Norton Critical Edition, W. W. Norton, 2002.

White, Deborah Gray. *Ar'n't I a Woman? Female Slaves in the Plantation South*. W. W. Norton, 1999.

Whitehead, Colson. *The Underground Railroad*. Anchor Books, 2016.

Whitsitt, Novian. "Reading between the Lines: The Black Cultural Tradition of Masking in Harriet Jacobs' *Incidents in the Life of a Slave Girl*." *Frontiers: A Journal of Women Studies*, vol. 31, no. 1, 2010, pp. 73–88.

Wiegman, Robyn. *American Anatomies: Theorizing Race and Gender*. Duke UP, 1995.

"William Crenshaw Papers." *ZSR Library*, Wake Forest University, wakespace.lib.wfu.edu/handle/10339/94114. Accessed 5 Sept. 2023.

Williams, Linda. *Playing the Race Card: Melodramas of Black and White from Uncle Tom to O. J. Simpson*. Princeton UP, 2001.

Wilson, Harriet E. *Our Nig; or, Sketches from the Life of a Free Black*. Penguin Books, 2009.

Wilson, John. "Pacific Rovings." *Blackwood's Edinburgh Magazine*, no. 61, 1847, pp. 754–67.

Windell, Maria A. *Transamerican Sentimentalism and Nineteenth-Century US Literary History*. Oxford UP, 2020.

Wood, Frances E. "Take My Yoke upon You." *A Troubling in My Soul: Womanist Perspectives on Evil and Suffering*, edited by Emilie M. Townes, Orbis Books, 1993, pp. 37–47.

Woodfox, Albert. "Albert Woodfox on Serving More Than Forty Years in Solitary Confinement." Interview conducted by Scott Simon. *NPR*, 2 Mar. 2019, www.npr.org/2019/03/02/699663270/albertwoodfox-on-serving-more-than-40-years-in-solitary-confinement.

Woolf, Virginia. "A Room of One's Own." Gilbert and Gubar, vol. 2, pp. 237–44.

Wright, Richard. *Native Son*. 1940. Harper Perennial, 2005.

Yaegar, Patricia. *Dirt and Desire: Reconstructing Southern Women's Writing, 1930–1990*. U of Chicago P, 2000.

Yellin, Jean Fagan. *Harriet Jacobs: A Life*. Basic Civitas Books, 2004.

———, editor. *The Harriet Jacobs Family Papers*. U of North Carolina P, 2008. 2 vols.

———. Introduction. *The Harriet Jacobs Family Papers*, edited by Yellin, vol. 1, U of North Carolina P, 2008, pp. xxix–xxvii.

———. Introduction. *Incidents in the Life of a Slave Girl*, by Harriet Jacobs, Harvard UP, 1987, pp. xiii–xxxiv.

———. "Texts and Contexts of Harriet Jacobs' *Incidents in the Life of a Slave Girl*." *The Slave's Narrative*, edited by Charles T. Davis and Henry Louis Gates, Jr., Oxford UP, 1991, pp. 262–82.

———. *Women and Sisters: The Anti-slavery Feminists in American Culture*. Yale UP, 1989.

———. "Written by Herself: Harriet Jacobs' Slave Narrative." *American Literature*, vol. 53, no. 3, 1981, pp. 479–86.

———. "Written by Herself: Harriet Jacobs' Slave Narrative." H. Jacobs, *Incidents* [Foster and Yarborough], pp. 213–19.

Zackodnik, Teresa C. *The Mulatta and the Politics of Race*. UP of Mississippi, 2004.

Zafar, Rafia. "Over-exposed, Under-exposed." Garfield and Zafar, pp. 1–10.

Zazzera, Elizabeth Della. "Incidents in the Life of Harriet Jacobs: A Virtual Tour of *Incidents in the Life of a Slave Girl*." *Lapham's Quarterly*, 15 Apr. 2019, www.laphamsquarterly.org/roundtable/incidents-life-harriet-jacobs.